ISLAM AND HOMOSEXUALITY

ISLAM AND HOMOSEXUALITY

Volume 2

SAMAR HABIB,
Editor

Foreword by Parvez Sharma

PRAEGER
An Imprint of ABC-CLIO, LLC

A B C ⬥ C L I O

Santa Barbara, California • Denver, Colorado • Oxford, England

Library of Congress Cataloging-in-Publication Data

Islam and homosexuality / Samar Habib, editor ; foreword by Parvez Sharma.
    p. cm.
  Includes bibliographical references and index.
    ISBN 978-0-313-37900-0 (set : alk. paper)   ISBN 978-0-313-37901-7 (set ebook)
ISBN 978-0-313-37902-4 (v. 1 : alk. paper)   ISBN 978-0-313-37903-1 (v. 1 ebook)
ISBN 978-0-313-37904-8 (v. 2 : alk. paper)   ISBN 978-0-313-37905-5 (v. 2 ebook)
  1. Homosexuality—Religious aspects—Islam. I. Habib, Samar.
  BP188.15.H65I75   2010
  297.5'66—dc22   2009022272

14   13   12   11   10   1   2   3   4   5

This book is also available on the World Wide Web as an eBook.
Visit www.abc-clio.com for details.
Praeger
An Imprint of ABC-CLIO, LLC

ABC-CLIO, LLC
130 Cremona Drive, P.O. Box 1911
Santa Barbara, California 93116-1911

This book is printed on acid-free paper (∞)
Manufactured in the United States of America

CONTENTS

VOLUME 1

Foreword by Parvez Sharma   ix

Acknowledgments   xv

Introduction: Islam and Homosexuality   xvii
    Samar Habib

1   Islam and the Politics of Homophobia: The Persecution
    of Homosexuals in Islamic Malaysia Compared
    to Secular China   1
    Walter L. Williams

2   Longing, Not Belonging, and Living in Fear   23
    Badruddin Khan

3   Public Displays of Affection: Male Homoerotic Desire
    and Sociability in Medieval Arabic Literature   37
    Jocelyn Sharlet

4   Islam and the Acceptance of Homosexuality:
    The Shortage of Socioeconomic Well-Being
    and Responsive Democracy   57
    Tilo Beckers

5   Gays under Occupation: Interviews with Gay Iraqis   99
    Michael T. Luongo

6   Reading and Writing the Queer Hajj   111
    Omer Shah

7   Sexual Orientation: The Ideological Underpinnings
    of the Gay Advance in Muslim-Majority Societies
    as Witnessed in Online Chat Rooms   133
    Max Kramer

8   "Because Allah Says So": Faithful Bodies, Female
    Masculinities, and the Malay Muslim Community
    of Singapore   163
    Nur 'Adlina Maulod and *Nurhaizatul Jamila Jamil*

9   Mithliyyun or Lutiyyun? Neo-Orthodoxy and the
    Debate on the Unlawfulness of Same-Sex
    Relations in Islam   193
    Barbara Zollner

VOLUME 2

10 The Social Construction of Religious Realities
    by Queer Muslims   223
    Christopher Grant Kelly

11 Is There a "Gay-Friendly" Islam? Synthesizing
    Tradition and Modernity in the Question
    of Homosexuality in Islam   247
    Christopher Grant Kelly

12 Neither Homophobic nor (Hetero) Sexually Pure:
    Contextualizing Islam's Objections to Same-Sex Sexuality   269
    Aleardo Zanghellini

13 Implied Cases for Muslim Same-Sex Unions   297
    Junaid Bin Jahangir

14 Queer Visions of Islam   327
    Rusmir Musić

15 Queer, American, and Muslim: Cultivating Identities
    and Communities of Affirmation   347
    Mahruq Fatima Khan

16   "You're What?": Engaging Narratives from Diasporic
     Muslim Women on Identity and Gay Liberation   373
     Ayisha A. Al-Sayyad

17   "Everywhere You Turn You Have to Jump into
     Another Closet": Hegemony, Hybridity,
     and Queer Australian Muslims   395
     Ibrahim Abraham

18   Marketing Diversity: Homonormativity and the
     Queer Turkish Organizations in Berlin   419
     Ilgin Yorukoglu

19   *Touch of Pink*: Diasporic Queer Experiences
     within Islamic Communities   445
     Ahmet Atay

20   Sexualities and the Social Order in Arab
     and Muslim Communities   463
     Rabab Abdulhadi

About the Editor and Contributors   489

Index   495

10

THE SOCIAL CONSTRUCTION OF RELIGIOUS REALITIES BY QUEER MUSLIMS

Christopher Grant Kelly

The blog "Eye on Gay Muslims" is targeted toward a number of audiences, most notably Muslims who experience same-sex attractions and/or who define themselves as "gay," "lesbian," "bisexual," "queer," or otherwise outside of heterosexuality (henceforth, simply "queer"). The blog describes its purpose and goals as follows:

> Here we discuss the concept and emergence of "Gay Muslims," considering that homosexual activity is clearly forbidden in Islam. We kindly advise Muslims struggling with same-sex attraction, affirming that nobody is sinful for what they feel inside. As for those people who try to distort the religion, we refute them soundly with evidence.[1]

From the preceding passage, we can glean a number of surface-level observations about the blog writers' position on homosexuality. They find the concept of a "gay Muslim" problematic. They regard the alleged prohibition of homosexual behavior in Islam as beyond debate. They consider same-sex attraction a burden. And, they regard evidence as being on their side. These are important points in themselves.

Going deeper, however, we can also detect a number of exclusions and concealed assumptions at play. For the prohibition to be defined as "clear," there must be a corresponding notion of the *unclear,* the ambiguous, the possibility of multiple meanings, which is systematically excluded from this text and the discourses in which it is embedded. The reference to "those people who try to distort the religion" implicates two hidden assumptions: (1) that there is a pristine original—which, of course, forbids homosexual activity—that is vulnerable to distortion and (2) that acceptance of their understanding is a precondition for intellectual honesty (hence, the phrase "*try* to distort [emphasis mine]"). These exclusions and concealed assumptions give the text an appearance of being sensible and correct.

At the same time, though, the text subtly undermines itself, and the best example is simply the fact that pronouncing the prohibition of homosexual activity as "clear" simultaneously raises the possibility of its ambiguity; similarly, the assertion that the blog authors "refute them [queer Muslims] soundly with evidence" introduces the possibility of their refutation being unsound and their evidence lacking. It is from within this space that many queer Muslims explore and promote alternative interpretations of Islam's main sources (the holy text known as the "Quran" and the teachings of Muhamad in the *hadith* tradition) in which homosexual activity is seen as not forbidden and may be undertaken as part of a romantic relationship between two men or two women.

These alternative interpretations can take a number of forms. Scott Siraj al-Haqq Kugle, for example, has produced the most extensive scholarly argument in this vein to date, questioning traditional interpretations of the Quran that forbid homosexual activity while offering alternative interpretations in their place.[2] In addition, he criticizes past scholars' (mis)use of Muhamad's teachings, as well as the authenticity of particular teachings and the overall reasoning used by those scholars. In response, Kugle offers an alternative, Sufism-based approach to homosexuality in Islam, an approach that regards sexual diversity as part of a divinely ordained diversity that is to be embraced.[3]

In contrast, queer Muslims without extensive scholarly training may refute Islamic scholars' arguments against homosexual activity in a manner that is much less elaborate than Kugle's but equally encompassing. In short, these individuals may insist upon an alternative position already articulated at length by queer Christians and Jews: "God made me gay [or 'lesbian,' 'bisexual,' etc.]." For example, gay Bosnian Muslim "Samir," who will reappear later in this chapter, states, "I think, from early on, I accepted that God created me the way he wanted to create me, and he created me as gay, so there's no reason why God shouldn't want me to be gay, no matter what any religious institution tells me." Here, whereas

Kugle challenges traditional Islamic views of homosexuality via engagement with sacred sources and pre-existing scholarship, Samir appears to bypass those sources and scholarship entirely, saying as much later.

What Scott Kugle and Samir have in common is that both of them, like many other queer Muslims, reject the ideas that homosexual activity or relationships are condemned or forbidden by Islam or are, in any way, incompatible with it. Considering that these views are at complete loggerheads with traditional and mainstream views of the issue, it is no surprise that it is sometimes difficult for the two sides to engage in dialogue about homosexuality. Whatever case one side might find completely sound may appear completely illegitimate, irrelevant, or incomprehensible to the other. It is almost as if each side inhabits an opposing reality.

In her examination of conversion to Charismatic Catholicism, Mary Jo Neitz invokes the notion of "social realities," in which people interpret their experiences differently, and choose different experiences *to* interpret according to which reality or set of realities each inhabits.[4] Neitz writes:

> A social reality . . . defines the meaning of persons and objects, and it designates the historical events and biographical identities that can be brought into play. It provides background expectancies in terms of which action can be understood. Furthermore, it is usually assumed that other people employ the same background expectancies, that is, that others "understand" words and events in the same way, and that others inhabit the same social reality.[5]

Obviously, Neitz is not referring to reality in a positivist sense but, rather, that which persons or groups *take* to be real and/or meaningful. In one social reality, inhabited by the architects of "Eye on Gay Muslims," a number of shared meanings (e.g., homosexual activity as "*clearly* forbidden [emphasis mine]") and background assumptions (e.g., the association between certain interpretations and intellectual honesty) are in play, as suggested by the previous discussion. In other realities, those inhabited by self-identified queer Muslims such as Kugle and Samir, with different meanings and assumptions, different understandings about how to interpret (and *what* to interpret) lead to different conclusions. It is no wonder, then, that communication across these realities would be a challenge!

This chapter will examine how lesbian, gay, bisexual, transgender, intersex, and queer (LGBTIQ) Muslims mobilize discourse to construct alternative, even oppositional, social realities—especially religious ones. The first section will review Berger and Luckmann's (1966) discussion of the legitimation of social realities, paying particular attention to what they call "universe-maintenance."[6] The next section will elaborate the social base of reality-constructing activities, including social relationships and cultural tools. The third section will examine this framework as it relates to the particular social and religious realities that Samir both invoked and constructed during our interview. The chapter concludes with a number of reflections and suggestions for further exploration of the main question.

REALITY LEGITIMATION AND MAINTENANCE

Human beings are unique in being born with underdeveloped instincts and with no natural environment, as most nonhuman animals have.[7] Instead, humans adapt to multiple environments, engaging with others in specific habitual activities that become particular *types* of activities. Similarly, their specific roles and relationships become general *types* of roles and relationships. In other words, these activities, roles, and relationships are *institutionalized,* which is the first phase of reality construction. For example, heterosexual pairing and procreation, on one level, is simply a particular activity in which many individuals happen to take part; however, because it has been done for so long and so widely, it becomes institutionalized.

This institutionalized world—especially as children are born and inducted into it—becomes an objective reality for its participants, taken for granted and existing prior to human activity: "This is how things are done."[8] Everything has its place and meaning in the order of things. Institutionalized heterosexuality is an especially ubiquitous example of that statement. However, new generations receive this world not as biographical memory, but as so many traditions—and stories about the traditions. Furthermore, just as human activity constructs this world and reproduces it on an ongoing basis, that same activity can also take the world apart via nonconformity, questioning, or anything else that introduces alternative possibilities. Therefore, this world must be explained and justified—or *legitimated.*

Broadly, legitimation is any kind of activity that renders an institutionalized order and its beliefs and practices integrated, ordered, and plausible to its members. Legitimation implies both values and knowledge that make the institutionalized order seem true and right. Berger and

Luckmann identify multiple levels of legitimation, ranging from pretheo-retical phenomena such as language and the mere familiarity of practice to complicated theories and "symbolic universes" that incorporate the insti-tutionalized order and all its beliefs and practices into a larger whole. Le-gitimations of institutionalized heterosexuality might include both basic claims ("God created Adam and Eve, not Adam and Steve") and theologi-cal beliefs in Man and Woman as a divine pair.

As a product of human activity, legitimations (in this case, of hetero-sexuality) are vulnerable and precarious and may become *problematic*. Individuals, certainly, may experience the social reality idiosyncratically, leading to occasional questions about it; in addition, subgroups within one reality may subscribe to a deviant definition of reality and challenge the existing one. Furthermore, the social reality and legitimations of one society may conflict with those of another, which can be even more prob-lematic than heretical alternative versions within one's own group because the former is more likely to have its own separate institutionalized and legitimated reality.

These possible and actual threats lead to the necessity of "conceptual machineries of universe-maintenance," which are essentially further elaborations of existing legitimations.[9] Two machineries exist for the ex-press purpose of neutralizing threats to that prevailing reality: therapy and nihilation. *Therapy* is designed "to ensure that actual or potential devi-ants stay within the institutionalized definitions of reality," by explaining why deviance occurs, diagnosing that deviance, and correcting it, ensur-ing conformity to social reality.[10] For example, a therapy might maintain institutionalized heterosexuality by pathologizing queer people, main-taining that same-sex desire is a result of bad parenting and curable via counseling.

Nihilation is a kind of legitimation in reverse, seeking to render *im*-plausible and *in*coherent anything outside of a social reality, and it takes at least two forms. First, nihilation (of an alternative reality) may occur by assigning a phenomenon an inferior status within the prevailing reality, by designating it as misguided, nonsensical, immoral, and so on. Thus, homosexuality may be dismissed as either a mental illness or a "perversion of the natural order." A second form of nihilation is the "translation" of "deviant definitions of reality in terms of concepts belonging to one's own universe."[11] What might appear to be an alternative reality is really one's own reality, merely conceptualized or institutionalized incorrectly. In this case, homosexuality might be regarded as merely a misguided attempt to realize one's own true gender identity—which, if accomplished properly, would presumably lead the person "back" to heterosexuality. In both these ways, nihilation maintains the prevailing reality through the "delegitimation" of alternatives.

Together, these activities—institutionalization, legitimation, and universe-maintenance—create entire social realities that appear unproblematic, unchangeable, justifiable, and true to their inhabitants. In addition, reality construction creates entire systems of belief that render that reality plausible to its members.[12] These systems include everything from language and lay beliefs to elaborate scholarly discourses and cosmologies. Institutional heterosexuality is legitimated—and homosexuality nihilated—through both cries of "Adam and Eve, not Adam and Steve!" and theological jeremiads on "Man" and "Woman" as a "sacred pair."

REALITY CONSTRUCTION AS A SOCIAL ACTIVITY

When examining how reality construction actually takes place as a concrete and contextualized social activity, Margaret R. Somers's concept of "relational setting" proves most valuable because the concept emphasizes identity and social behavior as ongoing, contextualized social processes rather than as fixed or reified phenomena.[13] Instead of simply looking at fixed statuses (e.g., race, class, and/or gender), Somers proposes an approach based on narrative identity[14] that stresses the particular "structural and cultural [i.e., institutionalized] relationships in which [individuals] are embedded" and "the [legitimating] stories through which [individuals] constitute their identities."[15] People's identities and actions are to be viewed in the context of their particular narratives and social relationships, which give meaning and coherence to their roles and behaviors.

In contrast to the essentialist conception of society, Somers proposes an alternative concept: "A *relational setting* is a pattern of relationships among institutions, public narratives, and social practices [emphasis mine]."[16] This concept not only recognizes actors' specific social relationships but also situates them within particular social institutions in a specific place and time. Those institutions may or may not harmonize, and the particular links among institutions and individuals may vary across places and times. We are "handed down" particular institutionalized roles, relationships, and practices, and their corresponding legitimations, but these settings also provide the ground for battles of both universe-maintenance and *universe-challenging,* the latter being very important to queer Muslims. Relational settings entail several elements that are germane to the construction of social realities. The most relevant ones here are the *audience* to which one makes a claim, the relevant *plausibility structures* for certain kinds of definitions versus others, and the *toolkit* for constructing definitions.

AUDIENCES

Charles Horton Cooley and George Herbert Mead have both established the central role of significant others in the establishment of identity. Cooley introduces the concept of the *looking-glass self,* arguing that individuals take on personal identities by defining themselves as they imagine that others see them.[17] Similarly, Mead contends that a person becomes a "self" by developing the ability to look at himself just as he might look at another person; a person develops this ability by learning to assume the perspective of an abstract *generalized other.* This reflection on oneself as an object, during interaction with others, leads to the development of a "self" as such.[18]

Similarly, Berger and Luckmann describe a third phase of reality construction: internalization. In the process of internalization, the individual comes to experience a social reality as personally meaningful; the individual is inducted, or socialized, into this reality. One enters these realities through learning and utilizing particular varieties of language and knowledge; she is able to participate in institutionalized social reality because it has become her own reality, as she has internalized the basic practices, social relationships, and legitimations. Like objective reality, subjective reality also requires maintenance because

> it is threatened by the marginal situations of human experience that cannot be completely bracketed in everyday activity. There is always the haunting presence of metamorphoses, those actually remembered and those only sensed as sinister possibilities. There are also the more directly threatening competing definitions of reality that may be encountered socially.[19]

The authors emphasize social interactions because one's significant others continually affirm the reality of everyday life, along with one's own role in this reality. Conversation, in particular, helps people give voice to various experiences and assigns them a place in their reality via a common language that orders that reality, reproduces it, and confirms it. These conversations take place within a world that makes sense and thereby confirms its reality.

In her work with an elderly Jewish community in Los Angeles, Barbara Myerhoff emphasizes the role of audience in affirming preferred narratives of one's life.[20] Many of these elderly Jewish people had lost relatives to the Holocaust, or were otherwise isolated, and felt their own lives were rendered invisible as a result. The community members resisted through what Myerhoff calls "definitional ceremonies," in which they would relate their life stories to an audience that would affirm their preferred identities. Myerhoff writes, "Definitional ceremonies deal with the problems of invisibility and marginality; they are strategies that provide opportunities for being seen and in one's own terms, garnering witnesses to one's worth, vitality, and being."[21] The audience both developed their own stories and contributed to each other's—developing a *collective* one, in the process. This example is especially important for its focus on narratives and other reality claims that do not have the benefit of recognition by larger social groupings and institutions. These audiences have the role of either confirming or disconfirming these claims, accepting or denying their validity. Depending on these audiences, one may be able to create and/or sustain one version of social reality or another, whichever the audience grants some level of plausibility.

PLAUSIBILITY STRUCTURES

The relational setting also provides the social conditions for particular claims about reality to appear more or less plausible. Berger and Luckmann write, "Subjective reality is thus always dependent upon specific *plausibility structures,* that is, the specific social base and social processes required for its maintenance [emphasis mine]."[22] Plausibility structures not only confirm the accepted social reality and ground specific social and personal identities, but also *discourage* doubt. People suspend doubt for fear of ridicule, either from other people or from the internal "generalized other."[23] Plausibility structures ensure that certain types of claims about (objective or subjective) reality can be accepted as valid, sensible, or "plausible," while others will be summarily dismissed as senseless or "implausible." Hence, every plausibility structure is, at the same time, an "*im*plausibility structure," relative to any claims that are contrary to the prevailing or preferred social reality.

Berger and Luckmann emphasize plausibility structures in "reality switching" or *alternation,* the paradigmatic case being religious conversion.[24] This necessitates socialization into a new reality and a *de*socialization from the old. Aside from adopting new legitimations (of the new reality) and nihilations (of the old), the prospective convert requires a new social base. Even though the convert himself makes the choice, Berger and Luckmann argue that a plausibility structure is necessary for the individual "to keep on taking it seriously; to retain a sense of its plausibility."[25] The convert requires a community that will reinforce the new identity and belief system, confirming their status as "reality." While taking on a new plausibility structure, the old one must be deauthorized, lest it reinforce the old reality or circumvent the new one. A new structure enables the convert to adopt and sustain a new identity and belief system.

While Berger and Luckmann's argument is useful for examining migrations to other complete realities, it does not clearly account for ideological mavericks—people who abandon the beliefs and theories, the legitimations, of their primary social reality in favor of various alternatives. How does one adopt and sustain an alternative identity and set of beliefs when there is no alternative plausibility structure?

DISCOURSES

Relational settings also provide the *tools* for reality construction. According to Ann Swidler, culture is a "toolkit" of language, symbols, stories, beliefs, practices, products of labor, relationships, institutions, and so on that individuals use in organizing their moment-to-moment conduct.[26] We can also situate toolkits within specific contexts in order to determine how different institutions intersect, creating unique assemblages of tools for people who inhabit those locations. James Paul Gee is helpful for elaborating the concept of a toolkit as part of a relational setting.[27] He uses "the term 'Discourse,' with a capital 'D,' for ways of combining and integrating language, actions, interactions, ways of thinking, believing, valuing, and using various symbols, tools, and objects to enact a particular sort of socially recognizable identity" and activity.[28] Discourses apply both to large societies and to smaller groups, so there can be Discourses for entire nations, regions, professions, religions, hobbies, families, and other social groupings.

A person in his or her relational setting may be fluent in many different intersecting Discourses, according to his various *milieux* and intersecting identities; each Discourse affords the user particular reality-construction resources. For example, being a gay Muslim convert from Christianity (Baptist and Anglican) and a sociology graduate student, I am more or less fluent in gay, Islamic, Baptist Christian, Anglican Christian, and sociological Discourses (among others!). "Discourse" draws our attention to the different resources, linguistic *and* nonlinguistic, available to a person or group for engaging in reality construction within a relational setting.

One important category of resources available by virtue of Discourses is that of language—vocabularies, meanings, and styles, to name a few. Gee introduces *social languages,* varieties of speaking that reproduce certain recognizable identities and activities in different settings.[29] An excellent example from religious studies is the practice of witnessing in evangelical Christianity.[30] According to Susan Friend Harding, witnessing has a particular rhetorical style, which sets up a dichotomy between the speaker and the listener; the speaker assumes a stance of authority and knowledge, while the listener assumes a stance of ignorance—or at least is expected to do so. In addition, there is the standard evangelical vocabulary of "lost," "found," "saved," "sin," and "conviction," among others; these terms are significant for the entire belief system that they imply—such as the use of words like "lost" and "found" to express someone's spiritual status (i.e., whether or not she has been "saved"). These terms correspond roughly to the lower levels of legitimation in Berger and Luckmann's scheme, as they are often used in a pretheoretical manner.

Narratives, imposing order and meaning on seemingly disparate experiences, also deserve special attention. Somers describes four modes of narrativity, three of which are relevant here.[31] *Ontological* narratives are personal stories that order one's life experience and help to guide action. Large and small groups can have *public* narratives—both general ones that center on their origins, their values, and their destinies (e.g., a Roman Catholic narrative about the origins of the church) and specific ones (e.g., an official clerical narrative about the sex abuse scandal). Finally, *metanarratives* are large abstract narratives spanning time and space, such as the Enlightenment narrative of scientific progress. Evangelical witnessing in Harding's research invokes all three types: a Biblical *metanarrative* about humankind's creation, fall into sin, opportunity for salvation through Jesus Christ, and eternal fate in Heaven or Hell; a *public* narrative about the unique role of one's denomination or congregation; and an *ontological* narrative about one's own salvation.[32] Queer Muslims, in particular, are likely to find themselves embedded in an number of narratives: their own personal, *ontological* narratives; the *public narratives* of their respective ethnic groups and nations of origin and, possibly, mainstream gay narratives, if exposed to Western culture or society; and the *metanarrative* of Islam. Therefore, they are likely to find themselves moving between and/ or negotiating various narratives that seem compatible at times and contradictory at others.

Providing various possible audiences, plausibility structures, and Discourses, the relational setting offers both the context and the tools of reality construction—enabling and constraining certain claims about social reality. In any setting, some claims will find an eager and accepting audience, favorable plausibility structures for appearing comprehensible and meaningful, and the necessary Discursive resources for articulating the claim in the first place. Other claims will lack a sympathetic audience, confront structures that deny them plausibility, and/or never even make it into language because necessary Discourse is simply not available. The following section will examine how these dimensions of relational setting affect Samir's claims about religious reality and personal identity.

CASE STUDY: "SAMIR"

"Samir" is a 23-year-old gay Bosnian Muslim immigrant and college student living in the Boston area since 2002. He currently lives with his family, who left Bosnia-Herzegovina because of the Bosnian War and its effect on the economy. He was recently enrolled in a premedical program and has since graduated. It is noteworthy that he identifies himself as not being religiously observant in the traditional sense, and he says that he did not receive much education in the Muslim religion. At the same time, he clearly believes in God, has an ethical and moral sensibility, and values his Muslim identity—which is largely connected to his national identity.

METHOD

I interviewed Samir in his laboratory on his campus. I asked him a series of open-ended questions about his life story, his religious history, the role of religion in his life, the role of his sexual orientation in his religious experience, experiences of God and spirituality, and life's ultimate ends and purposes.

In addition, I included several probes for each question. The questions were designed to (1) obtain basic biographical information about Samir and (2) elicit a "picture" of Samir's personal religious reality: that which he took to be true and real about Islam, God, and other aspects of religion. The whole interview lasted roughly one hour and was transcribed in full. In addition, I later asked Samir for clarification on a point he had mentioned during the interview, and I included his subsequent response in the transcript. All quotes from the transcript are italicized and edited here for clarity.

It is also important to point out that my reasons for focusing only on a single interview, rather than multiple ones. This chapter is not seeking to make any sweeping or generalizable knowledge claims about a particular population or to revise any existing theories. Rather, the chapter has three main purposes. First, one of my goals is to introduce a set of theoretical concepts and illustrate their applicability and usefulness for making sense of queer Muslims' religious realities and experiences, a goal that is not dependent upon the number of interviewees. Second, I am interested in providing the reader with in-depth understanding of how religious phenomena might figure into queer Muslims' life experiences, and to examine multiple interviews would be to sacrifice the deep understanding gained by focusing on Samir's interview; again, deep understanding, not generalizability, is the goal. Finally, a related goal is to provide readers with an example with which they might identify, to some extent; focusing on Samir alone, rather than on several interviewees, not only allows for deep intellectual understanding but also makes his experiences and even his person more accessible to the reader. For these reasons, an extended examination of a single interview is more than appropriate here.

ANALYSIS

Data analysis consisted primarily of identifying themes in the interview based upon a close reading of the interview transcript. Although as many themes as possible were identitfied, the main intent was to locate instances where Samir was invoking or actively constructing his social reality with respect to his religion and sexual orientation. An initial reading resulted in over 250 themes, though many of those were repetitive as similar ideas arose throughout the interview. The themes spanned a variety of topics, but the themes most directly related to the chapter's topic—a discursive construction of religious realities—became the center of analysis. Although that subset of themes was itself extremely nuanced, a number of larger overarching themes were present, three of which will be reviewed here.

Religion. One of the more striking aspects of Samir's understanding of religion is his disconnection of prayer from mainstream ritual technique in Islam. While Islamic prayer tends to consist of five daily prayers, undertaken at specific times of day according to a particular method, Samir does not define or practice prayer in ritualistic terms:

Chris: *Do you still ever do the prayers today?* [Referring to the standard five daily prayers]

Samir: *I do pray. Not in a prescribed way, like every day, five times. I know prayers that I just say. I don't do any of the rituals.*

Prayer is defined as a personal activity that does not have to be done in a particular way, and the "technique" appears to be up to the discretion of the person praying. At the same time, Samir does seem to believe in some obligation toward prayer:

Chris: *How important are religion and spirituality in your life today? You said you pray sometimes?*

Samir: *I tend to turn to religion and spirituality when I'm going through hard times. I'm not thinking about it as much when everything's okay. But, also, there's this sense of obligation to say prayers. If I don't say any prayers for a long time, then that's not good because I'm supposed to be saying at least some prayers. When I pray, I say some prayers, and then I pray for my family who died, my grandfather, or my cousin. It makes me feel good that I'm praying for them.*

I glean two inferences from this statement. First, there is some obligation to pray, but it is a very nonspecific obligation with no requirements for time or technique. Second, prayer seems to be interwoven with family commitment, which also points to his apparent pairing of religious identity with cultural identity, to be discussed shortly.

Second, Samir expresses his personal values and normative ends without reference to explicitly Islamic language or doctrine—seemingly the reverse of Harding's findings. His language about values and ends would be recognized as moral but not necessarily as religious. For example, he emphasizes being a "good person":

I think people do their best, and I generally think that you have to be a good person, and if you're a good person, you're also right with God. You don't have to do anything more.

Regarding the purpose of life, Samir discusses experiencing life and achieving happiness:

I think people are put here to experience life and gain experience, in general, of different things, and I think that in gaining experience, we learn how to be happy, and I think that the purpose of life is attaining happiness on some very basic level.

When asked how he would like to be remembered at the end of his life, he responds in similar generalities (which is only to point out a feature of his language use here):

I just want people to remember me as a kind person, a good person. I hope that I don't ever hurt anybody in any way. I don't want any great honors or anything. I just want to be remembered as a kind, lovable person.

While Samir clearly has ideas about what he values morally and what the purpose of life is, he expresses these without recourse to recognizably religious language. Rather, he speaks in broader generalities about being a "good person," "gaining experience," and "attaining happiness" in life. These are very different from mainstream Islamic themes of "submission" and the like.

When asked about religious (especially Islamic) condemnations of homosexuality and his feelings about them, Samir's apparent deemphasis on religious institutions and doctrines are even more pronounced. In regard to religion more generally, he argues that "religions are just a product of politics and other divisions that happened in the past." The assertion that religions are political (and social?) products would suggest that he does not recognize whatever authority religious institutions or clergy might claim for themselves. This suggestion is supported by Samir's earlier statement that "*there's no reason why God shouldn't want* [him] *to be gay, no matter what any religious institution tells* [him]." This understanding appears to extend to religious texts, to an extent, when I ask for his reflections on Islam's traditional sources regarding homosexuality:

Um, I don't know, I mean, all these religious books are written by people. I don't necessarily believe they're the words of God. Well, I mean, I do believe they're the word of God, but I don't believe that they were the word of God word-for-word. Just like with any story, if you just tell a story today, in 2,000 years, of course it's gonna change, it's gonna evolve, just like other people, changing and adding onto it. I don't know, there's like one mention of homosexuality being a sin in the Quran, but I haven't really concerned myself too much with it. I mean, I just take it to be a story.

Certainly, his claims about the divine origin of the Quran seem ambiguous. One could argue that he takes a liminal position on the Quran: It is not the word of God, but it is not *not* the word of God, either. For Samir, the authority of the Quran is apparently limited because it has been changed, or likely has been, and because it is "just a story;" this is in stark contrast to the tremendous authority of the Quran in mainstream Islamic scholarship and practice. The very claim "I haven't really concerned myself too much with it," along with the implicit suggestion that nonconcern is even an option to begin with, raises questions about the role of plausibility structures, or lack thereof. This is a major difference between Samir, on the one hand, and people like Scott Kugle and myself, who are *very much* concerned with the Quranic question.

GOD

Samir is clear about his belief in God: *"My belief in God has pretty much stayed constant. I think that believing in God and not* [being]*willing to change that is a very, very basic or necessary belief."* At the same time, his claims about God and his relationship with God, like prayer and personal values, seem to stand outside of any official Islamic scholarly doctrine or practice; he understands God as a personal God:

Over the years, I struggled with contemplating if I believe in God or not, and I realized that if I think of God in the context of religion, then I really had a hard time doing that there. I believe in God but I don't necessarily need to go to the mosque to pray to God or to have a connection with God. It's more like a personal level.

In fact, during the entire interview, we used the English word "God," never the Arabic equivalent "Allah." The relationship with God appears to be a rather individualistic endeavor in his understanding, outside of

Islamic religious institutions. At the same time, though, he does articulate beliefs about God and even seems to place a small amount of emphasis on religion:

> I think that you're always close to God. I can't say that I'm closer or further away from Him sometimes. Like I said, in times of need, you always turn to God more than you usually do, but I guess, if I think that I have been doing everything as I'm supposed to or as the religion thinks is appropriate, then I feel closer to God, like I have been less sinful. But then, I think that God's always close by.

There are two points worth raising here. First, God is understood as proximate, not distant—which contrasts with some more orthodox views that might place God at a distance. Second, Samir grants some credence to religious propriety or the distinctly religious notion of "sin." Thus, a definition of God as personal, proximate, and outside religion is paired with some recognition given to religion, inviting questions about how these two beliefs fit together.

Samir's distinction between God and religious institutions is perhaps the sharpest when he talks about being told by religious leaders and family that being gay is against God. He states the very opposite view:

> I think, from early on, I accepted that God created me the way he wanted to create me, and he created me as gay, so there's no reason why God shouldn't want me to be gay, no matter what any religious institution tells me [emphasis mine].

Here, Samir states a view exactly contrary to traditional and mainstream Islamic scholars' contention that God created "male" and "female" as a complementary pair.[33] More interestingly, though, he also positions God and religious institutions against each other, invoking God's name and authority against the institutions' condemnation of homosexuality, deauthorizing the latter. This statement and more are indices of Samir's nascent critique of institutional religion.

MUSLIM IDENTITY

While Samir does not practice Islamic rituals, study Islam extensively, or associate with Islamic organizations and institutions, he does adamantly claim and value his Muslim identity. He states, "*I tried to go* [to the mosque] *on many occasions, but I never really integrated myself into the religion. However, I still consider myself Muslim, and I think that has to do more with the, not like religious identification, but national and cultural identity.*" As the interview progressed, it became more and more apparent how significant his identity as a Muslim was to him, irrespective of his level of religious observance. In the excerpt below, he stresses the role of asserting a Muslim identity in the face of stereotyping and discrimination:

> *Although I don't follow every rule prescribed by the religion, I still consider myself Muslim. And, I think being perceived as Muslim in the society is also a very important part of my life . . . I mean, there has been discrimination against Muslim people in this country, especially after September 11th, and since then I actually have made a point about telling people that I am Muslim because I just think that, me being European and being white, I'm not the stereotypical Muslim that society in general has an image of.*

He frames his desire to be known as a Muslim in society in terms of resistance to stereotyping and discrimination post–September 11, 2001, which further reiterates and reinscribes the notion of "Muslim" as a social and cultural identity.

When I asked Samir a question about what it meant to him to be a Muslim, I was attempting to elicit some of his beliefs about what Islam is and the best way to follow its deeper principles, if not specific rules, but I got an even more striking and valuable insight:

> *It's part of who I am. Muslim is an identity that has caused Bosnian people to be a victim of a civil war and, you know, in a sense, just the fact that that happened is—It makes me cling on to my identity as Muslim. The war was a very defining experience in my life, and it happened because I was Muslim. I had to go through the experience because I was Muslim, and I can't just reject my religion, like, that part of myself because, in a sense, I'm rejecting everything that happened to me. Any of these major things that helped me become who I am.*

It was very important for me to hear this. As someone who converted to Islam because I agreed with the basic beliefs and practices, I needed to have my eyes opened wider to the multiple meanings that religion and religious identity can assume. While Islam has its own theological narrative based upon official traditions, it can take on different valences—different situated meanings—in the contexts of other relational settings and other narratives. In this case, in the Bosnian context, Muslim identity takes on different shades of meaning (e.g., different from what it means to someone like me) because of its role within a war. These meanings, associated with his experience of the war, are ones I would have liked to have explored more, though I was also concerned about Samir's own well-being and did not want to risk him inadvertently becoming saddened or upset.

LIMITATIONS

The two primary limitations of this analysis are the subject pool and the researcher's time constraints; this investigation is based upon one individual and because time has not permitted me to analyze this one interview in more detail. Thus, at this admittedly exploratory stage, neither codes nor themes are refined, nor is any kind of generalization possible. Everything is emergent. A large and diverse subject pool, and more coding and analysis, will be necessary in the future.

DISCUSSION

Nancy T. Ammerman emphasizes that identities emerge "at the everyday intersections of autobiographical and public narratives," which are "both structured and constructed" and intersectional.[34] People may find themselves embedded in both their own autobiographical narratives and a plethora of public ones. The above analysis suggests that Samir—who inhabits a relational setting that includes Bosnian society, Western society, family, queer communities, and scientific communities, among others—is "performing" for various audiences, negotiating plausibility structures, and mobilizing available Discourses to articulate and construct a religious reality that is meaningful to him and sensible in light of his personal experience and everyday life. In this reality, it would seem, religious institutions, religious leaders, specific practices, and even religious texts are not very significant or meaningful. What are meaningful are his personal modes of observance, individual values, his relationship with God (whom he believes created him gay), and Bosnian-Muslim identity.

Dynamics of legitimation and nihilation are ever-present in the interview and analysis. His Bosnian Muslim identity is legitimated through at least two narratives: that of the Serbo-Bosnian war and that of September 11th.

Both narratives help to order his various experiences of these historic events and render these identities true and meaningful. Similarly, his gay identity is legitimated by his own personal story ("Oh, oh, I'm different from other boys, I'm not interested in fighting or playing soccer with them") and possibly by modern, Western gay, and queer Discourses in which one might be "born gay," possibly by God's will.

Similarly, his statements about religious institutions and leaders and holy texts achieve the nihilation of clerical and textual authority, in general, and of condemnations of homosexuality, in particular. By citing a history of religious conflicts and human alteration of holy texts and by asserting the supremacy of God's will over religious authority, Samir invokes a culturally available critique of religious hierarchy that could possibly be connected to Protestant, American metanarratives and public narratives, regardless of whether he would voice, or even see, such a connection. According to Ammerman, religious narratives and schemata (i.e., Discourse models) are transposable from one setting to another; they can be uplifted from one context and moved to another. Although one can only speculate, it seems that Protestant approaches to religious interpretation that deemphasize clerical authority, once divested of specifically Christian entailments, would be very useful for the nihilation of religious hierarchical authority in another faith, while the separation of church and state offers an ideal plausibility structure for deauthorizing the hierarchy; both would be socially available to Samir, here in the United States.

What is not clear, however, is how his alternative religious reality—regarding prayer, values, and God—is legitimated and sustained. Who is his audience, and what are the plausibility structures? One possibility is his Bosnian background; in the interview, Samir pointed out that his family never pushed the religion on him and were not religious themselves, mentioning the influence of Communism. Thus, it could simply be that his relational setting left him free to develop whatever reality he wanted. Another likely possibility is the culture itself because Samir's beliefs sound very similar to what Christian Smith calls "moralistic therapeutic deism":

1. A God exists who created and orders the world and watches over human life on earth.
2. God wants people to be good, nice, and fair to each other, as taught in the Bible and by most world religions.
3. The central goal of life is to be happy and to feel good about oneself.

4. God does not need to be particularly involved in one's life except when He is needed to resolve a problem.

5. Good people go to heaven when they die.[35]

Samir's own statements about believing in God, being a "good person," finding happiness in life, and coming to God more when there are problems are all reminiscent of these five points. According to Smith, these beliefs are becoming more common among younger Americans, so perhaps Samir's very generation is functioning as his audience and providing a plausibility structure for his own extrainstitutional beliefs.

Also, it seems that Samir's Bosnian Muslim and gay identities are, in some ways, very separate from each other on a public level, if not the individual level. In the interview, he often discussed the two separately, except for when I asked specific questions about connections between the two. Certainly, he expressed that he really cannot talk about his gay identity in the Bosnian community: "Gay people are not really accepted into the Bosnian community, and society in general. It's a very taboo topic to even discuss. You know, it's very suppressed." After the interview, in fact, he pointed out that he has to use English to talk about it (even with his mother) because the Bosnian terms would be derogatory and because he is more used to discussing gay issues in English with his gay friends. Similarly, other comments suggest it might be difficult to talk about his Bosnian Muslim identity within the gay community:

> I think the gay community can be very judgmental, too. If somebody stays in the closet because being gay's not very accepted in their culture, they should have an understanding for that because it's not easy for that person. You don't know what they're going through and what that's causing them to feel, but you kind of judge those people, like "Aw, they're just afraid" or "They don't have enough courage," but we can't say that because I think that we are looking at that from our perspective or whoever's perspective. You know, we're looking from our own perspective at somebody else's situation, and you can't do that, and I think that happens a lot in the gay community.

Although I cannot say for sure, I get the distinct impression that he may be talking about himself, as he also mentioned him and a friend of his receiving negative reactions due to identifying themselves as Muslims. It seems that different communities offer opportunities to express some identities and make certain claims—to the exclusion of others. The interview data suggests that Samir, as others in his position might be, can be a Bosnian Muslim among Bosnian Muslims and gay among gays, but there may be no easily accessible relational setting—audiences, plausibility structures, or Discourses—in which to tell a story of being a gay Bosnian Muslim.[36] In either community, such a story may very well be "incommensurable."[37] It is my hope that I was able to be something of an audience.

CONCLUDING REMARKS

Although Samir is just one case (and a unique one, at that), his perspective is a rich and illuminating one around the topic of queer Muslims' religious realities. In particular, Samir's perspective suggests that I, as researcher, should keep an open mind to the various ways in which queer Muslims interact with and mobilize Islamic tradition and Muslim identity toward a variety of theoretical and practical ends. How do they negotiate their relational settings and utilize available resources in order to construct religious realities that are true and meaningful for them? And, are particular kinds of settings needed or desired?

This line of inquiry and corresponding research has important implications for any future efforts to establish *productive* dialogue between queer Muslims and mainstream and traditional Muslims around questions of sexualities and sexual identities in Islam. Queer Muslims, I hope, will be able to utilize this research to be more self-aware about how they talk about homosexuality and Islam, while their mainstream and traditional counterparts will have the opportunity to gain a better idea of what might and might not be meaningful to their queer interlocutors—and hopefully come up with a way to engage in actual dialogue instead of simply proclaiming "The Quran says so, and that's that!" In this way, it might be possible for queer Muslims to come to some understanding with that broader Muslim community, such that more could even find their own place within it.

NOTES

1. "Eye on Gay Muslims," http://gaymuslims.wordpress.com (accessed May 19, 2008).

2. Scott Siraj al-Haqq Kugle, "Sexuality, Diversity and Ethics in the Agenda of Progressive Muslims," in *Progressive Muslims: On Justice, Gender, and Pluralism*, ed. Omid Safi (Oxford: Oneworld Publications, 2003), 190–234.

3. Scott Sirajul Haqq Kugle, "Sexual Diversity in Islam," in *Voices of Islam, Vol. 5, Voices of Change,* ed. Vincent J. Cornell and Omid Safi (London: Praeger, 2007), 131–67.

4. Mary Jo Neitz, *Charisma and Community: A Study of Religious Commitment within the Charismatic Renewal* (New Brunswick, NJ: Transaction, 1987).

5. Neitz, *Charisma and Community,* 79.

6. Peter L. Berger and Thomas Luckmann, *The Social Construction of Reality: A Treatise in the Sociology of Knowledge* (New York: Anchor, 1966).

7. Ibid., 47–48.

8. Ibid., 59.

9. Ibid., 105.

10. Ibid., 113.

11. Ibid., 115.

12. Ibid., 92.

13. Margaret R. Somers, "The Narrative Constitution of Identity: A Relational and Network Approach," *Theory and Society* 23, no. 5 (1994): 605–49.

14. "Narrative identity" refers to the argument that identities, both group and individual, exist primarily as stories and narratives that those groups and individuals tell to themselves and others.

15. Somers, "Narrative Constitution of Identity," 624.

16. Ibid., 626.

17. Charles Horton Cooley, *Human Nature and the Social Order* (New York: Schocken, 1964), 183–85.

18. George Herbert Mead, *Mind, Self, and Society: From the Standpoint of a Social Behaviorist,* ed. C. W. Morris (Chicago: University of Chicago Press, 1934), 136–44, 196.

19. Berger and Luckmann, *Social Construction of Reality,* 147.

20. Barbara Myerhoff, "Life History among the Elderly: Performance, Visibility and Remembering," *A Crack in the Mirror: Reflexive Perspectives in Anthropology,* ed. J. Ruby (Philadelphia: University of Pennsylvania Press, 1982), 99–117.

21. Barbara Myerhoff, "Life Not Death in Venice: Its Second Life," in *The Anthropology of Experience,* ed. V. Turner and E. Bruner (Chicago: University of Illinois Press, 1986), 267.

22. Berger and Luckmann, *Social Construction of Reality,* 154.

23. George Herbert Mead, *Mind, Self, and Society: From the Standpoint of a Social Behaviorist,* ed. C. W. Morris (Chicago: University of Chicago Press, 1934), 136–44, 196.

24. Berger and Luckmann, *Social Construction of Reality,* 157.

25. Ibid., 158.

26. Ann Swidler, "Culture in Action: Symbols and Strategies," *American Sociological Review* 51 (1986): 277.

27. James Paul Gee, *An Introduction to Discourse Analysis: Theory and Method* (New York: Routledge, 2005), 32–33.

28. Ibid., 21.

29. Ibid., 20.

30. Susan Friend Harding, *The Book of Jerry Falwell: Fundamentalist Language and Politics* (Princeton, NJ: Princeton University Press, 2000), 40.

31. Somers, "Narrative Constitution of Identity," 605–49.

32. Harding, *Book of Jerry Falwell.*

33. Kecia Ali, *Sexual Ethics and Islam: Feminist Reflections on Quran, Hadith and Jurisprudence* (Oxford: Oneworld Publications, 2006), 94–95.

34. Nancy T. Ammerman, "Religious Identities and Religious Institutions," in *Handbook of the Sociology of Religion,* ed. by Michele Dillon (New York: Cambridge University Press, 2003), 215.

35. Christian Smith, "On 'Moralistic Therapeutic Deism as U.S. Teenagers' Actual, Tacit, De Facto Religious Faith." *Princeton Theological Seminary* n.d., http://www.ptsem.edu/iym/lectures/2005/Smith-Moralistic.pdf (accessed May 19, 2008).

36. Nancy Ammerman, May 1, 2008, personal communication.

37. Tom Boellstorff, "Between Religion and Desire: Being Muslim and Gay in Indonesia," *American Anthropologist* 107, no. 4 (2005): 575–85.

IS THERE A "GAY-FRIENDLY" ISLAM? SYNTHESIZING TRADITION AND MODERNITY IN THE QUESTION OF HOMOSEXUALITY IN ISLAM

Christopher Grant Kelly

According to "Mere Muslim," organizer of the Web site Mere Islam, he could no longer recommend a book he had previously endorsed (a translation of *Kitab al-Tanwir fi Isqat al-Tadbir* by Ibn Ata' Allah al-Iskandari) because of some information he learned about the translator that "clearly undermines his acceptability and integrity as a translator from an Islamic point-of-view." Supposedly, the translator "engages in intellectually dishonest conclusion-based hermeneutics that openly clash with the consensus of Sunni Muslim scholarship" and is guilty of "agenda-driven intellectual dishonesty," along with "exegetical charlatanism, hermeneutical acrobatics and bovine scatology."[1] All of this was in spite of the fact that the information about the translator had nothing to do with the actual translated text.

Who is the translator, and what did "Mere Muslim" learn about him that apparently disqualified him as a translator? The translator is a Muslim scholar, Scott Siraj al-Haqq Kugle, and he is responsible for the most systematic critique, to date, of the traditional and near-universal position that homosexual sex acts are forbidden in Islam.[2] Kugle has not only pointed out various weaknesses of the traditional position in his writing, but also advocated for the possibility of Islamically acceptable (and even commendable) same-sex relationships.[3] Needless to say, these kinds of arguments are entirely contrary to the almost unanimous consensus that homosexuality, and often nonheterosexuals themselves, have no place in the religion of Islam. Even many non-Muslims take this truism for granted and would react toward Kugle and his arguments in a similar sense of incredulity:

> Even "moderate" Muslims (whatever moderation means in this context) raise the issue [homosexuality] only to announce that it's not worth raising because the Koran is quite categorical on the matter. The sole exception to this rule was Leiden University's Dr Scott Siraj al-Haqq Kugle, an American-born convert who *busies himself looking for scriptural loopholes* that might, with enough *sophisticated paraphrasing* and *wishful thinking*, be enlarged until they're big enough to allow gay Muslims to show their faces in public [Emphasis added].[4]

Needless to say, in making his arguments, Kugle is fighting an uphill battle against long- and widely-held beliefs about this issue, as evidenced by reactions ranging from disbelief and skepticism to outright ire and personal attacks.

Certainly, neither of the examples provided here qualify as scholarly or specialist critiques of Kugle's arguments; in particular, speculations about his character or his intellectual honesty are beyond the scope of an academic discussion.[5] Still, they raise a number of questions that can stimulate a deeper discussion of his arguments and intellectual approach. First, for contextual purposes, what has historically been taken as "the official Islamic position" on homosexuality, based on the sacred texts?[6] Second, what alternative positions does Kugle derive by examining those same texts differently? Third, what kinds of general approaches to religious texts make traditional interpretations seem so obvious and interpretations like Kugle's seem like "sophisticated paraphrasing and wishful thinking," and what kind of alternative approach would lead us to take Kugle's interpretations seriously, instead? Fourth, how do Kugle's interpretations affect discussions of homosexuality in Islam? And finally, what are the theoretical and political consequences? These questions will be explored throughout the remainder of this chapter.

MAINSTREAM ISLAMIC VIEWS OF HOMOSEXUALITY

As mentioned earlier, it has become a truism of sorts that Islam and homosexuality are mutually incompatible. Certainly, the overwhelming majority of Muslims take it for granted that sex acts between two persons of the same gender (and same-sex relationships, by extension) are categorically forbidden. Even in the United States and the West, though, Islam is edging out Christianity as the quintessential homophobic religion, in the public mind; most Westerners have probably heard stories of people being abused, punished, tortured, and executed in Muslim-majority countries for homosexual behavior—such as a recent case in Iran that attracted substantial international outrage over the hanging of two young men.[7] Indeed, political conservatives in the West are, surprisingly, invoking human rights abuses against nonheterosexuals in their criticisms of Islam,[8] and advocates for Israel sometimes use Israel's ostensibly better treatment of gays and lesbians as proof of the Jewish state's moral superiority over its Palestinian neighbors.[9]

In Islamic theology and legal thought, the prohibition is on same-sex sexual acts—especially anal sex between two men.[10] This position is derived from the Quranic story of Lut and several reported sayings of the Prophet Muhamad, which serve as the basis for broader theological and juridical speculations and conclusions. Briefly, the story of Lut entails an incident in which some men, who were really angels in disguise, came to the Prophet Lut's city, visited him in his home, and faced the threat of sexual assault by the city's male citizens.[11] After trying to convince the men to desist, Lut took his family and fled the city, which was subsequently destroyed by God. This is taken as a condemnation of same-sex sexual activity because of verses such as the following: "You [the men of the city] approach men instead of women lustfully; you are rather a people given to excess" (7:81) and "Do you approach the males from all mankind and leave the wives that your Lord created for you? No, you are a transgressing people" (26:165–166).[12] Similarly, there are a number of sayings attributed to Muhamad harshly condemning anal sex between men and calling for a punishment of death, though these are of questionable authenticity.[13]

This view of homosexual sex acts is based upon a broader conception of men and women and their proper roles in relationships and in society.[14] God, according to this view, created men and women as a sacred pair, specifically designed for each other, in both the sexual and romantic senses. Each gender has its unique characteristics and appropriate social roles, and although men and women are equal before God, they are fundamentally different; there can be no blurring of this basic binary opposition. Some Muslim clerics—for example, in Iran—do permit sex-change operations for people who would be labeled as "transsexual" in Western society, but even that is in a context of affirming fundamental gender differences; this allowance functions as an affirmation of a core "true" gender in the individual.[15]

In Islamic jurisprudence, this understanding of gender grounds various positions on marriage and sexual expression. Sex acts themselves are understood in terms of their legality; they are either legal, if taking place between a man and his wife or female slave, or illegal, in any other context. For a sex act to be legal, it must at least take place within a legally recognized contractual relationship such as marriage. One might be compelled to ask, could sexual acts between two men or two women be *made* legal by letting the two be married? However, in mainstream Islamic jurisprudence, marriage has an inherently gendered quality in that a husband and a wife have distinct roles by virtue of the previously mentioned fundamental gender difference:

> Men are the only ones permitted to be "owners" in this [sexual] sense, and only women may be "owned." . . . The legal structure of Islamic marriage is predicated upon a gender-differentiated allocation of interdependent claims, which would be thrown into chaos by a same-sex union . . . [I]t would not be possible for one woman to adopt the "husband" role and the other to adopt the "wife" role in the marriage of two women. The self-contained logic of the jurisprudential framework does not permit such an outcome.[16]

Furthermore, even the notion of homosexual identities—or, for that matter, heterosexual identities—is essentially foreign to mainstream jurisprudence, which will be a major component of Kugle's arguments. Although some might recognize the possibility of an inherent sexual attraction to the same sex, it does not lead to the recognition of that attraction as a fundamental element of a person's identity, and it does not change the basic position on gender and sexuality.

SCOTT KUGLE'S CHALLENGE

Certainly, mainstream consensus is very powerful and treated as unquestionable. Any argument that there could be a place for same-sex sexuality and relationships in Islam is often regarded as a misguided absurdity, at best, and a heresy worthy of death, at worst. However, a small and recent minority within the Muslim community has begun arguing this very thing, seeking acceptance and validation of their nonheteronormative sexual identities, relationships, and lifestyles *within an Islamic framework*.[17] They are challenging the idea that same-sex sexual acts, including anal sex between men, are forbidden and insisting that the sacred texts have been misinterpreted and mainstream thought has been misguided, offering alternative views in their place. One such project, perhaps the most well-grounded in sacred texts and classical thought, takes place in the writings of Scott Kugle—two essays, in particular.

Kugle is a gay male Muslim scholar from the United States and a convert to Islam.[18] His training includes Quran, Prophetic tradition, and Islamic law, and he is able to read and translate texts in the Arabic, Persian, and Urdu languages. He identifies himself as a progressive Sunni and claims the Hanafi approach to law for its emphasis on rationality. Theologically, he approves of the work of Abu Mansur al-Maturidi for taking a middle ground between extremes of rationalism and dogmatism. Kugle aligns himself philosophically with Ibn Rushd, in terms of using science and reason to guide interpretation, and ethically with Nizam al-Din Awliya, a Sufi whom he reads as balancing justice and love. He specifies all this in the process of indicating his position as a writer and identifying "spiritual ancestors."[19] He positions himself within a Muslim community, both contemporary and historical, and within a gay community, as well. He engages this issue in both communities, in their classical *and* modern elements.

CHALLENGING TRADITION

"Sexuality, Diversity, and Ethics in the Agenda of Progressive Muslims" is the first essay on the subject that Kugle contributed to the edited volume *Progressive Muslims: On Justice, Gender, and Pluralism,* which was written largely in response to the events of September 11, 2001, and sought to express a politically engaged alternative to less progressive aspects of mainstream Islam. Here, Kugle's goal is to delineate the beginnings of an alternative approach to the sacred texts and classical thought that will lead to less heteronormative interpretations of Islam. This is motivated largely by the fact that sexuality has become a contentious issue, both spiritually and politically, among Muslims and has had detrimental effects on women and sexual minorities and his perception of a need for a critical approach to the topic.

Before describing the approach that he is advocating, Kugle outlines some basic background information. He starts by pointing out that Islam, unlike some other religions, generally takes a very positive attitude toward sexuality and sexual behavior, provided that it takes place within a contractually legitimate relationship. Scholars and clerics believe that sexuality has substantial spiritual value, and it is useful for cultivating the relationship between a husband and wife beyond its procreative purposes. He further points out that the Islamic tradition has generally valued diversity, in terms of such factors as tribe, ethnicity, nation, physicality, gender, and disposition; this, Kugle argues, raises the question of whether sexual diversity is also to be valued. He points out that the Quran probably "accepts the existence of diversity in sexuality and sexual orientation" and does not use a distinction between natural and unnatural.[20] He indicates that the Quran itself has no category of sexuality or sexual orientation, so it does not address anyone possessing a certain identity based on sexuality; it speaks, instead, of particular acts and moral attitudes. On this basis, Kugle questions whether one can really say that the Quran takes a negative stand toward homosexuality and homosexual persons, claiming that it is necessary to reevaluate the way the text has been read in the past, taking into account any preexisting prejudices and biases that might have affected this process. Instead, he insists that Muslims need to find new ways of reading the texts, outside of basic heteronormative and patriarchal biases.

Kugle suggests that gay and lesbian Muslims should start to engage in a "sexually-sensitive interpretation" of the Quran[21] that is attentive to social inequality and the oppression of certain people and entails asking critical questions, such as whether the Quran addresses sexual identities, relationships, or acts. He criticizes classical interpretations for analyzing the Quran in a literal, decontextualized manner and suggests that semantic and thematic analyses of the text would be more appropriate—not unlike Fazlur Rahman's approach to interpretation, which will be discussed later. The first, semantic, approach involves examining words in relation to other words to develop a fuller understanding of their meanings, while thematic analysis calls for the interpreter to look at a theme in its entirety, as it appears throughout the text in different contexts, to determine the unity underlying it. Most significantly, Kugle illustrates thematic analysis by offering an alternative interpretation of the story of Lut. He cites, at length, a classical commentary of the verses about Lut that emphasizes their underlying unity and places them in context, and uses this to argue that the sexual acts of Lut's people were significant not in their sexual nature but in their relevance to a broader context of unethical behavior toward others (versus hospitality), the rejection of Lut's prophethood, and a disbelief in God.

He goes on to critique the reasoning behind applying the death penalty to anal sex between men (in the Maliki, Shafi'i, and Hanbali schools of Islamic jurisprudence). Kugle illustrates various weaknesses in that position, such as drawing an analogy between that act and the act of adultery and the inattention to linguistic details regarding the Arabic term for "transgression." Kugle describes the Hanafi position that this act, although sinful, is not analogous to adultery and does not call for the same punishment. Jurists often use *hadith* to justify applying the death penalty to this transgression, but there are no reported cases of the Prophet Muhamad punishing anyone for it. Furthermore, the *hadith* in which he addresses the issue or calls for the death penalty are considered weak and are not present in any of the most authoritative *hadith* collections. In fact, there is a story of his Companions having to deliberate about how to punish someone because there was no Prophetic example. By critiquing both classical jurisprudence and *hadith* scholarship, Kugle undermines the basis for one of the practices that, in the popular mind, has been most emblematic of antihomosexual positions in Islamic thought.

In the place of the mainstream interpretation of the story of Lut, Kugle offers an alternative interpretation, in which the story is ethical rather than legal and emphasizes the role of "hospitality, generosity, and protection of the vulnerable" while prohibiting coercive and oppressive behavior.[22] He takes this into a denunciation of nominally Islamic governments that simultaneously punish homosexuals while protecting rapists (whose victims may be prosecuted for adultery)—as an example of gender injustice. In response to such double standards, Kugle suggests that sexual acts be judged by intention and the relationship, not by gender. Given that many Muslims are already challenging patriarchal norms with regard to gender, he claims it is appropriate to start challenging them on behalf of sexually diverse people as well.

DEVELOPING A POSITIVE ETHOS

In his subsequent essay "Sexual Diversity in Islam" in Volume 5 ("Voices of Change") of the series *Voices of Islam,* Kugle expands upon his claims from the previous essay, reiterating several points while also developing his argument in a new direction. Although he continues the work of challenging traditional interpretations of the sacred texts, he goes into greater detail elaborating *positive* arguments and visions of a different approach, as well. Indeed, he begins by establishing a vision of Islam that embraces diversity as a fundamental aspect of divine creation and necessitates an ethics of respect, compassion, and care for others, using the term "*tawhidic* pluralism."[23] This introduction sets the tone for the rest of the chapter.

After the previously mentioned biographical information, he explains the importance of understanding religious faith through the lenses of both tradition and reason. Lamenting the fact that ideologies of gender inequality have compromised the ethical message of the Quran, he says that this problem needs to be remedied by incorporating modern science and gay and lesbian Muslims' experiences into the process of interpretation. As in the previous essay,[24] Kugle emphasizes the importance of diversity in creation, adding that it has a moral purpose of overcoming egotism and chauvinism and encouraging compassion toward others and protection of the vulnerable; he once again insists this positive assessment of diversity be extended to sexuality, as a part of one's being, and sexual orientation. One particularly central element of his thought is modern psychiatry's conception of homosexuality, in which homosexuality is seen as innate and not subject to change, contrasting this to much of contemporary Muslim thought, which rejects this notion. He insists that a theory of personality is needed and finds inspiration for this in Sufi thought, identifying at least four in the Quran: "outer appearance, inward disposition, genetic pattern, and inner conscience."[25] These will become important in his developing a positive ethos.

He points out that desire and sex are only problematic when done in the wrong spirit or with the wrong intention, and brings this question to bear on the issue of sexual orientation, pointing out that the Quran does not address homosexuals, as we understand the term today. Kugle argues that interpretation should include a concept of sexual orientation—which would arguably promote a different interpretation of the story of Lut, an interpretation that emphasizes hospitable and ethical behavior toward others and forbids oppressive behavior. He further contends that understanding sexual orientation allows one to recognize Quranic references to people that would, today, be called "gay men" and "lesbians." But, the social and scientific factors leading to recognition of sexual orientation in the modern West have not affected mainstream Islamic thought as much, and Kugle sees a need to challenge this thought. Again, using an example of the Companions punishing anal sex between men, he argues that there was no Prophetic example and the justification was flimsy. Similarly, juridical arguments for the death penalty for this act are based upon weak and suspect *hadith*.

Kugle asks whether same-sex sexual acts could be made licit by a legal contract between the partners, in light of the weaknesses of the classical reasoning. To reexamine the issue of homosexuality, he wants to start the discussion with the notions of pairs and partners, which he argues is not limited to opposite-sex pairs. This leads back into his understanding of the four levels of personality, with which "we can understand how sexuality is woven deeply into our nature, regulating the union of self-and-other which shapes us at each level."[26] In this manner, sexuality and sexual orientation inhere deeply in that process.

To this end, such a theory of personality is necessary to interpret the Quran and formulate Islamic law justly. Moral guidelines such as those prescribed in the Quran should be interpreted and applied according to specific realities and the experiences of diverse communities. Kugle emphasizes the role of the sharia "as an ethical framework rather than a code of rules,"[27] and uses those ethics to call for human treatment of Muslim sexual minorities. Moreover, he calls for the development of positive sexual ethics for these minorities and asks "what would 'Islamic' gay and lesbian life be like?"[28] For Kugle, there are general sexual ethics that would simply be extended to same-sex partners: caring, selfless, and loving behavior toward one another, looking out for each others' interests. These would be applicable regardless of the partners' gender. Moreover, according to some Sufi thought, people return to God through various layers of the soul that correspond to the layers of the personality. If the return to God is through the personality, and if a human being's sexuality is part of that return, then he must be allowed to express it. People, including gay and lesbian Muslims, must be able to act in accordance with their natures, and this poses a moral challenge to all Muslims.

ALTERNATIVE APPROACHES TO INTERPRETATION

As suggested by the negative reactions to Scott Kugle and his work, which I described at the beginning of this chapter, it is tempting to read his argument as being nothing more than a strained attempt on his part to make the sacred and classical texts say something other than what they actually mean. The texts are supposedly clear and unambiguous about the issue of homosexuality and the fact of it being forbidden, and any attempt to say otherwise is misguided, at best, and "intellectually dishonest,"[29] at worst. One should not try to reconcile the two, it would seem. However, is this necessarily true?

Many recent scholars have expressed the importance of independent, critical thinking in Islamic scholarship. Kurzman identifies three "liberal" approaches to sharia, defined by him simply as Islamic law; the third approach is called "interpreted sharia," the notion "that the sharia is mediated by human interpretations" and, thus, open to reinterpretation.[30] According to this view, even the most historically accepted and/or orthodox scholarship is open to contestation; moreover, within this type of approach is often the contention that Quran and *hadith* can and must be reinterpreted according to new knowledge and the exigencies of new social contexts. Of all scholars promoting such innovative approaches to interpreting the sacred sources, probably the most influential and successful was Fazlur Rahman.

FAZLUR RAHMAN

According to Rahman, the Quran was revealed to Muhamad in response to the historical situation and unique challenges of the early Muslim community, according to particular timeless values and principles.[31] To interpret the Quran for a particular time, one must determine how the general principles can be applied differently. One must first comprehend the Quran as a unity and its specific pronouncements as responses to particular problems or questions and, then, extrapolate more basic principles and broader moral objectives from the specific ones, understanding their significance within the totality of the Quran. Next, one applies the basic principles in a manner that will actualize the broader moral objectives in the present. Because the Quran, when approached in this manner, is continually interpreted and reinterpreted according to the immediate historical and social context, it remains a source of fresh ideas and inspiration.

Rahman makes a similar argument about the Sunnah. He views *hadith* not as an objectively accurate historical record of what Muhamad said and did but, rather, as a collectively developed understanding of his principles and values. Rahman writes, "although Hadith, *verbally speaking* [italics his], does not go back to the Prophet, its *spirit* certainly does [italics mine]."[32] Therefore, interpreting *hadith* and deriving appropriate practices for the present is similar to interpreting the Quran. One must work backwards from the *hadith* to determine the general principles embodied and the broader objectives sought—recreating and actualizing them in ways appropriate to the present. The Sunna consists not of static legal pronouncements but of contextually specific (if not contextually bound) instantiations of timeless Islamic values and ideals.

RAHMAN'S PROGRESSIVE LEGACY

Fazlur Rahman's approach has become a mainstay of various contemporary and progressive approaches to the Quran and the *hadith*. His approach has become common sense among many current scholars.[33] All are linked by the contention that the Quran, though it is the literal word of God intended for all humanity, was addressed to the specific historical situation of the early Muslims and is best applied today by deriving general principles and applying them in new ways. Two contemporary, progressive scholars who have done this—and are briefly cited by Kugle—are Amina Wadud and Farid Esack.

Muslim feminist scholar Amina Wadud has criticized traditional Quranic interpretation for treating the text in a verse-by-verse manner and failing to confront the inadvertent gendering effects of language and its patriarchal approach, which reads the text through a gendered lens and excludes women as interpreters.[34] Wadud advocates an alternative approach in which the Quran is recognized as a coherent whole and as historically situated, thus making it possible to determine general ethical and moral principles that underlie the text, examine how they were realized in the historical situation, and apply them today in a manner appropriate to the situation. She also interrogates the role of sex/gender, both in the identity of the interpreter, insisting that women must play this role as well, and in the language of the Quran to determine whether grammatically gendered language is likewise restrictive of gendered persons.

Similarly, Farid Esack develops a Quranic liberation theology based upon the South African struggle against apartheid with an approach that is reminiscent of Rahman's, while going further.[35] For Esack, the person who approaches the holy text is inevitably shaped by her personal experience and sociohistorical context, and any interpretation will be similarly shaped by experience and context. No interpretation can be regarded as objective or innocent; on the contrary, it is contextually specific. In a situation of struggle for justice, such as the South African one, meaning and truth are discovered as part of that struggle; Muslims involved in that struggle will inevitably call on the Quran to speak to issues of liberation and justice and elicit new meanings from it. For example, in the South African struggle, it becomes a basis for interreligious cooperation—in stark contrast to other mainstream interpretations that are very unfavorable to non-Muslims.

Rahman, Wadud, and Esack's approaches reflect both a deep reverence for the Quran as a divinely revealed text and a political commitment to equality and social justice. Although the text is meaningful for all times and places, it is not necessarily meaningful in the same way that mainstream interpreters would argue or the same way across various social and historical contexts. Rather, for these scholars and those who follow their lead, the Quran is a repository of timeless moral and ethical principles that are meant to be applied in different ways in accordance with the demands of compassion and justice.

A NEW DIRECTION

Based on this alternative view of holy text, then, it is clear that Scott Kugle is actually doing something more profound that his detractors are willing to grant—much more than simply "looking for scriptural loopholes."[36] In fact, like Rahman, Esack, and Wadud, his approach is intimately bound with sacred texts and classical thought, while also using the social context itself as an interpretive tool. His method places him within this lineage of progressive, modernist, Muslim thinkers.

SYNTHESIZING THE CLASSICAL AND MODERN

Kugle's engagement of modernity is secondary to his *primary* engagement with the sacred and the classical, with the former serving as a springboard for the latter. Specifically, Kugle uses modernity (i.e., modern science, social science, and theoretical and political questions) in order to interrogate the sacred texts and classical thought so that they give new answers, creating a unique synthesis of classical and modern. The synthesis establishes the sacred and the traditional as resources to social justice for lesbian, gay, bisexual, transgender, intersex, and queer (LGBTIQ)

Muslims, to be understood and engaged in new ways instead of explained away; here, neither Islam nor traditional scholarship is necessarily an impediment. What is needed to integrate LGBTIQ Muslims into the broader *ummah* and guarantee their place is already present within the sacred texts and classical thought of Islam, so LGBTIQ Muslims and their supporters must only recognize them as such.

Perhaps the most prominent aspect of modernity that Kugle brings to his endeavor is a modernist conception of sexual orientation—"whether one is attracted to a partner of the same gender or the opposite gender (or perhaps to both and possibly to neither)."[37] He takes an explicitly essentialist view of homosexuality, seeing it as a transhistorical and transcultural reality that is simply called by different names that refer to the same basic thing, and he regards it as a fundamental component of someone's personality and identity. This conceptualization leads him to promote a sexually sensitive interpretation that is attentive to patriarchal and sexual oppression in society and Islamic scholarship and asks critical questions about the places where the Quran seems to address homosexuality or homosexuals. In addition, he lauds the very American and liberal notion of diversity, taken today to indicate a positive evaluation of difference in gender, race, class, sexual orientation, religion, and so on. By affirming a category of sexual orientation and the value of diversity and deriving new questions from those, he calls upon the sacred texts and classical thought in new ways, particularly the Quran, Sufi mysticism, and the Hanafi legal tradition.

Kugle draws different conclusions from the Quran by approaching it through the lenses of diversity and sexual orientation. First, a major theme pervading both writings is the positive valuation of diversity in Islam, in general, and the Quran in particular. This is based upon several verses that he quotes, in which human difference is treated either neutrally or positively. To this, he applies the term diversity, which has a certain resonance in Western discourse, and he discovers in the Quran a voice that echoes this theme and connects it to God Himself with a verse that identifies this difference as a sign from God. Thus, the Quran itself is induced to communicate a message of affirmation of difference, one that takes on a unique valence because of modern concerns with difference as a question of equality and social justice. Kugle demonstrates that the Quran is directly relevant to that question.

Second, he finds in the Quran a recognition of nonheterosexual sexual orientations—an oblique and indirect recognition but a recognition, nonetheless. By bringing a concept of sexual orientation and the findings of modern scientific sexuality research into the task of reading particular verses in the Quran, he finds new possibilities of meanings in those verses. For example, there is a verse mentioning certain men around whom women can relax their modesty, and another in which women who do not reproduce are excused from being modest in the presence of men. Some interpret these verses as referring to elderly men and women, but by including the assumption of a category called "sexual orientation" in his analysis, Kugle is able to identify a possible reference to people who might, today, be identified as gay or lesbian. This further establishes a basis for an authentically Quranic engagement with modern questions of sexual politics and diversity, and when combined with his conclusions about diversity, provides the beginnings of a case for the acceptance of *sexual* diversity in Islam.

Finally, Kugle reasons, if the Quran values diversity, acknowledges different sexual orientations, and perhaps even values sexual diversity, then it makes sense to reinterpret the story of Lut. These assumptions, when brought into the task of interpretation, lead the interpreter to question whether sexual acts were important as sexual or whether the gender of the actors is relevant. For example, this enables him to argue that the primary audience to which the Quran was addressed was heterosexual and that it never addressed homosexual people directly, there being no word in the Quran for such a concept. This enables him to remove homosexuality or certain sex acts as the focus and to take interpretation in a different direction, an ethical one that emphasizes an exhortation to compassion and condemnation of coercion and oppression. This interpretive move is also consonant with Western modernist efforts to challenge negative views of homosexuality to affirm gay and lesbian persons in their sexual difference—as well as progressive Muslim concerns of reading the Quran as a liberatory text.

This alternative view of the Quran sets the stage for interrogating classical thought with a new perspective and finding possibilities in that tradition for affirming gay and lesbian Muslim identities and lifestyles. One way Kugle accomplishes this is by engaging the Sufi tradition while bringing these ideas to bear on his analysis. Taking the given Sufi belief that human beings find their way back to God through the body, personality, and even sexuality itself, he adds the concept of sexual orientation as an innate personality trait and a dimension of divinely created diversity. This enables him to make the claim that being true to one's own nature—including one's sexual orientation—is a necessary precondition for returning to God. Kugle makes the further claim that recognizing the rights of gay and lesbian Muslims is necessary in order to honor this, making some kind of recognition morally obligatory upon *all* Muslims.

Kugle also finds liberatory possibilities for gay and lesbian Muslims in classical theology and jurisprudence. Most notably, he identifies himself with the Hanafi school of jurisprudence. In the first writing, Kugle invokes Hanafi scholarship in order to refute the application of the death penalty to anal sex between men, and it might seem to an outside observer (e.g., a traditional scholar or a non-Muslim reader) that he is only using Hanafi reasoning when it suits his purposes.[38] However, in the second reading, it becomes increasingly clear that something more substantial is going on; Kugle reveals that he values the Hanafi approach because of its emphasis on reason in the process of defining Islamic law, and he argues that, even though this school too regards homosexual sex acts as immoral, the emphasis on reason nonetheless makes it a promising starting place to reinterpret the sharia in accordance with the findings of modern scientific research into sexuality.[39] Similarly, he finds several exemplars in classical thought, such as al-Maturidi and Ibn Rushd, who provide theoretical frameworks that place reason, nature, and revelation in harmony—such that they can produce new conclusions in the present when new knowledge and ideas are brought to bear on the process of interpreting Islam and its sacred texts.

In these ways, Scott Kugle clearly grounds himself in those sacred texts and within the corpus of classical Sunni Islamic thought and Sufi mysticism—simply bringing new concepts and questions to the table. Far from engaging in "conclusion-based hermeneutics" or being "agenda-driven,"[40] Kugle is doing something more complex than any of his critics are giving him credit for. He is asking new questions of the sacred texts and bringing new knowledge to bear in the process of interpretation, validated by his own spiritual ancestors who place a high value on reason, and challenging past scholarship on the grounds of its reasoning and its interpretive approaches. He is synthesizing the modern and the classical in a way that opens the door for gay and lesbian Muslims everywhere to make claims upon their fellow believers and challenge patriarchal and heteronormative ideologies *on Islamic terms.*

THEORETICAL AND POLITICAL CONSEQUENCES

Scott Kugle's arguments, if taken seriously and accepted, have a number of consequences for the continuing debates over homosexuality, on both intellectual and political levels. The most obvious consequence relates to those who would argue that homosexual behavior is prohibited, especially those who insist that it merits a death sentence. Kugle makes *negative* arguments that challenge mainstream interpretations of the story of Lut, critiques juridical reasoning that calls for the death penalty, points out the lack of Prophetic example, and exposes the weakness of certain *hadith*. He also offers *positive* arguments about Quranic valuation of diversity and recognition of different sexual orientations, suggesting that sexual diversity is also to be valued. This places the burden of proof back onto the shoulders of those who argue mainstream positions, making it incumbent upon them to defend the validity of their conclusions.

Also, Yusuf Qaradawi, among others, deems it gravely wrong to call something that is allowed forbidden or vice versa, even equating it to the worst sin, *shirk* (assigning partners to God), and this is a commonly held belief among Islamic scholars.[41] Moreover, it is a severe injustice to apply the death penalty to a crime that does not warrant it. Thus, if there is a possible argument that homosexual behavior is not forbidden and/or does not warrant the death penalty, then people who would say that it is are morally obligated to engage with arguments like Kugle's and successfully refute them before continuing to forbid homosexuality and to call for it to be punished with death. Otherwise, they risk committing a grave sin themselves. Of course, such individuals likely will not engage Kugle, but it only renders their own positions that much more suspect.

Kugle's argument also has important consequences for Muslims who identify as gay, lesbian, or anything outside of heterosexuality. Kugle notes that many of these Muslims leave their faith behind when embracing their sexuality, regarding Islam as "antiquated, oppressive, or hopelessly corrupted by a patriarchal elite," and feeling that it has no place for them.[42] However, Kugle's work here has the benefit of placing gay and lesbian Muslims squarely back into Islam and its sacred texts and traditions, if they desire it. His arguments place them into the overall spectrum of God's creation as a valuable part of its natural diversity, and, by implication, he effectively defines those who persecute gays and lesbians as the true outsiders, for their violation of Islam's basic exhortation to ethically care for others and refrain from oppressive behavior. For LGBTIQ people, acceptance is *within* Islam.

Besides forging a basis for gay and lesbian Muslims to find a place in Islam, Kugle also establishes grounds for them to reclaim Islam's sacred texts and classical thought as their own, as a resource for affirming their dignity and worth and making moral claims upon the broader Muslim community. They do not need to reject the traditions of Islam, explain away the sacred texts, or borrow excessively from modern and Western thought in order to accomplish these goals because they already have the resources they need. Rather than simply being a vehicle for bigotry and homophobia, Islam is reestablished here as a force to contest both of those. "Islam is yours, too," Kugle seems to be saying to gay and lesbian Muslims.

CRITIQUE OF KUGLE'S PROJECT

In spite of the benefits that Kugle's work provides, there are also a number of weak points that merit further attention and suggestions for improvement. One point concerns the majority of Muslims worldwide. Because the belief that Islam forbids homosexual sex acts is so entrenched in the minds of most Muslims, many will not be persuaded differently, irrespective of the quality of his argument. They will likely continue believing that these acts are prohibited regardless. Thus, to reach them and make a case for allowing same-sex sexual acts and marriage, it may be necessary to argue on the grounds of their preexisting beliefs. One way to accomplish this would be through the very logic of Islamic jurisprudence, via a path missing from Kugle's work.

According to Khaled Abou El Fadl, "the purpose of the Sharia in jurisprudential theory is to ensure the welfare of the people;" one aspect of welfare is necessities, and five major necessities are "religion, life, intellect, lineage or honor, and property."[43] In fact, in Islamic legal reasoning, there is the maxim "*al-darurat tubihu al-mahzurat*," which can be translated as "Necessity overrides prohibition" (for example, even though eating pork is forbidden, it is permissible if necessary to prevent starvation). If one recognizes sexual orientation as a fundamental aspect of the personality, which a number of Muslims do, then one might argue that, even if same-sex sexual acts and marriage are technically forbidden, they could be *made permissible* on the grounds of necessity. That is, they could be permissible on the grounds that they are necessary for a homosexual person to live an honest and fulfilling life. Of course, there would be at least two problems with this approach: first, scholars have traditional applied "necessity" only to life-threatening situations; thus, it is questionable whether many Muslims would agree that same-sex sexual relations and relationships are actually necessary, and second, it involves temporarily acceding to the notion that they are forbidden in the first place, which might be unacceptable to many progressive Muslims. Nonetheless, it is a valuable line of reasoning to explore, even as a mere thought experiment.

Also, Kugle's use of a modernist conception of sexual orientation is somewhat questionable on at least two levels. First, it is not at all certain that one can identify what we call homosexuality as something that exists in all times and places, even if there is substantial overlap. In different social and historical contexts, desire and gender themselves may be structured in drastically different ways. For example, in Filipino culture, there are males who are normative in neither gender nor sexuality and who are called "*bakla;*" though this may seem similar to a "gay man," or even a "drag queen," it is not necessarily the same.[44] If concepts like homosexuality and categories like gay men and lesbians are going to be applied across times and places, this must be theoretically justified.

Second, even if one grants that sexual orientation is an inherent component of personality, Kugle's other claims may not follow. For example, would it have any bearing on whether same-sex sexual acts are forbidden? One might argue that, even if someone is gay or lesbian, he or she must still refrain from unlawful acts. Also, claiming that the Quran embraces sexual diversity because it positively evaluates other forms of diversity does not necessarily follow; after all, the Quran clearly condemns some forms of religious diversity—including polytheism, paganism, and according to some, even Judaism and Christianity. So, even if some diversity is Islamically commendable, there is still room to argue that other forms, such as sexual diversity, are not.

Certainly, none of these weak points are fatal errors of any sort. Rather, they are areas that scholars who are interested in cultivating a place for gay and lesbian Muslims must continue to confront if they are to spread their views in the wider Muslim community and be seen as credible.

FUTURE DIRECTIONS

In addition to serving Kugle's own goals on the level of interpretation, his work also leads us in several directions for future intellectual and academic explorations aimed at the goal of achieving social justice for Muslim sexual minorities. These directions are both intellectual and political, and I will briefly suggest two that I find to be the most relevant.

First, there needs to be a set of dual critiques of both Muslim communities and gay and lesbian communities because both perpetuate ideologies and practices that can be damaging to gay and lesbian Muslims. Muslim communities often engage in any number of homophobic and bigoted practices that are harmful—ranging from extremes, like the death penalty and honor killings, to subtler ones, such as discrimination at the mosque, rejection by one's family, or even juvenile homophobic banter in university Muslim Students' Associations. More research needs to be done in order to identify these practices and their consequences and to devise strategies for educating Muslim communities about the needs and welfare of their gay and lesbian members.

Similarly, non-Muslim gay and lesbian communities often harbor subtle racist and antireligious prejudices that can make them seem like nonwelcoming environments to Muslims, and even the process of coming out often involves setting oneself apart from family and community, something that is rarely an acceptable option for Muslims. Moreover, much of gay male culture is pervaded by hypersexuality and alcohol consumption, which is contrary to Islamic values of modesty and moderation. A systemic, Islamically grounded critique is needed to identify such issues in gay and lesbian communities and work toward solutions to make them more hospitable and morally responsible environments for gay and lesbian Muslims.

Another important goal is to develop a more comprehensive political agenda or agendas for gay and lesbian Muslims. This agenda should include support services for gay and lesbian Muslims who are having psychological, spiritual, or familial difficulties; plans for educating mainstream Muslim communities about homosexuality and homosexual persons; public service messages to disseminate in those same communities; ways for gay and lesbian Muslims to participate in mosques and Islamic organizations without having to hide their sexual orientations; better organizing opportunities for Muslim sexual minorities; and ideas for rudimentary activism in Muslim-majority countries, starting with more tolerant ones like Turkey and Tunisia and eventually working toward nations like Pakistan and the Persian Gulf states.

CONCLUDING REMARKS

If nothing else, Scott Kugle's arguments demonstrate that it is rarely either reasonable or prudent to let the persistence of traditional Islamic thought lead us to assume that that is the only possible interpretation of the faith. No matter how long the Quran has been interpreted a certain way, it is always open to reinterpretation, and when someone does this it does not mean that they are "intellectually dishonest" or engaged in "wishful thinking."[45] This would also apply to the interpretation of religious texts in general. Even if one vehemently disagrees with Kugle's methods or conclusions, surely he should be commended for his commitments to intellectual engagement and to justice. Rather than degrading or devaluing the faith, it is this kind of interaction with text and tradition that keeps Islam lively, dynamic, and relevant across time and locale.

NOTES

1. Mere Islam, "The Fons Vitae Ibn 'Ata' Allah al-Iskandari Series." [http://www.mereislam.info/2005/05/fons-vitae-ibn-ata-allah-al-iskandari.html (accessed December 13, 2007; now discontinued).

2. Words like tradition and traditional should be taken to refer to whatever is the most historically normative (allowing for diversity within the normative) within the body of work that Kugle is engaging.

3. Scott Siraj al-Haqq Kugle, "Sexuality, Diversity and Ethics in the Agenda of Progressive Muslims," in *Progressive Muslims: On Justice, Gender, and Pluralism,* ed. Omid Safi (Oxford: Oneworld Publications, 2003), 190–234; Scott Sirajul Haqq Kugle, "Sexual Diversity in Islam," in *Voices of Islam,* vol. 5, *Voices of Change,* ed. Vincent J. Cornell and Omid Safi (London: Praeger, 2007), 131–67.

4. Thomas Sutcliffe, "There's a Lot of It Going On." http://findarticles.com/p/articles/mi_qn4158/is_20060124/ai_n16014404 (accessed December 17, 2007; now discontinued).

5. Though this question will be approached from a different angle when addressing Kugle's biography.

6. However, as the reader will soon see, there are differences among various scholars' positions on same-sex sexual acts, in spite of their agreement that they are immoral.

7. Paula Ettelbrick, "IGLHRC Op-Ed: Holding Iran Accountable for Violating Human Rights." http://www.iglhrc.org/site/iglhrc/section.php?id=5&detail=587 (accessed September 3, 2007; now discontinued). The article can now be accessed via the ukgaynews.org.uk Web site. See http://www.ukgaynews.org.uk/Archive/2005sept/2301.htm (accessed June 6, 2009).

8. "A Student's Guide to Hosting Islamo-Fascism Awareness Week," 2007, http://media.terrorismawareness.org/files/Islamo-Fascmism-Awareness-Week-Guide.html (accessed December 17, 2007).

9. Paul Varnell, "Why Does Israel Look Like Paradise to Gay Palestinians?" *Stand with Us* August 28, 2002, http://www.standwithus.com/pdfs/flyers/why doesIsrael.pdf (accessed September 1, 2007).

10. Kecia Ali, *Sexual Ethics and Islam: Feminist Reflections on Quran, Hadith and Jurisprudence* (Oxford: Oneworld Publications, 2006), 76–77.

11. According to Kecia Ali, the "sexual assault" interpretation is not directly indicated in the text (however, Samar Habib argues that one can infer non-consent because Lut offered up his daughters instead). (Personal communication)

12. Majid Fakhry's translation.

13. Kugle, "Sexuality, Diversity, and Ethics," 219–22.

14. Ali, *Sexual Ethics and Islam,* 91–95.

15. Kecia Ali, personal communication. See also Samar Habib, *Female Homosexuality in the Middle East: Histories and Representations* (New York: Routledge, 2007), 14–15.

16. Ali, *Sexual Ethics and Islam,* 94.

17. Ibid., 78–79.

18. Kugle, "Sexual Diversity in Islam," 132–33

19. Ibid.

20. Kugle, "Sexuality, Diversity, and Ethics," 197.

21. Ibid., 203.

22. Ibid., 224.

23. Kugle, "Sexual Diversity in Islam," 131.

24. Kugle, "Sexuality, Diversity, and Ethics," 195–97.

25. Kugle, "Sexual Diversity in Islam," 137.

26. Ibid., 155.

27. Ibid., 158.

28. Ibid., 159.

29. Mere Islam, "The Fons Vitae."

30. Charles Kurzman, "Liberal Islam and Its Islamic Context," in *Liberal Islam: A Sourcebook,* ed. Charles Kurzman (New York: Oxford University Press, 1998), 16.

31. Fazlur Rahman, *Islam and Modernity: Transformation of an Intellectual Tradition* (Chicago: University of Chicago Press, 1982), 1–11.

32. Fazlur Rahman, *Islamic Methodology in History* (Islamabad: Islamic Research Institute, 1965), 80.

33. Kecia Ali, personal communication.

34. Asma Barlas, "Amina Wadud's Hermeneutics of the Quran: Women Rereading Sacred Texts," in *Modern Muslim Intellectuals and the Quran,* ed. Suha Taji-Farouki. (London: Oxford University Press, 2004), 97–123.

35. Farid Esack, *Quran, Liberation & Pluralism: An Islamic Perspective of Interreligious Solidarity against Oppression* (Oxford: Oneworld Publications, 2002), 1–15.

36. Sutcliffe, "There's a Lot."

37. Kugle, "Sexual Diversity in Islam," 136.

38. Kugle, "Sexuality, diversity, and ethics," 190–234.

39. Kugle, "Sexual Diversity in Islam," 131–67.

40. Mere Islam, "The Fons Vitae."

41. Yusuf al-Qaradawi, *The Lawful and Prohibited in Islam* (al-Halal wal Haram fil Islam). [Translator unknown] http://www.witness-pioneer.org/vil/Books/Q_LP/ (accessed December 17, 2007).

42. Kugle, "Sexuality, Diversity, and Ethics," 195.

43. Khaled Abou El Fadl, "Islam and the Challenge of Democracy," in *Islam and the Challenge of Democracy,* ed. Joshua Cohen and Deborah Chasman (Princeton, NJ: Princeton University Press, 2004), 23–24.

44. Martin F. Manalansan IV, *Global Divas: Filipino Gay Men in the Diaspora* (Durham, NC: Duke University Press, 2003).

45. Sutcliffe, "There's a Lot," and Mere Islam, "The Fons Vitae."

12

NEITHER HOMOPHOBIC NOR (HETERO) SEXUALLY PURE: CONTEXTUALIZING ISLAM'S OBJECTIONS TO SAME-SEX SEXUALITY

Aleardo Zanghellini

The charges leveled against Malaysian opposition leader Anwar Ibrahim in July 2008 are illustrative of the politically motivated uses to which sodomy offenses lend themselves; or at least it seems hard to quarrel with this view, given the timing of Ibrahim's arrest, which followed a period of intensified political engagement and heightened rhetoric on Ibrahim's part and occurred the very year his disqualification from political office came to an end.[1] However, speaking of Ibrahim's arrest merely as an example of the politicization of prohibitions against same-sex sexuality may understate the case. Rather, I think the arrest of a political figure highly respected in the West and even rumored, by his detractors, of being close to Zionist interests needs to be understood in light of a more profound fact about the politics of early 21st-century Western-Muslim relationships. That fact is that homosexuality has become one of the principal battlegrounds over which normative contemporary Western identity and its Muslim counterpart are being enacted and consolidated, following an oppositional logic that bears out less the descriptive accuracy of a rhetoric insisting on the inevitability of the "clash of civilizations,"[2] than its current prescriptive power.[3]

The viability of this us against them logic (which makes no conceptual space to accommodate a multiplicity of Western, Muslim, and Western-Muslim identities) is contingent upon what Judith Butler would call a performative reiteration of identity.[4] In other words, Muslim identity and Western identity—each of which is purported to ground both a certain ontology (a mode of being) and a certain epistemology (a way of knowing the world)—remain, as discursive constructs, always open to failure. The purported irreducibility of one to the other requires continuous reinstatement through appropriate speech acts. But why have so many of those speech acts now come to concentrate on homosexuality? That is, why has homosexuality become so prominent as a discursive field for the ideological construction of Islam and the West as two discrete, homogenous wholes irreducible to each other?[5]

Joseph Massad explains the etiology of this phenomenon essentially by arguing that a Western gay nongovernmental organization's (NGO) mafia-like group—which he calls "the Gay International"—is trying to promote itself, as well as Western modes of same-sex sexuality, on a global scale, through a culturally imperialist project that amounts to an "incitement to discourse" about homosexuality in Muslim countries. He goes on to argue that "[t]he Gay International is aided by two other phenomena accompanying its infiltration into the international public sphere: the spread of AIDS on an international scale . . . and the rise of Islamism in the Arab and Muslim worlds."[6]

Albeit not lacking in insight in its analysis of the problematic nature of the strategies adopted by lesbian, gay, bisexual, transgender, intersex, and queer (LGBTIQ) NGOs, Massad's thesis remains ultimately unpersuasive in its caricaturization of their agenda. Massad's argument is predicated on the dubious premise that Muslim homosexual ontologies are radically different from Western ones (to the point that calling them "homosexual" would be incorrect)—a premise that Samar Habib's recent work makes difficult to maintain.[7] More importantly for the purposes of my argument, while I agree that the rhetoric of what he calls the Gay International may have, more or less unwittingly, contributed to the identity politics game described above, it is implausible to suppose that it could have produced all the "incitement to discourse" that Massad credits it with. If homosexuality has risen to such prominence in discourse about Western and Muslim identities, it is not essentially as a reaction to a Western gay conspiracy aimed at universalizing its epistemology and ontologies. Rather, homosexuality happens to be, for conceptual, demographic, strategic, and historical reasons, a particularly suitable field on which to enact the contest of identity politics.

HIJAB AND HOMOSEXUALS

This contest of identity politics will become clear if we compare the issue of homosexuality with that of the hijab. The latter has, for at least a couple of decades, been one of the crucial issues around which the narrative of Western and Muslim irreducibility has been constructed.[8] However, homosexuality is likely to have begun to supersede the hijab in this role. To begin with, Muslim feminist contributions to the debate on hijab have revealed how ethnocentric and naïve the assumption is that the headscarf is an incontrovertible sign of Islam's barbarism and oppressiveness to women. There is also the fact that the vast majority of Muslim countries do not feature any legal requirement that the hijab be worn; this makes it awkward for Western critics to argue that Islam's essence is all about the oppression of women as exemplified in the denial of their freedom of choice.[9]

More importantly, perhaps, the hijab question suffers from a crucial asymmetry: it has only ever offered a discursive opportunity for Western identity to construct and assert itself in opposition and as superior to Muslim identity, but not the other way around. With women constituting approximately half of the world's population, and feminism having become a significant force to contend with in the intellectual, political, and legal arena, many Muslim women choosing not to wear the headscarf, and centuries of European stigmatization of Islam as misogynistic, as well as Muslims' own sensitivity to that charge (also thanks to Muslim feminist scholarship and work), few Muslims could seriously entertain the idea of discrediting the Western way of life by decrying the scarfless heads of Western women.

In contrast to the headscarf, homosexuality offers a perfect discursive field for the representation of the West as respectful of human rights or, from the perspective of the other side, dysfunctional and decadent, and of Islam as irredeemably oppressive or, from the perspective of the other side, morally wholesome. Why is this so?

Same-sex sexual activity is lawful throughout the West, and in an ever-growing number of Western countries lesbians and gay men enjoy protection from discrimination and an increasing number of family rights. That sexual orientation is a prohibited ground of discrimination is becoming an entrenched principle in international human rights law—a system of normative standards for which the West takes, expressly or implicitly, much of the credit (no doubt aided in this effort by the rhetoric of human rights' Eurocentricity, as expressed throughout the 1990s both by some Western academics and by political leaders in the Global South and developing countries). Indeed, even many conservative voices in the West and, for that matter, the Catholic Church, concede the undesirability of the criminalization of same-sex sexual activity, however much they oppose family rights for lesbians and gay men.[10]

In short, the mainstream Western ethos, far though it may be from accepting the view that lesbians and gay men are fully entitled to the rights accorded to heterosexuals, does subscribe to, and significantly invests in, the view that homosexuality shouldn't be criminalized, and that doing so would be an infringement of fundamental rights.

On the other hand, "Islamic legal thought . . . does not seriously consider the possibility that any same-sex relationships could be lawful" and the "near totality of Muslim thinkers [denies] that homoerotic desire is *innate* and that its satisfaction through lawful means is possible."[11] This view is reflected in the content of the sharia[12] and tends to dominate public discourse about homosexuality.[13] Since the orthodox and official view in the Muslim world is that the sharia is essentially an extension of the fundamental sources of Islam (the Quran and the Sunna of the Prophet), the legal proscription of homosexuality is (mainstream) Islam's own proscription of homosexuality. To put it differently, according to mainstream accounts, the law and (Muslim) morality coincide in the sharia: therefore, according to these accounts, if the sharia condemns homosexuality so does Muslim morality.[14]

The fact that the sharia speaks more strictly with respect to the question of homosexuality than it does with respect to the hijab, coupled with the fact that at least a minimum common denominator of toleration is easily detectable when it comes to Western attitudes toward homosexuality, makes homosexuality a firmer ground on which to enact the contest of identity politics for both Islam and the West.

Another reason why homosexuality provides an ideal arena for the game of identity politics is mundanely demographic in nature. Regardless of how widely practiced same-sex sexual activity may be (and the conventional view is that it has been very widely practiced in Muslim countries),[15] the people who are ready to admit openly to being same-sex attracted, and recognize a *direct* stake in laws or policies that oppress LGBTIQ people, are currently a minority, both outside and inside Muslim states. Targeting homosexuality, then, does not expose mainstream Islam—in terms of sheer numbers—to the same backlash risks that a focus on women's issues such as the hijab has the potential for doing.

Furthermore, while it is true that legal opinion has traditionally discouraged prosecutions for homosexuality on the grounds of the doctrine of overlooking the vices of other fellow Muslims,[16] the fact is that the sharia does condemn homosexuality. From the West's perspective, therefore, it is unlikely that any self-identified LGBTIQ Muslims, or Muslims openly acknowledging same-sex attraction, will stand up to defend mainstream or official Islam's stance on homosexuality in the same way in which Muslim women have proved willing to do with respect to mainstream or official Islam's approach to the issue of the hijab. Therefore, for the West, the charge of a homophobic Islam seems easier to defend than that of a misogynist Islam—it does not have to contend with critiques coming from the parties directly interested.

Finally, while Islam's sensitivity to the charge of misogyny is at least in part, as I have suggested, the result of a historical tradition of Western discourses about Islam's oppressiveness to women, until recently the West has stigmatized Islam not as sexually puritanical and intolerant but rather as sexually licentious, and indeed as catamitically inclined.[17] In this connection, Dror Ze'evi speaks of an "Occidentalist counternarrative" generated by 17th- and 18th-century European travel literature stereotyping the Ottoman Middle East as sexually licentious.[18] This being the case, it is not surprising that the collective unconscious of Muslims would be particularly preoccupied with reclaiming for itself the badge of (hetero)sexual purity and integrity, and that such a preoccupation would have survived the West's belated, and relatively sudden, waking up to the rights of sexual minorities and the attendant change in Western rhetoric about Islam. This too accounts, I would argue, for the centrality of the issue of homosexuality to the contemporary construction of Western and Muslim identities.

Just as the West's self-congratulatory homophilic self-conception calls for careful scrutiny, so it is necessary to undermine mainstream Islam's representation of the West as (homo)sexually decadent. Similarly, we need to challenge, as I shall do in this chapter, mainstream Islam's self-conception as heterosexually pure/purely heterosexual, as well as the Western idea that Islam is inherently and necessarily homophobic. This is not only because the Islamic tradition is capable of being characterized as nonhomophobic and because that characterization does greater justice to, and provides a morally attractive understanding of, Islam. It is also because, if we fail to do so, we become complicit in the identity politics that is at the heart of the troubled relationship between Islam and the West. If the content of Western and Muslim identity is problematized beyond current orthodoxies, the radical irreducibility of one identity to the other is questioned and the tendency to invest one with a value denied to the other is undermined.

In challenging the representation of Islam as inherently homophobic or heterosexually pure/purely heterosexual, this chapter will not focus on whether or not same-sex sexual activity has existed and was de facto tolerated in Islamic societies. De facto tolerance cannot be conclusive of the question of Islam's relation to homosexuality; as Kecia Ali notes, "for contemporary Muslims grappling with same-sex attraction the key question is not: what have (some) Muslims done? but rather: what may Muslims do? or even more generally: what does 'Islam' allow?"[19]

Some progressive Muslim scholars have addressed these questions in recent years. Their arguments tend to center on the Quranic passages relating the story of the Prophet Lot,[20] "which is the constant referent of both classical and contemporary [Islamic] discussions of all same-sex sexual activity."[21] The passages refer to the men who attracted God's punishment when they sought same-sex intercourse with Lot's guests, who were God's Messengers. Progressive scholars have made a "compelling case for understanding the sexual transgressions of Lot's people in a larger context of disbelief and moral turpitude" and they have argued that "the townsfolk's behavior was objectionable not because they sought same-sex intercourse but due to other considerations including their lack of concern for Lot's visitors' consent."[22]

In what follows, I too shall challenge the orthodoxy that Islam objects to homosexuality per se, but I shall pursue a different line of argument. I shall argue that, properly understood, mainstream Islam's preoccupation with same-sex sexual acts has been traditionally limited to same-sex anal penetration, and only to the extent that, quite regardless of the consent or lack thereof of those involved, this was socially intelligible as paradigmatic of practices of subordination.

LIWAT AS ANAL SEX

The people of Lot are described in the Quran as using to "commit foul deeds" (11:78), "exceeding all bounds" (26:166), "commit[ting] this outrage" (27:54), "practis[ing] outrageous acts" and "commit[ting] evils in [their] gatherings" (29:28–29). These references to misdeeds and excess are very generic, and they need to be read in the context of the relevant passages, each of which makes a reference to same-sex desire, describing the people of Lot as "lust[ing] after men rather than women" (7:81), "want[ing]" Lot's male guests rather than his daughters (11:79), "lust[ing] after males and abandon[ing] the wives that God ha[d] created for [them]" (26:165–166), "lust[ing] after men instead of women" (27:55), and "lust[ing] after men [and] waylay[ing] travellers" (29:29).[23]

Since these passages leave unspecified the misdeeds committed by the people of Lot but give the clue that same-sex desire is key to their evil, sinful, or outrageous quality, an outsider might easily infer that the passages effectively proscribe all sexual activity between or among males. S/he might then be surprised to find out that, although contemporary mainstream or conservative commentators do tend to identify *liwat*—the sin of the people of Lot[24]—with homosexuality broadly understood, the classical jurists' discussions on the subject (on which contemporary mainstream or conservative commentators profess to base their opinions), actually tend to identify it specifically with anal intercourse.[25]

Indeed, even some contemporary legal scholars, although speaking of the crime of "homosexuality," actually use it as a synonym for anal intercourse between men rather than in its broader usual sense, testifying that this has been the traditional position within Islam. Yahaya Yunusa Bambale's book on Islamic crimes, for example, explains "homosexuality is a great sin in Islam and . . . arises in a situation when a man engages another man through the anus to satisfy his sexual urge."[26] If this weren't enough to clarify how focused on the specific act of anal intercourse Islamic jurisprudence on same-sex sexuality has traditionally been, Bambale, in a taxonomical move that could not fail to leave Western readers bewildered, goes on to include within the sin of "homosexuality" anal sex between a man and a woman and clarifies that "homosexuality with one's wife is regarded as minor sodomy."[27]

This might leave one under the impression that Islam objects to same-sex anal intercourse *purely* on the basis of the fact that the anus (considered a place of impurity) is involved. Although it is true that, according to Islamic jurisprudence, "in the case of anal sex, the act itself may be an enormity, regardless of who engages in it,"[28] the gender of the participants in an act of anal intercourse is not irrelevant: the crime of the people of Lot involves males lusting after males. Indeed, anal intercourse *between males* provides, even within Bambale's classificatory scheme, the paradigm of anal sex as a sin and a crime—indeed, it has been argued, the paradigm of all perversions and depravities in Islam.[29]

In short, the sort of sexual activity implied in the people of Lot's lustful approach toward other males, that is, the desire to anally penetrate or be penetrated, is as relevant to the proscription of *liwat* as the fact that the object of the penetrator's desire and/or the subject desiring to be penetrated is male. This classical meaning of *liwat* is of great significance to a proper understanding of Islam's relation to homosexuality.

Could it be, however, that in interpreting the story of Lot the classical jurists arbitrarily singled out anal intercourse from the rest of same-sex sexuality in contrast to the intention of the Quran, which, as we have seen, is relatively unspecific about the misdeeds of Lot's townfolk? To draw such a conclusion would be to ignore that the Quran was not revealed in a vacuum. As M.S.A. Abdel Haleem points out:

> An important feature of the Quranic style is that it alludes to events without giving their historical background. Those who heard the Quran at the time of its revelation were fully aware of the circumstances. Later generations of Muslims had to rely on the body of literature explaining the circumstances of the revelation . . . and on explanations and commentaries based on the written and oral records of statements by eyewitnesses.[30]

The point can be extended: the Quran assumed knowledge not only about particular events, but also more generally about the sociocultural conventions of pre-Islamic Arabia and the social context in which the first Muslims functioned. What part of that social context entailed, and some of those sociocultural conventions codified, was a certain understanding about the semantics of same-sex anal intercourse. The Quran's preference for conciseness means that it neither explicitly states that the sin of the people of Lot was anal sex, nor elaborates on the significance of anal intercourse between adult males in pre-Islamic Arabia. There would have been no point: The Quran's 17th-century audience already shared in the sociocultural conventions that signified same-sex anal intercourse in a certain way; thus, there was no need for the Quran to dwell on the reasons why this sexual practice was, given the sociocultural context of the time of the revelation, objectionable.

In identifying *liwat* with same-sex anal intercourse, the classical jurists interpreted the story of Lot more accurately than contemporary Muslim commentators who identify the sin of the people of Lot more generally with "homosexuality." They were able to do so precisely because they shared the understanding of anal sex presupposed by the Quran itself—an understanding that permeated, among others, Mediterranean societies at the time the Quran was revealed.

ANAL SEX AS SUBORDINATION

As a number of studies have now argued, the organization of same-sex desire in ancient Rome and Greece differed in significant ways, but both civilizations subscribed, by and large, to a hierarchical model of male same-sex relationships focused on anal (and, by extension, intercrural) intercourse, where the penetrator had to enjoy higher social status than the penetrated. Thus, it was acceptable for a free citizen to sodomize a slave, but not the other way around. Similarly, if a free adult male allowed himself to be penetrated by another, he attracted social opprobrium; at a minimum he risked becoming the butt of jokes. In other words, a polarity of evaluation invested the penetrator/penetrated dichotomy with the former being valued more highly than the latter. In both cultures, penetration was intelligible as an assertion of the penetrator's virility and dominance at the same time as sanctioning or enacting the subordinate status of the penetrated, effecting or reinforcing his emasculation and submission. This understanding of same-sex activity played out differently in Greece and Rome when it came to man–boy sex. Because in Greece the practice of man–boy sex was contextualized as part of a pedagogical relationship essentially directed at turning a boy into a fully responsible adult male enjoying full citizenship rights, the sexual penetration of boys by their adult lovers was accepted as a normal practice. In Rome, however, for a variety of reasons, pederastic relationships *à la grecque* never really took hold, and a man sodomizing a boy or youth carried with it societal censure, as it amounted to the violation of a free citizen—or at least a potential one, regardless of any issue of consent.[31]

The available evidence suggests that analogous models provided a framework of intelligibility for male same-sex sexual activity in ancient Mesopotamian societies, Egypt and "all the ancient cultures of the Mediterranean basin" (though it is safe to assume that, just as the framework played out differently in Rome and ancient Greece, so it would have manifested itself in variable forms in different places).[32] As Khaled El Rouayheb notes, "[t]he same could more or less be said of contemporary Arab, southern European, or Latin American culture, or, for that matter, the culture of . . . Viking-age Scandinavia, or pre-Meiji Japan."[33] One could add that this understanding of same-sex sexuality remains a distinctive motif in Western discourses about male homosexuality at a variety of levels, including, and especially, that of pornography.[34]

In an essay included in a collection that has been rightly criticized for its marked Orientalist overtones,[35] Arno Schmitt refers to work in psychoanalysis and developmental psychology to explain the prevalence of this model in Southwest Asia and North Africa.[36] His analysis, however, reads as rather crude (partly because of its brevity); likewise, the reflections Schmitt presents under the rubric of "Sociology of Cultural Interaction" appear essentially unsubstantiated. Much more interesting is Schmitt's sociolinguistic analysis.[37]

Albeit unnecessarily polemic, the analysis demonstrates quite convincingly that, despite the relatively recent coinage of Arabic terms translating the concept of "same-sex attracted people" (essentially used only in writing[38] or at most by urbanized elites), the dominant lens through which male same-sex sexuality has been read in Arabic, Turkish, and Farsi is one that "reflects a sharp separation between penetrator and penetratee and a preoccupation with anal intercourse," at the same time as tending to connote the passive partner negatively as not fully a man.[39]

Other analyses (albeit couched partly as critiques of other claims made by Schmitt)[40] mostly confirm Schmitt's conclusions reported here, attesting to the actual, though not necessarily widespread, existence of same-sex sexualities that are not centered on anal sex and the active/passive dichotomy, but on the near absence of a social vocabulary to refer to them.[41] To be sure, Stephen O. Murray was able to identify one Arabic and one Farsi term denoting versatility.[42] This indicates that, however "sharp" the separation of sexual roles may be, it does break down both linguistically and socially (to do him justice, Schmitt does specify that he is "not saying that men never take turns in fucking each other").[43] In this sense, the two terms identified by Murray might be taken to disprove Schmitt's point that "there is no social role of male-wants-to-fuck-male-and-wants-to-get-fucked-by-another-male, neither a tolerated role nor a condemned role, neither a pitied role nor the role of a psychologically ill person, neither

a nonconformist role nor a defiant one of a self-conscious minority—
although we find traces of the latter in medieval folk literature."[44] Nevertheless, it seems clear from a reading of just about all the literature on the
subject that terms designating exclusively active or passive roles provide
the *basic* framework of intelligibility for male same-sex sexuality in Southwest Asia and North Africa. Furthermore, both of the terms denoting versatility identified by Murray clearly emphasize the idea of "taking turns" at
being anally active and passive;[45] in this sense even these terms reinforce,
rather than contradict, Schmitt's point that a sociolinguistic analysis of
Persian, Arabic, and Turkish terms relating to male same-sex sexuality reveal a focus on anal sex.[46]

In sum: there is evidence that a certain framework of intelligibility
(where male same-sex sexual activity is largely reduced to anal sex, anally
penetrating another points to an intact, if not reinforced, masculinity, and
the indignity of being anally penetrated signifies submission or subordination) largely organized same-sex sexuality in the ancient civilizations
of Greece, Rome, the rest of the Mediterranean basin, and Mesopotamia.
There is also evidence of the contemporary currency of that framework
throughout North Africa and Southwest Asia, among others. Indeed, applying that framework of intelligibility helps us make sense of the attitudes
toward same-sex sexuality throughout Islamic history, as revealed by a variety of primary sources from this geographical area.

Ze'evi, for example, discusses manuals on the interpretation of dreams.
In manuals from the very first centuries of Islamic history, "male dreams
of penetrating other partners, male or female, are good omens," although
"homoerotic sex may be good for the penetrated *in certain cases.* For instance, a jailed man who dreams he is the penetrated party in male intercourse will be freed."[47] This might appear to partially disrupt the polarity
of evaluation investing the active/passive dichotomy, but it could just as
easily, and I think more reasonably, be read according to a nonevaluative
penis = key/anus = lock metaphorical imagery; alternatively, it could be
read in the sense that submitting to penetration is a way of humbling oneself and hence atoning for one's misdeeds by acknowledging one's guilt
(assuming that the man has been jailed for a good reason).

In a later Ottoman compilation, dreaming of being penetrated by an
unknown man portends to being vanquished by an enemy, or to caus-
ing damage to one's honor; or, if the penetrator is known to the dreamer,
that they will cooperate to commit something heinous.[48] In the second

scenario, the dream cannot be a good omen for either party, despite the fact that being the penetrator is generally nowhere near as shameful as being penetrated: knowledge of the penetrator and cooperation suggest that sodomy is willed by both parties, but it would be morally repugnant for a man to wish to undergo the humiliation of being penetrated and for his friend or acquaintance to make him undergo such indignity.

Ze'evi also discusses at length Sufi man–boy love practices and the *ulama's* reaction to them during the Ottoman period.[49] An interesting parallel could be drawn between the Sufi celebration of master–disciple relationships and man–boy love in classical Athens on the one hand, and the *ulama's* and Roman condemnation of the practice on the other. In any case, pederasty, especially if an institutionalized practice as in classical Greece, medieval Japan, or, indeed, Sufi Islam during the Ottoman period, makes sense in terms of what Will Roscoe calls "status-differentiated homosexuality."[50] The correlative of the acceptability of man–boy sexuality is the perceived problematic quality of role-noncompliant, status-undifferentiated, male same-sex sexuality. In these contexts, those who (like the majority of the *ulama* or Roman official morality) condemn man–boy sexuality, do so less because they do not share in the understandings surrounding status-differentiated homosexuality than because they are keenly aware of the indignity of being penetrated, which they see as afflicting, albeit in a toned down way, sodomy among social unequals.

Habib's discussion of medieval literature is similarly revealing of the significance of same-sex anal sex in Islamic culture of the time.[51] For example, in a 12th-century work by al-Asfahani, anal penetration is presented by a religious leader caught *in flagrante delicto* as the best way of aggravating an infidel. In another anecdote, a man falsely confesses to having killed a man so as to induce the dead man's friend to punish him by sodomizing him. In yet another example, a bottom answers a top's assertion that he is better by virtue of being closer to the sky with the retort that he is closer to the earth and humbler.[52] While "humble" has positive connotations and the bottom's retort clearly relies on such connotations, ultimately the anecdote makes sense inasmuch as it presupposes that the reader can see that the bottom is humbler less because of his physical proximity to the earth than due to the fact that being sodomized is humiliating. As Habib notes, the literature reveals that Medieval Islamic culture understood same-sex sexuality and desire through a variety of social constructs and ideologies. The second anecdote reported above, for example, attests to a cultural awareness that "what is considered punishment for one man is another man's paradise."[53] Still, this does not displace the dominant cultural understanding surrounding male same-sex sexuality detailed above; after all, in all of the above anecdotes, the pleasure of penetration is articulated through the social vocabulary of aggravation, punishment, and humiliation, even by the penetrated.

Khaled El-Rouayheb also offers ample evidence of the predominance of this cultural mode of intelligibility in the Arab-Islamic world between 1500 and 1800. For example, he reports a 17th century poem in which a Damascene judge defames a contemporary through the violent imagery of penetration (where the object of his derision is, however, presented as a willing receptive partner), while at the same time disclaiming any actual sexual desire to sodomize the man. El-Rouayheb takes the judge's assertions at face value and draws what, to me, is an implausible distinction between sodomy as a practice of, and metaphor for, subordination and sodomy as a sexually pleasurable practice,[54] but this is beside the point— sexually pleasurable or not, the understanding of anal penetration as a form of subordination of the passive partner is clear.

El Rouayheb provides additional evidence supporting the thesis about the hierarchical view of male same-sex sexuality during the Ottoman period. He notes, for instance, that accounts of battles in classical Arabic tend to evoke an imagery of penetration;[55] that a 19th century Egyptian scholar claimed that the sin of the people of Lot "was resurrected after the Islamic conquest of the Middle East" as a form of situational homosexuality when, in an all-male environment, soldiers turned to "native, *subservient* males";[56] and that from the 10th century and well into the Ottoman age, passive sodomy, unlike active sodomy, was rationalized as a pathological condition[57]—for how could a healthy person actively seek an experience that dominant social scripts equated to subordination and degradation?[58]

ANAL SEX AS SUBORDINATION IN PRE-ISLAMIC ARABIA

It is clear that this understanding of male same-sex sexuality (which made anal sex central to it, heavily relied on the distinction between active and passive roles, and subjected those roles to specific value judgments) has been dominant in the central lands of Islam throughout Islamic history;[59] it is more difficult to establish whether a similar understanding had some currency in pre-Islamic Arabia. However, it seems plausible to suppose that it did.

On the one hand, the conceptualization of same-sex sexuality discussed here could well have been an indigenous construct, given that, as El-Rouayheb notes, "[o]ne is clearly dealing with a conceptualization that is very widespread, both geographically and historically."[60] Indeed, one could go further and assert that such a conceptualization has been almost inescapable for any culture. This is, at least, the implication of Bersani's argument that "human bodies are constructed in such a way that it is, or at least has been, almost impossible not to associate mastery and subordination with the experience of our most intense pleasures."[61]

Even without appealing to Bersani's radical claim, the proposition that pre-Islamic Arabia is likely to have subscribed to the conceptualization of same-sex sexuality described above can be plausibly defended. A study of Bedouin honor by Frank Henderson Stewart can be used to give some texture to my conjectures about the currency of the understanding of same-sex anal sex as a practice of subordination in pre-Islamic Arabia (including the settled populations of Mecca and Medina, given that "sedentary people which have come under strong Bedouin influence" tend to share in Bedouin understandings of honor).[62] Stewart's book concentrates on ideas of honor ('ird) among the Bedouins of the central Sinai, that he argues are broadly shared by the Bedouins of Arabia.[63] He also emphasizes that the main difference between those ideas and those of pre-Islamic Bedouins has to do with the fact that the latter "used the word 'ird in a much wider sense."[64] The implication is that, although the reverse is not true, an offence against 'ird for contemporary Bedouins would have also counted as an offence for pre-Islamic Bedouins.[65]

Assuming, therefore, that contemporary understandings of an 'ird offence provide an insight into its pre-Islamic equivalent, the 'ird offence of having sexual relations with a woman who is not one's wife can throw some light on pre-Islamic understandings of same-sex penetrative anal sex. (Unfortunately, Stewart's account does not include a treatment of same-sex sexual activity.) As Stewart explains, this sexual relationship is an offense against the honor of the woman's guardian (her closest adult male agnate),[66] rather than the woman's own honor, because in "societies where honor is important, it tends to be mainly something for men."[67] Stewart also explains (and his remarks here are not confined to Bedouin 'ird) that it is characteristic of sexual honor that, often, the guardian's honor is undermined not only by the man's seduction of the woman, but also by the woman herself, who is seen as having behaved disgracefully.[68] This is, no doubt, because a woman's personal honor, to the extent that she is socially recognized as having any at all, is generally made to coincide with chastity.[69] Finally, Stewart also notes that the offending man, although directly impugning the honor of the woman's guardian, is not acting dishonorably—in other words, his own honor remains intact despite his having acted wrongly.[70]

I want to argue that the structure and inner logic of the offence against *'ird* just discussed makes it plausible to assume that pre-Islamic Arabia shared in the understanding of same-sex anal sex as a practice of subordination. Wherever different-sex intercourse is the normative point of reference for all sexual practices, the association between passive homosexuals and women, and hence their feminization, is inescapable. Yet, if passive male partners make themselves, or are made, women through penetration, and women either "have no honor at all (as among many Bedouin tribes)" or their honor is reducible to chastity,[71] then passive males necessarily lose their honor in the act of penetration.

Here it should be noted that, just as one impugns a woman's guardian's honor by seducing her, so one can damage a man's honor by offending against another male who has put himself under the protection of the former.[72] However, the general rule is that an adult man is his own protector and guardian; hence, a male who penetrates another male is, through penetration, impugning the passive partner's own *'ird*. Drawing out all the implications of the analogy with illicit different-sex intercourse, it can be further argued that the penetrator, although acting wrongly, is not acting dishonorably; that is, his own *'ird* remains untainted, paralleling the view, discussed in this chapter, that anal sex subordinates the passive partner but not the active one. Just as a woman, by succumbing to seduction, may be seen as dishonoring her guardian, so in being penetrated (seduced), a man is acting dishonorably; he is acting in a way that causes him to lose his own honor.

Finally *'ird* is a form of "personal honor." "Personal honor," as Stewart intends it, is the kind of honor that is owed to an equal rather than a superior; for which there is a specific vocabulary; and which requires, in order for it not to be lost, adherence to certain standards of behavior.[73] Stewart points out that it is a distinctive trait of personal honor that the standards one must adhere to in order not to lose it "are viewed as being of central importance in judging a person's worth."[74] To this extent, losing one's honor through anal sex can be meaningfully related to the idea of anal sex as a practice of subordination, that is one that has the effect of impairing the passive partner's personal worth.

Furthermore, if, as Cantarella comes close to implying, the Romans perfected the understanding of anal penetration as a practice of subordination and this may be more than contingently connected with the Roman aggressive political ethos,[75] then it may be more likely than not that a similar conceptualization of same-sex sexuality would be developed by warlike people like the Bedouins of pre-Islamic Arabia. We know, for example, that the Bedouins subscribed to an ethical code (*muruwwa*) often translated as "manliness,"[76] and were focused on ideas of valor in battle and raiding and the satirical denigration of rival tribes,[77] especially through poetry. Admittedly, we lack literary records indicating that references to sodomy were part of the metaphorical repertoire through which such denigration was accomplished, but this may be due simply to the fact that pre-Islamic Bedouin poetic conventions may have ruled out a thematic concentration on same-sex sexuality in any form,[78] unlike Islamic poetry, which, starting with the eighth-century poet Abu Nuwas, has been known both for celebrating man–boy love and for the use of the imagery of an opponent's passive anal penetration as a defamatory tool.

Finally, even if not originally a part of indigenous culture, the conceptualization of same-sex sexuality discussed above might well have penetrated into significant areas of Arabia by the seventh century. As noted above, the civilizations surrounding pre-Islamic Arabia (including the ancient Roman and Mesopotamian cultures) subscribed to this conceptualization; furthermore, the Eastern Roman Empire had some dependencies in the Arabian Peninsula[79] and commercial routes led from southwestern Arabia through Mecca and Medina to Mesopotamia (and beyond).[80]

UNDERSTANDING THE STORY OF LOT AND ITS JURISPRUDENTIAL ELABORATION

An awareness of the symbolic significance of anal sex as a practice of subordination allows us to read Lot's story in a different, and I would argue more accurate, light. The sin of the people of Lot was neither homosexuality (broadly understood in the sense of same-sex attraction/ desire/love/sexuality) nor necessarily rape. Rather, as indeed the classical commentators insisted,[81] it was same-sex anal sex; this was because, at the time of the revelation and for considerable time afterwards, the essential valence of same-sex anal sex (regardless of its consensual or non-consensual nature) was that of enacting relationships of mastery and subordination. The foreign identity of the male Messengers who were approached "lustfully" by the people of Lot may have added poignancy to Lot's story once it is interpreted in this way: according to pre-Islamic Bedouin ethical codes, it appears that foreigners were potential rivals and hence fair game, and the denigration of rivals was not only acceptable but praiseworthy.

I would also argue that this interpretation better fits the text of the Quran than the idea, put forward by contemporary progressive exegetes, that the fundamental sin of the people of Lot was rape—in this case, the rape of messengers who happened to be male. The rape thesis, as Ali has argued, is difficult to maintain in light of the fact that the same-sex quality of the misdeeds of the people of Lot does not appear simply as an accidental aspect of the story, but rather is repeatedly stressed in the relevant Quranic passages.[82] Furthermore, even if the people of Lot's intention to have sex with the Messengers was indeed in disregard of their consent, sura 29:28 refers to Lot reproaching his townfolk for "commit[ting] evil in their gatherings"—a misdeed which reads as separate from, and indeed chronologically prior to, the intended violation of the people of Lot. Given the earlier, emphatic, references to lusting after males in the relevant Quranic passages, the word "gatherings" in sura 29:28 has clear orgiastic undertones,[83] conjuring up scenes of Roman-style same-sex consensual debauchery, rather than rape. One could add that this interpretation—which makes another's subjugation, even if they themselves will it, key to the moral repugnancy of the acts of the people of Lot—accords with fundamental principles of the Islamic faith. In particular it has distinct affinity with the idea that submission is owed to God and God alone (sura 3:19).

The fact that same-sex desire, or same-sex sexuality, more broadly understood, lacked, in and of themselves, the symbolic significance that same-sex anal intercourse had (in terms of enacting relationships of mastery and subordination) explains why, for the medieval jurists, the sin of *liwat* had a narrow meaning: it referred not to all same-sex sexual activity, but only to same-sex anal sex (albeit occasionally extending to different-sex anal sex).[84] Indeed, even the reasons, or at least some of the reasons, they provided when elaborating on the sinfulness of *liwat* make more sense once they are read in light of the conceptualization of anal sex as a practice of subordination. This is true, for example of the frequently voiced claim that *liwat* was "repulsive to 'people of sound character.'"[85] A 17th-century Egyptian scholar elaborated upon this in terms that conceived of passive sodomy as a psychological or physiological pathology and of active sodomy as "subservience to animal desires."[86] According to the conceptualization of male anal intercourse as a practice of subordination, it makes some sense to think of the desire for passive sodomy as pathological (why would anyone healthy desire his own subordination?) and of the desire for active sodomy—a desire to subordinate—as animalistic.

Admittedly, not all of the reasons used by scholars to rationalize the sinfulness of *liwat* can easily be reconciled with the idea that anal sex was conceived of as a practice of subordination (but my argument is not that the jurists always said the correct things about *liwat*; rather, that the conceptualization of anal sex described above helps us make sense of much of what the jurists said, and to show it in its best light, as well as provides us with a more insightful understanding of relevant Quranic passages).

For example, the jurists' argument that *liwat* is bad because it jeopardizes the continuation of the species does not quite square with the idea that *liwat* is objectionable essentially as a practice of subordination. However, in some of its formulations, that argument is couched in terms of reversing the natural order of things and is related to ideas of male disposition toward sexual activity and female sexual passivity;[87] this framework of intelligibility can, in fact, be related to the idea that same-sex anal sex is bad because it subordinates the passive male through the dishonor effected by his "emasculation."

The fact that women were seen by the jurists as "naturally" sexually passive explains perhaps why three of the four Sunni traditions of jurisprudence viewed *liwat* with a male slave, but not intercourse with a female slave, as just as impermissible as *liwat* with a free man.[88] On the one hand, there was always the risk that same-sex *liwat* would be committed with the master as the passive party. On the other hand, the jurists may have thought that, although slavery involves, by definition, a relationship of mastery and subordination, sodomizing a male slave was going too far and amounted to an affront to the slave's humanity because of the special significance that same-sex anal sex had come to assume, whether or not the slave was a willing participant.

An awareness of the conceptualization of same-sex anal sex as a practice of subordination explains why nonpenetrative male same-sex sexual activity—and for a minority of scholars, even gazing at beautiful beardless youths—was considered by the four Sunni schools a minor sin subject to chastisement, rather than a major sin on a par with *liwat*.[89] These acts did not have, in and of themselves, the specially problematic quality of anal intercourse in terms of their social intelligibility as practices of subordination: however, those who engaged in them were on a slippery slope to committing *liwat,* and hence the acts needed proscribing in their own right because they might lead one into temptation.[90]

Finally, the fact that the penetrative-anal-sex-as-subordination rationale is inapplicable to female same-sex grinding[91] may explain why this activity was generally regarded as not requiring legal punishment[92] (however much it may have been condemned by appealing to *hadith,* often of dubious authenticity, in which the Prophet had directly or obliquely spoken against it).[93] Grinding tended to be considered a sin of minor gravity than either *liwat* or heterosexual fornication (*zina*),[94] which, on the contrary, were normally treated jointly as the sexual crimes of greatest gravity,[95] with *liwat* generally seen as the worse.[96]

IMPLICATIONS AND CONCLUSIONS

An awareness of the special meaning attached to same-sex anal intercourse assists our interpretation of the Quran, throwing light on relevant passages dealing with same-sex sexuality. Such an awareness provides us with an understanding that is more satisfactory than either the interpretation that the Quran opposes homosexuality broadly understood, or that the story of the people of Lot is really about the badness of rape. Similarly, it helps us make sense of much of what Islamic legal and other scholars have had to say about same-sex sexuality in past centuries.

From the fact that both relevant Quranic passages and legal scholarship can be understood in light of the framework of intelligibility that associates same-sex anal sex with practices of subordination, it does not necessarily follow that those passages ineluctably generate those scholarly positions via the medium of that shared framework of intelligibility. In other words, classical and Ottoman-period scholars have not always, or even frequently, drawn the correct conclusions when interpreting the story of Lot. For example, it may have been a keen sense of the significance of same-sex sodomy as a practice of subordination that led the Maliki, Hanbali, and Shafi schools of law to regard *liwat* as a serious crime subject to *hadd* (punishment) even where the Quran does not prescribe a punishment for it; but the schools' conclusion runs counter to the general principle that a *hadd* crime is, by definition, one for which the Quran prescribes a preestablished punishment. Similarly, as I argued, the same keen sense of the problematic nature of anal sex may well account for the jurists' arguments that nonpenetrative same-sex sexual activity is a minor crime subject to discretionary punishment; but the basis for finding these activities reprehensible at all is extremely weak—by its very nature, the "temptation" argument precludes a reasonable assessment of the interests and values at stake, thus disabling a conscientious employment of *ijtihad*.

Indeed, I would argue that, while the story of the people of Lot reveals the Quran's condemnation of nonegalitarian sexual activity—whether consensual or nonconsensual—and illustrates this condemnation through the case of same-sex sodomy, which at the time was widely and predominantly intelligible as a practice of subordination, it is fatally flawed to conclude that same-sex sodomy—let alone other forms of consensual same-sex sexual activity—should be legally proscribed. For a start, the Quran does not object to same-sex sodomy in itself, but only inasmuch as it is engaged in as an inegalitarian sexual practice. Whereas at the time of the revelation and during the centuries that followed it, a near universally shared semantics of same-sex anal intercourse might have made it relatively unproblematic for this sexual activity to stand as a paradigm of inegalitarian sex, this is clearly no longer the case—not even where that traditional conceptualization of anal sex remains prevalent, and despite the fact that it may remain ubiquitously relevant.

Furthermore, there is no way for one to be reasonably certain about whether two consenting others are engaging in same-sex penetrative anal intercourse as a practice of subordination or not: an "asymmetrical" sexual practice may appear inegalitarian to an observer while carrying no such connotation for those who participate in it. In light of these considerations, the fact that the Quran refrains from prescribing *hadd* (a preestablished punishment) can be taken to indicate, in the specific case of *liwat*, that it is inappropriate to punish it by law at all. On the reading proposed here, the story of Lot makes it clear that inegalitarian sex—even if consensual—is morally reprehensible, while at the same time clearly implying that consensual sex—even if apparently inegalitarian—should not be prohibited or punished by law. The last point applies *a fortiori* to consensual same-sex sexual activities (such as grinding or nonpenetrative male same-sex sex) that not even historically were clearly intelligible as practices of subordination.

NOTES

1. Anon., "Malaysia's Opposition Leader Anwar Ibrahim Arrested," *ABC Radio Australia* July 16, 2008, http://www.radioaustralia.net.au/news/stories/200807/ s2305621.htm (accessed January 21, 2009).

2. Samuel P. Huntington, *The Clash of Civilizations and the Remaking of the World Order* (New York: Simon & Schuster, 1996).

3. Edward W. Said, "The Clash of Ignorance," *The Nation,* October 4, 2001; Amartya Sen, *Identity and Violence: The Illusion of Destiny* (New York: W. W. Norton & Company, 2006).

4. Judith Butler, *Gender Trouble: Feminism and the Subversion of Identity* (New York: Routledge, 1990).

5. It may be impossible to "prove" that homosexuality has acquired the central status I claim for it in discourse about normative Muslim and Western identities; but assuming that the Internet is a rough barometer of the topicality of certain issues, one can come up with some interesting figures. If, for instance, one Googles the word "Islam" coupled first with "headscarf," then with "scarf," and finally with "*hijab,*" and eliminates the effect of any double counting, one gets approximately 1,629,700 hits in total. If, however, one Googles "Islam" with, respectively, "lesbian," "homosexuality," and "gay" and, once again, avoids any double counting, one will come up with a total figure of 11,820,000 hits! The fact that the term "gay" has come into common use in many languages might artificially inflate the search results; therefore, I have limited the "Islam AND gay" search to English language pages.

6. Joseph Massad, "Re-Orienting Desire: The Gay International and the Arab World," *Public Culture* 14, no. 2 (2002): 361, 374.

7. Samar Habib, *Female Homosexuality in the Middle East: Histories and Representations* (New York: Routledge, 2007).

8. Joan Wallach Scott, *The Politics of the Veil* (Princeton, NJ: Princeton University Press, 2007).

9. A critic bent on proving the superiority of the Western way of life by relying on the issue of the hijab would then have to argue along either of two lines. He could say that women who wear the headscarf are de facto, even if not legally, forced to wear it, but this would be an unconvincing argument, for the conceptual inseparability of sharia and morality from within mainstream Islam's own point of view means that mainstream Islam cannot sanction social compulsion in the absence of a legal requirement, and hence that any de facto coercion to wear the headscarf could not be imputed to a distinctively *Islamic* way of life. Alternatively,

the critic could argue that women who wear the hijab have been socially conditioned to do so and that Islam is responsible for creating the climate in which such social conditioning occurs, but this is a false consciousness argument and accepting it opens the door to applying such arguments also in the Western context, which is just what Muslims have done when they argued that Western women's attire shows they are socially conditioned into being sexually objectified. This undermines the West's own claim to superiority, which relies on an unproblematic idea of free choice as the cornerstone of Western identity—an idea that is imperiled if any conceptual space is made for the notion of false consciousness.

10. John Finnis, "Law, Morality and 'Sexual Orientation,'" *Notre Dame Journal of Law, Ethics & Public Policy* 9 (1995): 11–39; Joseph Card. Ratzinger and Angelo Amato, SDB, "Considerations Regarding Proposals to Give Legal Recognition to Unions between Homosexual Persons," *Congregation for the Doctrine of the Faith* n.d., http://www.vatican.va/roman_curia/congregations/cfaith/documents/rc_con_cfaith_doc_20030731_homosexual-unions_en.html (accessed January 21, 2009). Of course, the West does have its own Christian fundamentalists who would happily criminalize gay and lesbian sex, but they appears to be, currently, a marginal position—they represent neither the official stance of state authorities nor that of mainstream society. Interestingly, this sort of Christian fundamentalism inverts the terms of the identity politics game, stigmatizing Islam first and foremost as rampantly homosexual. (See, for example, "Islam: Religion of Homosexuality?" Shelley the Republican, http://www.shelleytherepublican.com/2008/04/24/islam-religion-of-homosexuality.aspx (accessed January 21, 2009).

11. Kecia Ali, *Sexual Ethics & Islam: Feminist Reflections on Quran, Hadith, and Jurisprudence* (Oxford: Oneworld, 2006), 81, 90.

12. Note that, in Arab-Muslim countries, the legal provisions prohibiting homosexuality that are practically enforceable (albeit not necessarily frequently enforced) owe their content as much to colonial influences as to sharia. Brian Whitaker, *Unspeakable Love: Gay and Lesbian Life in the Middle East* (London: Saqi, 2006), 122–23, 139.

13. For example, IslamOnline.net, one of the largest and most prominent Web sites devoted to Islam, states unequivocally in a number of fatawa that Islam condemns homosexuality as a grave sin and heinous crime. The Web site presents itself as mainstream; two of its policies being "adopting the middle ground of Islam, avoiding extremism or negligence, rejecting deviant or eccentric opinions" and "striving for accuracy, adopting neutrality and avoiding pre-judgments and preconceptions." Brian Whitaker argues that, although Yusuf-al-Qaradawi, the head of the scholarly committee that scrutinizes the Web site content, "is often described as an extremist in the West . . . [i]n the Arab world . . . he is regarded as relatively moderate." Whitaker, *Unspeakable Love,* 146.

14. The proposition that homosexuality is thus un-Islamic has also led some—most recently and notoriously, the president of Iran at Columbia Law School—to argue that it is quintessentially Western in the sense that it all but fails to occur in the Muslim world.

15. Abdelwahab Bouhdiba, *Sexuality in Islam,* trans. Alan Sheridan (London: Routledge, 1985), 200.

16. Khaled el-Rouayheb, *Before Homosexuality in the Arab-Islamic World, 1500–1800* (Chicago: University of Chicago Press, 2005), 123; Ali, *Sexual Ethics & Islam,* 85.

17. Scott Siraj al-Haqq Kugle, "Sexuality, Diversity, and Ethics in the Agenda of Progressive Muslims," in *Progressive Muslims: On Justice, Gender, and Pluralism,* ed. Omid Safi (Oxford: Oneworld, 2003), 190–234, 198; Joseph Massad, "Re-Orienting Desire," 361–85.

18. Dror Ze'evi, *Producing Desire: Changing Sexual Discourse in the Ottoman Middle East, 1500–1900* (Berkeley: University of California Press, 2006), 168–69.

19. Ali, *Sexual Ethics & Islam,* 80.

20. Suras 7:80–84, 11:77–83, 26:160–73, 27:54–58, 29:28–35. It is rather more controversial whether another passage, which I won't discuss here (sura 4:15–16), deals with same-sex sexuality; Habib, *Female Homosexuality in the Middle East,* 60–61; Ali, *Sexual Ethics & Islam,* 81; el-Rouayheb, *Before Homosexuality in the Arab-Islamic World,* 122.

21. Ali, *Sexual Ethics & Islam,* 82.

22. Ibid., 83.

23. Here, and in the rest of the chapter, I rely on the following English translation: *The Quran,* trans. M.A.S. Abdel Haleem (Oxford: Oxford University Press, 2004).

24. On the etymology of *liwat,* see Charles Pellat, "*Liwat,*" in *Sexuality and Eroticism among Males in Moslem Societies,* ed. Arno Schmitt and Jehoeda Sofer (New York: Haworth Press, 1992), 151–68, 151.

25. el-Rouayheb, *Before Homosexuality in the Arab-Islamic World,* 125. This difference between contemporary mainstream or conservative scholarship and classical scholarship on *liwat* is ironic, given that one of the standard rhetorical strategies used by the former to discredit contemporary progressive Muslims is to argue that their accounts of Islam fail because their authors are not conversant and fail to engage with classical Islamic scholarship.

26. Yahaya Yunusa Bambale, *Crimes and Punishments under Islamic Law* (Ibadan, Nigeria: Malthouse Press, 2003), 40.

27. Ibid., 40 and 42.

28. Ali, *Sexual Ethics & Islam,* 77.

29. Bouhdiba, *Sexuality in Islam,* 31.

30. M.A.S. Abdel Haleem, "Introduction" to the *Quran*, trans. M.A.S. Abdel Haleem (Oxford: Oxford University Press, 2004), ix–xxxvi, xii.

31. Eva Cantarella, *Bisexuality in the Ancient World* (New Haven, CT: Yale University Press, 2002); David M. Halperin, *One Hundred Years of Homosexuality: And Other Essays on Greek Love* (New York: Routledge, 1990); Craig A. Williams, *Roman Homosexuality: Ideologies of Masculinity in Classical Antiquity* (Oxford: Oxford University Press, 1999).

32. Will Roscoe, "Precursors of Islamic Male Homosexualities," in *Islamic Homosexualities: Culture, History, and Literature,* ed. Stephen O. Murray and Will Roscoe (New York: New York University Press, 1997), 55–86, 61, 62.

33. el-Rouayheb, *Before Homosexuality in the Arab-Islamic World,* 22.

34. John Stoltenberg, "Gays and the Propornography Movements: Having the Hots for Sex Discrimination," in *Men Confronting Pornography,* ed. Michael S. Kimmel (New York: Crown Publishers, 1990) 248–62; Christopher N. Kendall, "Gay Male Pornography after *Little Sisters Book and Art Emporium:* A Call for Gay Male Cooperation in the Struggle for Sex Equality," *Wisconsin Women's Law Journal* 12 (1997): 21.

35. Massad, "Re-Orienting Desire," 365–67.

36. Arno Schmitt, "Different Approaches to Male-Male Sexuality/Eroticism from Morocco to Usbekistan," in *Sexuality and Eroticism among Males in Moslem Societies,* ed. Arno Schmitt and Jehoeda Sofer, 1–24, 2–3 (New York: Haworth Press, 1992).

37. Ibid., 8–13.

38. el-Rouayheb, *Before Homosexuality in the Arab-Islamic World,* 161.

39. Arno Schmitt, "Different Approaches to Male-Male Sexuality/Eroticism," 12, 13.

40. Stephen O. Murray, "Islamic Accommodations of Male Homosexuality," in *Islamic Homosexualities: Culture, History, and Literature,* ed. Stephen O. Murray and Will Roscoe (New York: New York University Press, 1997), 14–54, 29.

41. Ibid., 29–31, 34–35. The South-Asian term *"gandu,"* which can be applied to active as well as passive partners in anal intercourse seems initially to disrupt the neatness of the argument, but the analysis of the term provided in Murray's essay actually reveals that the penetrator/penetrated dichotomy, together with the polarity of evaluation that invests it, remains intact: "Many insertees grow up to become insertors, so the label must incorporate a certain flexibility so as not to besmirch the reputation of a boy destined to become an insertive man." Badruddin Khan, cited in Ibid., 30.

42. Ibid., 34.

43. Schmitt, "Different Approaches to Male-Male Sexuality/Eroticism from Morocco to Usbekistan," in *Sexuality and Eroticism among Males in Moslem*

Societies, ed. Arno Schmitt and Jehoeda Sofer (New York: Haworth Press, 1992), 1–24, 6.

44. Schmitt, "Different Approaches to Male-Male Sexuality/Eroticism," 6.

45. Murray, "Islamic Accommodations of Male Homosexuality," 34.

46. The prevalence of "top/bottom" terminology within Anglophone Western gay sexual cultures (especially, perhaps, North American ones) suggests a similar preoccupation with sexual roles and anal sex; however, the widespread use of terms such as "gay" and "homosexual" or even "queer"—which tends to be the terminology used in public discourse about homosexuality—does reveal the existence and even dominance of a different conceptual framework accounting for a different order of intelligibility of same-sex sexuality.

47. Ze'evi, *Producing Desire,* 118 (emphasis added).

48. Ibid., 120.

49. Ibid., 77–98.

50. Roscoe, "Precursors of Islamic Male Homosexualities," 56.

51. Habib, *Female Homosexuality in the Middle East,* 48–55.

52. Ibid., 49–50.

53. Ibid., 48.

54. el-Rouayheb, *Before Homosexuality in the Arab-Islamic World,* 14.

55. Ibid., 15.

56. Ibid., 17 (emphasis added)

57. Ibid., 19–20.

58. It is important to note that none of the above takes a stand in the debate about whether Islamic same-sex sexuality was only conceptualized in terms of acts or whether it made any room for identities, behavioral inclinations, and psychological orientations. While the most accurate view seems to be the latter (Habib, *Female Homosexuality in the Middle East,* 48), the point need not be resolved for the purposes of this discussion, whose sole concern is to demonstrate the prevalence of a certain understanding of male same-sex sexuality in the central lands of Islam throughout Islamic history.

59. Independent scholar Armstrong-Ingram makes essentially the same point in a paper available on the Internet, where he considers the discussion of illicit sexuality in the Kitab-i-Aqdas—the "Mother-Book" of teachings of the Bahá'í faith. Since the language of revelation of the Bahá'í faith was Arabic, this uses the term *liwat* and builds on understandings thereof derived from Islam and based on Middle Eastern socio-cultural practices. Although the paper, unfortunately, does not include references, it is worth quoting:

"The Mediterranean emphasis on intromissive ejaculation is associated with an instrumental attitude toward sexual activity. A man *does* sex to another person for his own pleasure, to prove his masculinity . . . The essentially aggressive nature of *liwat* can be seen in the tradition of dabib, or 'crawling,' where sexual access to another individual is gained through getting him drunk or drugging him and then perpetrating liwat while he is unconscious . . . That *liwat* is conceptualised first and foremost as exemplifying dominance can be seen in the mainstream Saudi legal opinion that a non-Muslim who perpetrates *liwat* on a Muslim must always be put to death . . . Liwat does not encompass fellatio or mutual masturbation. The latter is common in the Middle East but generally considered simply one of those things young men do that does not need to be acknowledged or discussed . . . Although egalitarian relationships between pairs of adult men that involved mutual sexual activity have not been unknown in Middle Eastern societies, there was no specific term to cover such liaisons before recent decades. They fell outside regular sociocultural categories, and they were not subsumable under *liwat*." R Jackson Armstrong-Ingram, "The Provisions for Sexuality in the Kitab-i-Aqdas in the Context of Late Nineteenth Century Eastern and Western Sexual Ideologies," 1996, http://bahai-library.com/conferences/sex.aqdas.html (accessed January 21, 2009).

60. el-Rouayheb, 22.

61. Leo Bersani, "Is the Rectum a Grave?," *AIDS: Cultural Analysis / Cultural Activism* 43 (1987): 197, 216.

62. Frank Henderson Stewart, *Honor* (Chicago: The University of Chicago Press, 1994), 102.

63. Ibid.

64. Ibid., 103.

65. Ibid.

66. Ibid., 82.

67. Ibid., 107.

68. Ibid., 109.

69. Ibid., 107.

70. Ibid., 83.

71. Ibid., 107.

72. Ibid., 96.

73. Ibid., 54–58.

74. Ibid., 146.

75. Cantarella, *Bisexuality in the Ancient World,* 217.

76. Irving M Zeitlin, *The Historical Muhammad* (Cambridge: Polity, 2007), 20.

77. Julie Scott Meisami and Paul Starkey, *Encyclopedia of Arabic Literature* (London: Taylor and Francis, 1998), 146.

78. Ibid., 547.

79. Irving M. Zeitlin, *The Historical Muhammad* (Cambridge: Polity, 2007), 50.

80. Ibid., 25.

81. Kugle, "Sexuality, Diversity, and Ethics," 204, 216; el-Rouayheb, *Before Homosexuality in the Arab-Islamic World,* 125, 137.

82. Ali, *Sexual Ethics & Islam,* 83.

83. But see Kugle, "Sexuality, Diversity, and Ethics," 211.

84. el-Rouayheb, *Before Homosexuality in the Arab-Islamic World,* 131.

85. Ibid., 127.

86. Ibid., 128.

87. Ibid., 129.

88. Ibid., 124.

89. Ibid., 111–18, 137–38.

90. Ze'evi, *Producing Desire,* 90.

91. As Habib explains, the original term for female same-sex sexual activity in Arabic is *Suhaq,* which literally translates the idea of "grinding" (as in the grinding of peppercorns), used as a metaphor for non-penetrative external genital stimulation, seen, according to patriarchal scripts, as the only plausible sexual activity between two women. Habib, *Female Homosexuality in the Middle East,* 17–18.

92. el-Rouayheb, *Before Homosexuality in the Arab-Islamic World,* 137.

93. Habib, *Female Homosexuality in the Middle East,* 59–60.

94. Ze'evi, *Producing Desire,* 55; Habib, *Female Homosexuality in the Middle East,* 59.

95. Ali, *Sexual Ethics & Islam,* 75–76.

96. el-Rouayheb, *Before Homosexuality in the Arab-Islamic World,* 126.

13

‒‒‒◆‒‒‒

IMPLIED CASES FOR MUSLIM
SAME-SEX UNIONS

Junaid Bin Jahangir

Surely it is the nature and quality of a relationship that matters: one must not judge it by its outward appearance but by its inner worth. Homosexual affection can be as selfless as heterosexual affection, and therefore we cannot see that it is in some way morally worse. . . . Homosexual affection may of course be an emotion which some find aesthetically disgusting, but one cannot base Christian morality on a capacity for disgust.

—*The 1963 Quaker statement*

Concerning contemporary homosexuality, are we Moslems reading the holy verses and Hadith in a way that calls upon all our knowledge and spiritual resources? Putting aside extreme penalties, mainstream Muslim opinions on the subject of how our communities should deal with homosexuality are made up of counseling reparative therapy and marriage or prescribing celibacy. Neither scientific consensus nor human suffering seems to have motivated a re-evaluation of the Muslim scriptures. While inter-sexuals have been accommodated by the highest of both Sunni and Shia scholarly bodies, gays and lesbians continue to be viewed as having made a deliberate morally wrong choice.

Some contemporary scholarly works challenge long-held mainstream opinions. Siraj Kugle[1] questions the traditional interpretation of the

Quranic passages on the "People of Lot," by drawing on the Qisas al Anbiya texts to understand the story as that of greed, rape, and coercion.
Amreen Jamal[2] employs semantic analysis to indicate that each key Arabic
word that occurs in the Quranic passages on the People of Lot has multiple meanings and therefore the entire story can be understood alternatively. Both these seminal works echo the approach indicated by Rabbi
Gershom Barnard,[3] who stated that for change in Conservative Judaism
on the issue, the paradigm needs to be changed such that the same material may be looked at in a different way, like drawings that one may see
either as a vase or as two people looking at each other.

While mainstream Judaism has sanctioned same-sex unions and
blessed gay Rabbis, no change has occurred in the case of mainstream
Islam, despite the voices raised by Imams like Mohsin Hendricks[4] and
Daayiee Abdullah,[5] writers like Faris Malik[6] and Pamela Taylor,[7] scholars like Ghazala Anwar[8] and Farid Esack,[9] and more recently Siti Musdah
Mulia.[10] Perhaps the reason behind all these heroic efforts, with the exception of the articles by Pamela Taylor, is that the case for same-sex unions
is not placed within the framework of traditional Islamic jurisprudence.
Opening a dialogue with the mainstream Muslim community and scholars requires a concerted effort to exhaustively address the relevant *hadith*
and jurisprudential literature on the subject. Mainstream scholars need to
be engaged in their jargon despite the fact that contemporary writers and
scholars are not confined by the traditional texts.

This chapter attempts to fill this lacuna in the literature by comprehen-
sively addressing the scriptural texts and establishing the case for Muslim same-sex unions based on Islamic jurisprudence. The chapter begins
by delineating current mainstream Muslim opinions on the subject and
the subsequent consequences of the intransigence of the general Muslim
community. Two fundamental misconceptions that bias the reading of
the scriptural texts are addressed followed by a comprehensive analysis
of the relevant Quranic passages and *hadith* literature. Having established the silence of the scriptures on the issue, and based on the rules
of Islamic jurisprudence, three cases are derived for Muslim same-sex
unions. More specifically, it is stated that the case for Muslim same-sex
unions can be made through the jurisprudential treatment of marriage,
intersexuality, and necessity. An attempt is also made to delineate the
evolution of positive Muslim thought on the subject and it is concluded
that the case for same-sex unions is only an extension of that evolution.

CURRENT MAINSTREAM MUSLIM OPINIONS

Most scholars, including those who espouse democracy and human rights, will cite the Quranic passages on the destruction of the people of Lot to substantiate their claim that homosexuality is unnatural, a perversion, and a deliberate, morally evil choice.[11] Homosexuality is considered a crime in the same manner as adultery and murder. For instance, the scholar Dr. Muzammil Siddiqi, former president of the Islamic Society of North America, while having received the Humanitarian of the Year Award in 1999 from the National Council of Christians and Jews, states:[12]

> Homosexuality is a moral disorder. It is a moral disease, a sin and corruption . . . No person is born homosexual, just like no one is born a thief, a liar, or murderer. People acquire these evil habits due to a lack of proper guidance and education.

Perhaps the reason behind such strong opinions lies in the inability to understand both homosexuality and the Quranic passages that are purported to address it. For instance, writer Dr. Abu Ameenah Bilal Philips states:[13]

> Islam considers homosexuality to be the result of a choice. It is inconceivable that God made people homosexuals then declared it a crime and prescribed punishments for it in both this life and the next. To accept such a proposition is to accept that God is unjust.

Other writers would equate homosexuality with bestiality and pederasty[14] or as an outcome of promiscuous Western societies.[15] The constellation of Muslim scholars and writers at the popular Muslim Web site islamonline.net paraphrase similar strong opinions, and while they are strictly against capital punishment for homosexuals, they do preach a strong social ostracism of gays and lesbians.[16] Furthermore, through the articles of Dr. Nadia El-Awady, the scientific and expert studies conducted by the National Association for Research and Therapy of Homosexuality (NARTH) are heavily cited.[17] It also appears to be the case that, just like the opinions of the experts at NARTH, Muslim scholars have a strict focus on male homosexuals and anal sex, for instance, when Dr. Yusuf Qaradawi states that "Lesbianism is not as bad as homosexuality, in practical terms."[18]

Other scholars, considered moderates, will perhaps claim that even the innateness of homosexuality does not provide the license of its sanctioning and, in fact homosexuality must be considered as part of the grand scheme of the trial of life wherein each person works with a set of problems that have fallen in his or her lot. Just like the blind, the crippled, the mute, and the ones suffering with chronic diseases, a homosexual is undergoing a similar form of trial (i.e., that of patience).[19] In short, while there may be a difference of contemporary mainstream scholarly opinion from some of the traditional opinions on issues such as the head cover (hijab), women leading prayers, the charging of interest, blasphemy, apostasy, testimonial, and inheritance laws, there is not a single mainstream opinion that calls for a reevaluation of the long cherished stand on gays and lesbians, let alone that which sanctions same-sex unions. The opinions of the over-whelming majority of the Muslim masses are no different from those of the scholars.[20]

Technically speaking, many of the contemporary voices above would not support the execution of homosexuals. In fact, even Imams like Rexhep Idrizi who have called for homosexual beheadings during sermons paradoxically state that they are against killings.[21] However, Bishop John Shelby Spong states:[22]

> Words shape consciousness and therefore words have consequences. When religious voices claim to speak for Christ suggest in their prejudiced igno-rance that homosexual people are sinful, abnormal, unclean or subhuman, we do nothing less than to sow the seeds that are used to justify hate, and even murder.

It is, therefore, a consequence of the verbal assault led by scholars and the Muslim masses that one reads of cases of excommunication,[23] verbal threat,[24] bullying,[25] physical abuse,[26] and even suicide.[27] In fact, one may note that the verbal assault on gays and lesbians seems to have a back-ground in Muslim history when the Sunnis have belittled Shiites and vice versa for having proclivities toward homosexuality or, more specifically, as they understood it as indulging in anal sex.[28]

The above illustrates that mainstream scholarly opinion is moved more by the law than by human plight, as is true for Orthodox Christian and Jewish circles. They consider homosexuality to be a result of a choice and predominantly equate homosexuality with anal sex. The more sympathetic scholars, while avoiding the choice and unnatural rhetoric, distinguish between orientation and sexual acts and prescribe celibacy. However, according to an excerpt from one of the Judgments of the Supreme Court of Canada:[29]

> Madam Justice Rowles: "Human rights law states that certain practices cannot be separated from identity, such that condemnation of the practice is a condemnation of the person" . . . [I]t is possible to condemn a practice so central to the identity of a protected and vulnerable minority without thereby discriminating against its members and affronting their human dignity and personhood.

This, then, entails that before the scriptures are engaged, the two fundamental misconceptions regarding homosexuality should be addressed, that is, the element of choice and the predominant understanding of the issue as that of anal sex.

ADDRESSING TWO FUNDAMENTAL MISCONCEPTIONS

Homosexuality and Anal Sex

The traditional discourse on homosexuality has predominantly revolved around anal sex, as is evident from the following definition:[30]

> Homosexuality means having intercourse with males in the back passage. This was the action of the accursed people of the Prophet Lot. In Sharia terminology it refers to inserting the tip of the penis into the anus of a male.

The same holds true for medieval discourses in Christianity and Judaism. According to Rabbi Gershom Barnard, the discussions around gays and lesbians have suffered, to use his words, "an improper (and prurient) fixation on male homosexual anal intercourse."[31] However, studies indicate that 33 percent to 50 percent of gay couples do not practice anal intercourse.[32] In fact, extrapolating from Rabbi Gershom Barnard's article, just as in the case of orthodox Jews, traditional gay Muslims would make a special effort to avoid anal sex. One sex expert columnist states:[33]

> While many people stereotypically view anal stimulation as a homosexual male act, anal sex is a sexual behaviour, not tied to a group of people . . . Much of the pornography available, marketed toward people of

any sexual orientation, provides extreme and stylized examples of fantasies. Anal sex is portrayed as quite normal in porn imagery, but, in reality, it occurs much less frequently than other sexual behaviours.

Homosexuality and Choice

Almost inevitably, preconceptions shape a person's assessment of evidence, whether the evidence is criminal, scientific, religious, or legal. Although they have preconceptions, people who are fair, loving, considerate of others, caring, and wise with a sense of social justice do not approach evidence with closed minds.

Already there is a wide body of scientifically disciplined study on homosexuality. The entire corpus of the studies[34] that has been done, including gene studies, twin studies, brain, and pheromones studies and significant studies in zoology, is too often discarded by some religious scholars of several faiths with claims that the studies do not provide a shred of evidence concerning homosexuality. On the other hand, these same scholars tout poorly conducted studies by organizations like NARTH as somehow bolstering the conclusion that homosexuality is completely unnatural. As noted earlier, Dr. Nadia El Awady's articles at the Islam-Online Web site is one illustration of this sad reality.

Since mainstream scholars tend to promote reparative therapy, it may be noted that in 1999 a constellation of prestigious organizations—the American Academy of Pediatrics, American Counseling Association, American Association of School Administrators, American Federation of Teachers, American Psychological Association, American School Health Association, Interfaith Alliance Foundation, National Association of School Psychologists, National Association of Social Workers, and the National Education Association—jointly issued a document titled: "Just the Facts about Sexual Orientation" wherein they condemned reparative therapy as potentially harmful and of little or no efficacy.[35] Leaving aside the statements of the American Psychological Association,[36] which came under criticism for bowing to gay and lesbian activists, even the Academy of Pediatrics and the Council on Child and Adolescent Health have stated that homosexuality is not a choice and cannot be changed.[37]

Perhaps arguments for the innateness of homosexuality may even be deduced from the Quran itself from verse 30:22 in light of the argument brought forth by Irshad Manji that, according to the Quran, God made nothing in vain.[38]

And one of His signs is the creation of the heavens and the earth and the diversity of your tongues and colors; most surely there are signs in this for the learned.

Verse 30:22 may also be viewed in light of the following excerpt by a religious scholar:[39]

There are some people who are born extroverts, and there are others who are introverts by their natural inclination. It is neither possible to change the nature of individuals nor is it the purpose of the Almighty's message that our personalities be artificially changed. We are expected to operate within the boundaries of our personalities. The diversity in human nature is a beauty and it would be a disaster if it is attempted to be bulldozed by a system for its own narrow purposes. We can only come up with the best of our potential if we are given to perform in accordance with what we are.

It also appears that the argument that homosexuality is predominantly a choice seems to have stemmed only recently and that, among early Muslims, it was viewed as a natural disposition. For instance, Nathan Bassem indicates that, from amongst the three theories prevalent among Medieval Arab physicians, one clearly stated that homosexuality results when the maternal sperm prevails over the paternal sperm.[40] In fact, scientific writers like Qusta Ibn Luqa have distinguished men on the basis of the disposition toward men, women, or both.[41] In some instances in Muslim history, homosexuality was even sanctioned within certain societies, such as that of the Oasis of Siwa.[42] Murray and Roscoe's seminal collection "Islamic Homosexualities"[43] and Samar Habib's *Arabo–Islamic Texts on Female Homosexuality*[44] include more illustrations of such accommodation of same-sex relationships in Muslim societies.

All of this then begs the question, why did previous Muslim societies fail to address the issue of the naturalness of same-sex relationships, despite the fact that a whole school of Muslim scientific thought treated homosexuality as a natural phenomenon? Perhaps the answer may lie in the observation that even liberal Muslim thinkers treated the subject based on their personal tastes rather than on the basis of dispassionate thought. For instance, even a physician like Ibn Sina, who allegedly indulged excessively in wine and sex,[45] categorized homosexuality as nothing more than a nasty phenomenon that merits punishment. It seems that this view greatly shaped the opinions of later doctors throughout Muslim history.

The theories on the innateness of homosexuality never attained prece-
dence in Muslim history, thus one cannot blame the overwhelming majority of the Muslim scholars of the previous ages for having failed to provide a
reasonable stand on same sex relationships. However, this does not excuse
the contemporary scholars from their failure to reevaluate the scriptures
despite having access to much more information than their predecessors
were ever exposed to. As the Salaf scholar Rashid Rida states:[46]

> The laws governing mu'amalat (social relations) should conform to Islamic
> ethics but on specific points may be continually reassessed according to
> changing conditions of different generations and societies.

Having addressed the two fundamental misconceptions of contemporary Muslim scholars, it is clear that the Muslim scriptures require a
reevaluation without the bias that has predominantly influenced Muslim
thought regarding same-sex relationships.

REVISITING THE QURANIC PASSAGES

As Siraj Kugle has pointed out,[47] there is no Quranic verse that deals
with homosexuality, let alone same-sex relationships. Any prohibition
is derived indirectly from the passages on the people of Lot. In fact, as
previously mentioned, even these passages are technically understood as
pertaining to anal intercourse between males who may have abandoned
their wives. This it is surprising that, when contemporary writers claim
homosexuality as a major sin, they are basing their opinion on a derived
rule as opposed to a clear-cut law found within the Quran, as in the case
of intoxicants (2:129), pork (5:03), fornication (17:32), and incest (4:23).
Pamela Taylor states:[48]

> One canonical position throughout the history of Islam has been that what-
> ever is not expressly forbidden is permissible.

Some scholars therefore attempt to quote other verses to bolster the case
that homosexuality is expressly forbidden. One such attempt, by Ahmad
Shafaat, seems to invoke verses 4:15–4:16 to provide evidence for the express prohibition for same-sex intercourse.[49] However, most scholars of
both the present and past seem to refute this understanding. For instance,
Rowson states:[50]

Only one maverick commentator, the Mutazilite Abu Moslem Esfahani (d. 934), understood two highly ambiguous verses (4:15–16) as referring to, respectively, female and male homosexual behaviour . . . while otherwise there was unanimous consent that the subject of both verses was heterosexual fornication.

This statement finds support in both Maududi's commentary on the Quran[51] and in Khaled El Rouayheb's seminal work.[52] However, still other scholars are of the opinion that if anal intercourse has been forbidden in a heterosexual context (2:222), then the prohibition extends to homosexuality, however this opinion incorrectly assumes that same-sex relationships are synonymous with anal intercourse. Moreover, even the prohibition of anal intercourse is contested; for instance the Grand Ayatollah Ali Sistani, the highest Shiite cleric in Iraq, has stated that heterosexual anal intercourse, although undesirable, is permissible.[53]

The above indicates that not a single verse exists that expressly prohibits same-sex relationships. This entails revisiting the passages on the people of Lot, without the two fundamental misconceptions addressed earlier, to ascertain whether these passages prohibit same-sex relationships indirectly. In the following, Shakir's translation[54] of the Quranic verses is used and, where necessary, supplemented by other translations. Each verse will be studied separately and the focus will be on the verses that are directly relevant and quoted to prohibit same-sex relationships.

Verses 7:80 and 29:28

Verse 7:80, which is similar in its content to 29:28, with the exception that the latter translation replaces "any one in the world has not" with "none of the nations," and for which Yusuf Ali and Pickthal's translations use the words "no people in creation" and "no creation ever," states:

And (We sent) Lut when he said to his people: What! Do you commit an indecency which any one in the world has not done before you?

If one went by the conventional understanding, two understandings emerge from the above, that is, homosexuality was never practiced by either individuals or nations before the people of Lot, however this stands in contrast to archaeological findings, as the men of Sodom have been dated to have lived around 1800 B.C., whereas the lovers King Neferkare

Pepy II and General Sisenet are dated around 2300 B.C.,[55] and the tomb of the same-sex Egyptian couple Niankhkhnum and Khnumhotep is dated around 2450 B.C.[56] While the two Egyptian examples are those of individual couples and may be dismissed as an aberration, the Mesopotamian society as a whole is depicted to have been quite tolerant of same sex practices. Wenham's article states:[57]

> From iconographic evidence dating from 3000 B.C. to the Christian era it is clear that homosexual practice was an accepted part of the Mesopotamian scene. This conclusion is confirmed by many literary and legal texts in which homosexual activity is mentioned.

Likewise, in Sierra Da Capivara National Park in Brazil, archaeologists have discovered paintings on rocks that depict graphic illustrations of Stone Age homosexual sex practices. These paintings are dated as far back as 12,000 years, clearly before the time of the People of Lot.[58] All of this evidence then indicates that verse 7:80 is referring to something other than loving same-sex relationships.

Verses 7:81, 26:165–166, and 27:55

The four verses have a similar content and Verse 7:81, as translated by Shakir, is as follows:

> Most surely you come to males in lust besides females; nay you are an extravagant people.

The words "besides females" are replaced with "in preference to women" and "instead of women" by Yusuf Ali and Pickthal, respectively. In verses 26:165–166, the words used by the three translators are "leave your mates" or "leave your wives," whereas the words used in verse 27:55 are "rather than women" or "instead of women."

According to the understanding of most exegetes and jurists, all these verses—(7:80–81; 26:160–166, 27:54–55, 29:28–29)—refer specifically to anal intercourse between males, and hence this particular act is condemned as a major sin.[59] Taken at face value, the variants of verse 7:81 do seem to suggest that men who prefer men over women have been reproached as transgressors; however, on closer inspection, this conclusion seems to falter on many grounds.

First, these verses seem to suggest that a majority of the people of Lot were engaging in exclusive same gender sexual activities and leaving behind their wives or womenfolk of the town. Given the absence of statistics in Muslim countries and acknowledging the Family Research Report that indicates that only two to three percent of men are homosexual,[60] it is clear that the people whom the verses are addressing are heterosexual men. This argument can be bolstered by both Maududi's opinion that the Quran deals with only fundamental questions and Bilal Philips's opinion that God cannot make people homosexuals and then punish them as criminals. If the people of Lot were indeed homosexual, as the opinion is held in contemporary circles, then it really sounds quite unreasonable.

Second, since the word *fahisha* has been used to denote indecency in verse 7:80, and the terms "extravagance" or "transgressing bounds" have been used in 7:81, it is important to understand that both these words are related. Daryabadi explains the word *fahisha* as follows:[61]

> in its general significance [it] is "an excess; an enormity; anything exceeding the bounds of rectitude." But when particularized, signifies "adultery or fornication."

This means that indecency and extravagance are, in fact, interrelated, as both are referring to a practice conducted in excess, especially given the alternative of lawful substitutes. This understanding also emerges from Ibn Hazm's writings when he states that nothing has been forbidden without the provision of an excellent substitute.[62] Thus, it seems reasonable to understand that the Quran is condemning the predominantly heterosexual males of the people of Lot for indulging in an excessive act of male anal intercourse when a lawful substitute of sex with their wives/potential wives was available.

Third, it would be a folly to generalize these verses by equating gays today with the people of Lot, just as it would be an error to equate the Jews and Christians today with the Jews and Christians of seventh-century Arabia, especially given the context of verse 5:51, which orders seventh-century Muslim believers to avoid taking Jews and Christians as friends.

Fourth, it seems that Rabbi Gershom Barnard's observation on the Jewish tradition not recognizing sexual orientation[63] perhaps holds true for the Muslim tradition as well, which is perhaps why contemporary Muslim

scholars equate gays with the people of Lot. The following verse corrobo-
rates the argument that the two are entirely different entities.

Verse 29:29

*What! Do you come to the males and commit robbery on the highway,
and you commit evil deeds in your assemblies?*

Verse 7:80 is synonymous with verse 29:28, and if the latter is understood in the light of verse 29:29 and the understanding applied to
verse 7:80, then a more holistic picture of the people of Lot emerges. While
the text of the verse is clear about robbery and subsequent assault on travelers, the evil deeds committed in assemblies are open for interpretation.
The history of al-Tabari[64] contains narratives in the context of verse 29:29,
traced back to the Prophet and His Companions that shed light on the de-
meanor of the people of Lot. Invariably, most of these narratives supposedly attributed to Ikrimah, Ibn Masud, Aishah, Mujahid, Ibn Zayd, and
Umm Hani paint a picture of acts of violence and coercion. The acts in the
assemblies are described as ranging from passing wind, sexual intercourse,
and mounting and mocking travelers to shortening them. Shortening refers to a practice wherein they would have a procrustean bed in which they
would put the traveler and, if he was too long, they would shorten him,
and if too short, stretch him, resulting in his death.

The narratives therefore indicate that the phrase "evil deeds in assemblies," has had multiple explanations, of which one possibility is that of
consensual and nonconsensual male anal intercourse. It may be noted
that even if verse 29:29 stretched to include consensual homosexual activity, it is clear from the word "mounting" found in the narratives that it
refers to one specific sexual act. In fact, another narrative confirms this
argument.[65]

> God's statement, "such as no one did before you in both worlds," refers to
> the fact that no male jumped upon a male before the people of Lot.

Siraj Kugle's referencing of Al Kisai and Al Rawandi's *Qisas Al Anbiya*
(*Stories of the Prophets*) texts only corroborate the Tabari narratives in that
the acts of the people of Lot are depicted as those of greed and coercion.[66]
While the Qisas texts indicate that the people of Lot sodomized travelers
during a period of famine, commentators like Jalal al Din al Mahalli and
Jalal al Din al Suyuti state that the people of Lot sodomized travelers to

drive them away from their prosperous land.[67] Despite the difference of opinion of various commentators, and notwithstanding the authenticity issue of these narratives, the holistic picture that emerges is that of coercion and, even if stretched by a long way, the only other remote possibility is that of male anal intercourse.

Verses 11:78–79 and 15:67–72

Portions of verses 11:78–79, as reproduced below, contain the words "no claim," which are replaced by "no need" and "no right" by Yusuf Ali and Pickthal, respectively.

> He said: "O my people! These are my daughters—they are purer for you . . ." They said: "Certainly you know that we have no claim on your daughters, and most surely you know what we desire."

These verses have raised a difference of opinion in whether Lot offered his daughters to the wanton crowd to protect his guests and whether he offered them for marriage or whether he offered the women folk of the whole town or whether the offer of his own daughters was merely to prick the conscience of the people.[68] Notwithstanding this difference of opinion, by the offer of his daughters, it seems reasonable to conclude that the people of Lot would have been satisfied with either the male visitors or with Lot's daughters. This opinion is also supported by Rabbi Gershom Barnard in the context of the Jewish scriptures.[69]

The other point to note is that two of the translations use the words "right" and "claim" as opposed to "need," which indicates that perhaps the issue was one of coercion of travelers as opposed to the "need" of molesting travelers. Finally, parallels from the Old Testament, specifically Judges 19 and Genesis 34 that depict the destruction of Gilbeah[70] and Shechem's hometown for heterosexual rape,[71] indicate the need to derive reasonable conclusions[72] from scriptural texts as opposed to those based on personal distaste and emotions.

In short, it may be stated that, based on a holistic picture of the people of Lot from the Quranic texts, the contemporary prohibition of same sex relationships suffers from many shortcomings. This, then, entails a closer look at the *hadith*, which are also used in condemnation of same-sex relationships.

REVISITING THE *HADITH* LITERATURE

Most *hadith* that are used to condemn same-sex relationships are of dubious nature, and most opinions of jurists indicate a lack of appreciation of the issue. For instance, *hadith* like "When a man mounts another man, the throne of God shakes," and opinions like "The lesbian's testimony is unacceptable because she is an evildoer"[73] clearly leave much to be desired.

Hadith that indicate capital punishment for same-sex activity[74] have been shown to be suspect even by mainstream scholars at Islam Online.[75] Such *hadith* usually come from secondary *hadith* texts as opposed to the more accepted Bukhari Muslim and Malik Muwatta texts. Moreover, when such *hadith* motivate capital punishment for gays and lesbians— whether by burning, throwing off a cliff, stoning, or by burying under a wall—they grossly violate Quranic verse 5:32, a portion of which is reproduced below.

> whoever slays a soul, unless it be for manslaughter or for mischief in the land, it is as though he slew all men.

It may also be noted that when the *hadith* use words like "the one who does it and the one to whom it is done," it is clear that male anal sex is being specifically indicated and that the prohibition of same-sex relationships is merely an unreasonable derivation from the supposed prohibition of male anal intercourse. Likewise, the extension of the prohibition to lesbian sexual activity by labeling such activity as fornication[76] goes against the grain of mainstream traditional jurisprudence wherein fornication is strictly defined as vaginal intercourse between a man and woman and does not include any other sexual activity within its definition.[77]

There are other *hadith* and narratives that indicate the Prophet mentioning God's curse on those who try to resemble the opposite gender and males who practice anal intercourse with other men.[78] Elsewhere, the Prophet is reported to have cursed the practice of the people of Lot, or expressed fear of his *ummah* following in their lead.[79] Still other narratives have the Prophet cursing effeminate men and banishing them from Medina.[80] In other narratives, normative statements are attributed to Ali—the fourth Caliph—wherein he is either reported as relating the onset of natural calamities with same sex behavior, or he is presented as stating that same-sex behavior among males leads to the diminution of their desire for women.[81]

These narratives contradict other narratives and juristic opinions and, like the narratives that support capital punishment for gays, they sound dubious. The effeminates of Medina would visit the Prophet's home and, only in one instance, was an effeminate exiled, and that was for conduct unrelated to his disposition.[82] This indicates that the Prophet's conduct stood in stark contrast to some of these narratives that have him and God cursing effeminates. So far as the narratives on the Prophet cursing the practice of the people of Lot or expressing fear for his *ummah* are concerned, many issues arise including those of authenticity, of equating the people of Lot with gays and lesbians, and of the nature and definition of the conduct of the people of Lot. The statements attributed to Ali simply negate common sense and present knowledge on natural calamities and sexual orientation. In short, at most the conclusion that can be stretched is that of the prohibition of male anal intercourse. However, given the established weaknesses of similar texts cursing heterosexual anal intercourse,[83] the conclusion of the prohibition of homosexual anal intercourse through these dubious texts does not hold much water either.

In the absence of the two fundamental misconceptions of contemporary scholars, the Quranic passages were revisited and discovered to contain no injunction for gays and lesbians. Likewise, the narratives in *hadith* literature were found to be dubious, contradicting the Quran or other narratives and/or negating common sense and current scientific knowledge. Perhaps, given the silence of the Quran and the weakness of the *hadith* literature in this regard, some scholars indicate that rather than a religious prohibition, homosexuality is a natural prohibition.[84] However, it has been expressed that most theologians do not accept arguments based on "natural prohibitions" and that perhaps such arguments were first developed to counter arguments that could not be rationally refuted.[85] Thus, given the alternate opinion that homosexuality is not religiously prohibited, coupled with the silence of the Quran and the dubious nature of the relevant *hadith,* the case for same sex unions may be derived just as the condemnation of same-sex unions is also a derived position.

THE IMPLIED CASE FOR MUSLIM SAME-SEX UNIONS

The implied case for same-sex unions will be made by noting the evolution of Muslim thought on homosexuality and by placing it as part of the trend of that evolution. The case itself can be separately built based on the jurisprudential treatment of intersexuality, marriage, and necessity.

Evolution of Muslim Thought

Amongst the four schools of Islamic jurisprudence, three prescribe severe punishment for homosexuality, which is understood as male anal intercourse. The Hanafi school left punishment to the discretion of the courts based on the reasoning that homosexuality is not synonymous with adultery.[86] This opinion appeared to be the first departure from the traditional understanding that homosexuals deserve to be killed in the worst possible manner, as evident from the *hadith* literature. Three centuries after Imam Abu Hanifa, Ibn Hazm distinguished between nonpenetrative sexual acts between two men and male anal intercourse on the basis of the penalty merited by each. While Ibn Hazm prescribed no more than 10 lashes for the former transgression,[87] on the latter he never provided his own opinion, and merely stated that God has not forbidden anything without the provision of excellent substitutes.[88]

Four centuries after Ibn Hazm, Muslim scholars, including those at al-Azhar until the 19th century, appeared to have made remarkably liberal statements based on contemporary Muslim standards. Khaled El Rouayheb documents how several Muslim scholars have supported the permissibility of male anal intercourse in Heaven by reasoning that such a place would be devoid of filth or reproduction. Others supported the narrative that the death of a chaste same-sex lover confers martyrdom upon that individual. Both these opinions have been recorded by Rectors at al-Azhar.[89]

Still others, similar to Ibn Hazm, distinguished nonpenetrative sexual acts as minor sins, with some claiming that such sins, even if deliberately and repeatedly committed, could be compensated for by simply avoiding major sins or by supererogatory works, even if the perpetrator did not repent. In fact the words "venial faults" in verse 53:32 were specifically understood as referring to nonpenetrative sexual acts.

Khaled El Rouayheb also documents the opinion of the Hanafi Mufti of Aleppo al-Kawakibi who seemed to have mentioned the possibility of interpreting the word "right hand possesses" in verses 23:6 and 70:30 as referring to, amongst others, male slaves. Another jurist, Al Ramli, is documented to have stated that, given the medical theory of the day, the kissing of a same-sex beloved would become an obligation if one feared the inevitability of death if passion remained frustrated.

It may be noted from the above that the juristic treatment of homosexuality evolved from a focus on male anal intercourse to considering non-penetrative sexual acts that were deemed to be minor sins. Moreover, the tone of the jurists appeared to have changed from that of condemnation to one of rational speculation. Finally and most importantly, opinions based on the possible interpretation of "right hand possesses" and on the prevalent medical theory of the day seem to indicate that jurists had begun to set the stage for the case for same-sex relationships, if not same-sex unions.

Based on this pattern, the case for Muslim same-sex unions can now be derived based on the juristic treatment of marriage, intersexuals, and necessity.

THE JURISTIC TREATMENT OF MARRIAGE

Contrary to contemporary opinions relegating the main purpose of marriage to reproduction, several traditional authorities, according to Vardit Rispler-Chaim (2006), understood the concept quite differently. Among the five main purposes of marriage, the traditional authority al-Ghazzali includes the satisfaction of sexual desire. In fact, in one of the Shiite lexicons, the main purpose of marriage is considered to be included in the meaning of the word *nikkah,* deemed equivalent to the word *wat,* which means sexual intercourse between a man and a woman sanctioned by marital contract. Vardit Rispler Chaim writes:

> More pivotal for the preservation of marital relations than bearing children a child seems to be that the couple are both healthy enough to engage in physical and emotional intimacy and in sexual intercourse.[90]

Several *hadith* invoking the sayings of the Prophet have also been used to underscore the importance of marriage in Islam. Some narratives even have the Prophet ostracizing those who fail to uphold this tradition.[91] The reason perhaps has to do with the regulation of human sexual needs, as one contemporary opinion states that marriage safeguards the chastity of spouses[92] and anything that jeopardizes that chastity, including the refusal of spouses to engage in marital sex, is disliked by God.[93] Hence, anyone who refuses to marry has been counseled to not fight against human nature.[94]

So strong is the recognition of humans' sexual needs, individuals have not only been granted permission to marry based on aesthetics[95] they have also been given leave to do so when the male falters and falls in love with another woman.[96] According to traditional authorities, while the wife may not dissolve the marriage contract even if the husband suffers from leprosy, she is allowed a divorce if her husband can no longer serve the primary purpose of marriage[97]—sexual intercourse. One of the reasons stated for the dissolution of marriage is *unna* (asynodia, or impotence), understood by Dr. Ahmad Kanan as a man's inability to penetrate a woman for psychological reasons that may include revulsion. According to traditional authorities, *unna* is established by a confession or oath.[98]

Given the importance attached to the provision of a legitimate avenue for sexual intercourse, and the acceptance of the traditional authorities on issues as *unna* stemming from revulsion on the basis of a confession or oath, the next step may be to take a holistic view of both marriage and *unna*. This holistic view could then set the stage for same-sex unions. Invoking the silence of the scriptures on same-sex unions, if homosexuals can be classified as individuals with *unna* or its variant, and given the importance of marriage in safeguarding chastity, perhaps gays and lesbians can be allowed to form same-sex unions[99] as opposed to being counseled to adopt the foreign value of celibacy.

The Juristic Treatment of Intersexuality

While one case for same-sex unions can be potentially derived from the juristic treatment of marriage, another may be implied from the juristic treatment of intersexuality. Muslim authorities, both Shiite and Sunni, have been extremely mindful of the plight of intersexuals in that they have been allowed to undergo gender reassignment surgeries. In fact, even transgendered individuals have been accommodated with this allowance. While Sunni scholars base their ruling on medical grounds,[100] Shiite scholars base their opinion on the juristic principle that what is not expressly prohibited is, in principle, permissible.[101]

Vardit Rispler-Chaim states that, in permitting gender reassignment, Shiite authorities like Ayatollah al Khaminai have a broader definition of individuals that would include males who are emotionally and sexually inclined toward female behaviors or appearance. Vardit Rispler-Chaim also states that, in the determination of gender, psychological and emotional inclinations need also be examined apart from external organs, chromosomes, and hormonal levels.[102] Traditional authorities, in fact, went beyond issues of gender determination to consider the possibility of the marriage of intersexuals with the typical population. Paula Sanders states that traditional jurists did not consider the marriage of an intersexual to a typical individual to be prohibited and, in fact, casually considered the error of marrying an intersexual to a woman if the former turned out to be a woman.[103]

Invoking the silence of the scriptures, given the juristic treatment of gender as dependent not only on physical organs but also emotional and psychological inclinations, and given the possibility of the marriages of intersexuals, if homosexuals can be classified as variants of intersexuals, then perhaps gays and lesbians can be allowed to form same-sex unions.

The Juristic Treatment of Necessity

While two cases for same sex unions can be potentially derived from the juristic treatment of marriage and intersexuality, another may be implied from the juristic treatment of necessity. According to one jurisprudential ruling, necessity trumps prohibition.[104] Traditional jurists, by referring to verses 2:185 and 22:78,[105] reason that Islamic law is mindful of genuine public or private needs and allows overstepping even the clear scriptural text under exceptional situations. The Ottoman Civil Code Majallah incorporated this notion in articles 17 and 21, and jurists like al-Mawardi even considered the maxim "necessity trumps prohibitions" as one of the pillars of Islamic jurisprudence.[106]

However, traditional jurists did not define "need" except by indicating it occurs in the absence of things that are essential for a healthy, respectable, and dignified life. In fact, the traditional jurists left it for the future Muslim generations to define need according to circumstances and changing times.[107] Perhaps this is why some contemporary scholars have allowed interest-based loans for lodging in the absence of alternatives,[108] and in other cases they have also facilitated left-handed people based on their natural orientation.[109]

Invoking the silence of the scriptures, and given that marriage—as defined by physical and emotional intimacy—is a basic necessity for a healthy life, any contemporary position against same-sex unions can be overruled to facilitate the hardships faced by gays and lesbians by allowing them to form same-sex unions. In the traditional context, Ramli's opinion on allowing the homosexual lover to kiss the beloved under dire circumstances perhaps appears to be a precursor for the contemporary case for allowing same-sex unions.

CONCLUDING REMARKS

Scholarly efforts have been made by the likes of Kugle and Jamal to help Muslim gays and lesbians reconcile their orientation with their faith. Imams like Daayiee Abdullah have even supported same-sex unions.[110] Many others have also added their voice to the plight of gay and lesbian Muslims; however, mainstream Muslim scholars continue to counsel reparative therapy or celibacy. Two fundamental misconceptions behind mainstream thought include treating same-sex desire as a choice and equating homosexuality with anal sex and are highlighted as having biased the contemporary readings of the scriptures. Having addressed these misconceptions, the scriptures are revisited to ascertain that not a single verse or *hadith* exists that prohibits same-sex unions. Given the silence of the scriptures, the juristic rule that what is not expressly forbidden is allowed and, based on the juristic treatment of issues of marriage, intersexuality, and necessity, three cases for same-sex unions were delineated and placed in the context of the evolution of traditional Muslim thought. It is hoped that this exercise in analogical deduction would support initiatives that aim to address the plight of gay and lesbian Muslims.

A major change, according to Rabbi Gershom Barnard, would not only require a strong position that affirms same-sex unions but also as many voices as is possible that support that position.[111] However, sympathetic contemporary mainstream authorities may find the task of accepting same-sex unions to be quite daunting simply because of the absence of rules that regulate such unions. For instance, issues of modesty, praying in the congregation, rules of inheritance, divorce, adoption, and artificial insemination by same-sex couples may not have direct and simple answers within the current Islamic framework. However, if the traditional authorities have richly dealt with complexities such as intersexuality, then it is hoped that likewise contemporary scholars would chart new territories of independent reasoning. As such, much more remains to be done, especially in inviting mainstream authorities to revisit their stance on gays and lesbians. Rabbi Harold Schulweis puts it quite well when he states:

We have little control over natural catastrophes: earthquakes, floods, hurricanes, tornadoes. But there are catastrophes over which we have control because we have created them. The curse upon the gay person we have pronounced. This tragedy we have imposed on our children is not the will of God. It is our doing. The blessing and curse, life and death given us is our choice. We are not coerced to silence.[112]

NOTES

I am grateful for the editorial assistance of Hadi Hussain, the critical input of Jay Smith, and above all the discussions with my friend Husseini.

1. Siraj Kugle, "Sexuality, Diversity and Ethics in the Agenda of Progressive Muslims," in *Progressive Muslims: On Justice, Gender, and Pluralism,* ed. Omid Safi (Oneworld Publications, 2003), 190–234.

2. Amreen Jamal, "The Story of Lut and the Quran's Perception of the Morality of Same-Sex Sexuality," *Journal of Homosexuality* 41, no. 1 (2001): 1–88.

3. Rabbi Gershom Barnard, "Homosexuality," *Northern Hills Synagogue* 2003, http://www.nhs-cba.org/Homo03.htm (accessed January 14, 2009).

4. Muhsin Hendricks, "What Is Homosexuality," *Behind the Mask* http://www.mask.org.za/article.php?cat=islam&id=729 (accessed January 14, 2009).

5. Metro Weekly, "A Man for All Seasons," *Metro Weekly* December 21, 2006, http://www.metroweekly.com/feature/?ak=2458 (accessed January 14, 2009).

6. Faris Malik, "Queer Sexuality and Identity in the Quran and Hadith," *Born Eunuchs* http://www.well.com/user/aquarius/Qurannotes.htm (accessed January 14, 2009).

7. Pamela Taylor, "Gay People Are People. Like Anyone Else," *Washington Post* March 5, 2007, http://newsweek.washingtonpost.com/onfaith/pamela_k_taylor/2007/03/gay_people_are_people_like_any.html (accessed January 14, 2009); Pamela Taylor, "Equal Rights for All Include Marital Rights," *Washington Post* May 2008, http://newsweek.washingtonpost.com/onfaith/pamela_k_taylor/2008/05/equal_rights_for_all_includes.html (accessed January 14, 2009).

8. Ghazala Anwar, "Islam, Homosexuality and Migration" (Yoesuf Foundation Conference on Islam in the West and Homosexuality—Strategies for Action, 2000). Yoesuf Foundation is a Dutch organization based in Utrecht.

9. Farid Esack, *On Being a Muslim—Finding a Religious Path in the World Today.* (Oxford: Oneworld Publications, 1999), 136.

10. Abdul Khalik, "Islam 'Recognizes Homosexuality,'" *The Jakarta Post* March 28, 2008, http://www.thejakartapost.com/news/2008/03/27/islam-039-recognizes-homosexuality039.html (accessed January 14, 2009).

11. This section excludes the extreme opinions that call for capital punishment for gays and lesbians.

12. Muzammil Siddiqi, "Islam and Homosexuality," *Mission Islam* http://www.missionislam.com/knowledge/homosexuality.htm (accessed January 14, 2009).

13. Bilal Philips, "Islam's Position on Homosexuality," *Official Web site of Dr. Bilal Philips* July 6, 2006, http://bilalphilips.com/bilal_pages.php?option=com_content&task=view&id=370 (accessed January 14, 2009).

14. "Bestiality and pederasty are certainly natural as well. Every society has men who use children sexually. Everywhere sheep or goats are kept, they are used for sex. So the argument that homosexuality is natural or inborn has little persuasive power for Muslims." Mikail Tariq, "Islam and homosexuality," *Mikail Juma Tariq* June 16, 2002, http://www.geocities.com/mikailtariq/homo.htm (accessed January 14, 2009).

15. "One must keep in mind that the nature on which the Almighty has created human beings tends to get perverted in societies where promiscuity and nudity are rampant" Shehzad Saleem, "Homosexuality," *Renaissance: A Monthly Islamic Journal* September(2000), http://www.monthly-renaissance.com/issue/content.aspx?id=618 (accessed January 14, 2009).

16. "The Muslim needs to take precautions against these deviants and not to give them any opportunity to mix with and corrupt their children. Furthermore, they are neither fit to establish *masajid* and frequent them, nor are they fit to lead those who frequent the *masjid* whoever they may be." Taha Jabir al-'Alwani, "Islam's Stance on Homosexual Organizations," *Fatwa Bank, Islam Online* May 17, 2004, http://www.islamonline.net/servlet/Satellite?pagename=IslamOnline-EnglishAsk_Scholar/FatwaE/FatwaE&cid=1119503545314 (accessed January 14, 2009).

17. Nadia El-Awady, "Homosexuality in a Changing World: Are We Being Misinformed?" *Islam Online* February 17, 2003, http://www.islamonline.net/english/Contemporary/2003/02/Article01.shtml (accessed January 14, 2009).

18. Yousuf al Qaradawi, "Homosexuals Should Be Punished Like Fornicators but Their Harm is Less When not Done in Public," *The Middle East Media Research Institute,* no. 1170 (2006), http://www.memritv.org/clip/en/0/0/0/0/0/100/1170.htm (accessed January 14, 2009).

19. "If He has deprived people from some faculty or some ability, it is to test them. He has created children who are born blind or handicapped in some other way. If God is unfair to you, then perhaps He is even more unfair to such children." Shehzad Saleem, "Genetic Homosexuality," *Renaissance: A Monthly Islamic Journal* February (2001), http://www.monthly-renaissance.com/issue/query.aspx?id=428 (accessed January 14, 2009).

20. See the huge array of comments received on Faris Malik's Web site *Queer Jihad.* Faris Malik, "Archive of Comments," *Queer Jihad* http://www.well.com/user/queerjhd/comments.html (accessed January 14, 2009).

21. Ian Haberfield, "Imam Accused of Promoting Gay Hate," *Muslim Village* December 8, 2003, http://muslimvillage.com/forums/lofiversion/index.php/t2654.html (accessed January 14, 2009).

22. John Spong, "A Statement from The Rt. Rev'd John S. Spong on the Death of Matthew Shepard," *Baptist Watch* October 22, 1998, http://www.baptistwatch.org/content/spomatletter.html (accessed January 14, 2009).

23. "Because of her [Itrath Syed] beliefs in equality for all Canadians, she and her elderly parents were effectively excommunicated from the Richmond mosque her parents helped build and that she has been attending since her youth." Disabled Women's Network Ontario, "Equality—What it Means, How it Works," *Disabled Women's Network Ontario* June 16, 2004, http://dawn.thot.net/election2004/issues61.htm (accessed January 14, 2009).

24. "Dr. Yusuf, in England, was due to call for an 'Islamic Reformation' to an audience primarily made up of gay men and women. The engagement has allegedly provoked the wrath of senior Islamic clerics, who warned they could not guarantee his safety if the lecture went ahead." Benjamin Cohen, "Liberal Islamic Scholars Forced to Pull out of Gay Rights Speech by Muslim leaders," *Pink News* March 20, 2006, http://www.pinknews.co.uk/news/articles/2005-864.html (accessed January 14, 2009).

25. "Boys call each other 'gay' without any understanding of what this means ... I was surprised that teachers at my sons' 'Islamic school' allowed this kind of abuse to rage among their students unchecked and unchallenged." Commenter, on "Hamid Natosh," *Monotheizm LGBT Issues Forum* April 19, 2007, http://www.monotheizm.com/bb/viewtopic.php?f=50&t=425 (accessed January 14, 2009).

26. "Ahmed told of a friend whose father discovered he was having a gay relationship and, after a beating, bundled him off to a psychiatrist ... The treatment involved showing him pictures of men and women and giving him electric shocks if he looked at the men." Brian Whitaker, "Homosexuality on trial in Egypt," *The Guardian* November 19, 2001, http://www.guardian.co.uk/world/2001/nov/19/worlddispatch.brianwhitaker (accessed January 14, 2009).

27. "Hamid Natosh was a fourteen year old in Vancouver from an Afghan family who was driven to suicide on March 11, 2000 ... Schoolmates persistently bullied him with accusations of being gay and he found no consolation or protection in his religious tradition as it had been presented to him." Kugle, 190–234.

28. AllahuAkbar, "Al-Kafi: The Most Reliable Shia Book," *Allahuakbar*, http://allaahuakbar.in/article_read.asp?id=223 (accessed January 14, 2009); Answering Ansar, "The Nasibi Assault on the Sahaba and Salaf Imams," *Answering Ansar*, http://www.answering-ansar.org/wahabis/en/chap11.php (accessed January 14, 2009).

29. Judgments of Supreme Court of Canada, "Trinity Western University vs. College of Teachers," May 17, 2001, http://csc.lexum.umontreal.ca/en/2001/2001scc31/2001scc31.html (accessed January 14, 2009).

30. Muhammad Salih al-Munajjid, "Why Does Islam Forbid Lesbianism and Homosexuality?" Fatwa No. 10050, *Islam QA* http://www.islamqa.com/en/ref/10050 (accessed January 14, 2009).

31. Barnard, "Homosexuality."

32. Sexual Health Info Center, "Anal Sex," Sex Health.org, http://www.sexhealth.org/bettersex/anal.shtml (accessed January 14, 2009);

Tiscali Lifestyle, "Anal Sex," *Tiscali Lifestyle,* http://www.tiscali.co.uk/lifestyle/healthfitness/health_advice/netdoctor/archive/000594.html?page=2 (accessed January 14, 2009).

33. Alice, "Not All Gay Men Love Anal Sex," *Go Ask Alice* June 13, 2008, http://www.goaskalice.columbia.edu/0900.html (accessed January 14, 2009).

34. Simon LeVay, "The Biology of Sexual Orientation," *Simon LeVay*, http://www.simonlevay.com/the-biology-of-sexual-orientation (accessed January 14, 2009).

35. B. A. Robinson, "Professional Associations' Statement about Homosexuality," *Religious Tolerance.org,* February 11, 2006, http://www.religioustolerance.org/hom_prof.htm (accessed January 14, 2009).

36. "The American Psychological Association released a *Statement on Homosexuality* in 1994-JUL. It states: 'The research on homosexuality is very clear. Homosexuality is neither mental illness nor moral depravity. It is simply the way a minority of our population expresses human love and sexuality. Study after study documents the mental health of gay men and lesbians. Studies of judgment, stability, reliability, and social and vocational adaptiveness, all show that gay men and lesbians function every bit as well as heterosexuals.'" Ibid.

37. Ibid.

38. John Glassie "In Good Faith," *The New York Times* December 21, 2003, http://www.irshadmanji.com/news/nytimes-dec21-03.html (accessed January 14, 2009).

39. Khalid Zaheer, "Are We Accountable for Personality Differences?" *Renaissance: A Monthly Islamic Journal* December (2005), http://www.monthly-renaissance.com/issue/query.aspx?id=86 (accessed January 14, 2009).

40. Nathan Bassem, "Medieval Arabic Medical Views on Male Homosexuality," *Journal of Homosexuality* 26, no. 4 (1994): 37–9.

41. John Boswell, "Revolution, Universal and Sexual Categories," in *Hidden from History: Reclaiming the Gay and Lesbian Past,* ed. Martin Duberman, Martha Vicinus, and George Chauncey (New York: Meridian, 1989), http://hem.passagen.se/nicb/boswell.htm (accessed January 14, 2009).

42. Stephen Murray and Will Roscoe, *Islamic Homosexualities: Culture, History and Literature.* (New York: New York University Press, 1997), 37, 40.

43. Ibid.

44. Samar Habib, *Arabo-Islamic Texts on Female Homosexuality 850–1780 A.D.* (New York: Teneo, 2009), 17, 42.

45. Petri Liukkonen. "Avicenna," http://www.kirjasto.sci.fi/avicenna.htm (accessed January 14, 2009).

46. Sohail Hashmi, "Rashid Rida," in *Encyclopedia of Islam and the Muslim World,* ed. Richard Martin (New York: MacMillan Reference, 2004), 597.

47. Siraj Kugle, "Sexuality, Diversity and Ethics in the Agenda of Progressive Muslims," in *Progressive Muslims: On Justice, Gender, and Pluralism,* ed. Omid Safi (Oxford: Oneworld Publications, 2003), 190–234.

48. Pamela Taylor, "Gay People are People."

49. Ahmad Shafaat, "Death Penalty For Homosexuality, Incest, and Bestiality," *Punishment for Adultery in Islam: A Detailed Examination* March 6, 2005, http://www.islamicperspectives.com/Stoning5.htm#Chapter5 (accessed January 14, 2009).

50. E. K. Rowson, "Homosexuality In Islamic Law," *Encyclopaedia Iranica* http://www.iranica.com/newsite/index.isc?Article=http://www.iranica.com/newsite/articles/v12f4/v12f4026b.html (accessed January 14, 2009).

51. "Even less convincing is the opinion expressed by Abu Muslim al-Isfahani that the first verse relates to lesbian relations between females, and the second to homosexual relations between males. It is strange that al-Isfahani ignored the basic fact that the Quran seeks merely to chart a broad code of law and morality and hence deals only with fundamental questions." Sayyid Abul Ala Maududi, *Towards Understanding the Quran,* trans., Zafar Ishaque Ansari, http://www.tafheem.net/tafheem/surah4.html (accessed January 14, 2009).

52. "Not all scholars understood the verse (4:16) as applying to homosexual intercourse. In fact, even Hanafi commentators, whom one might expect to have exploited the verse in defence of their school's peculiar ruling on *liwat,* interpreted the verse as applying to fornication between a man and a woman." Khaled El Rouayheb, *Before Homosexuality in the Arab-Islamic World, 1500–1800* (Chicago: University of Chicago Press, 2005), 122.

53. Brian Whitaker, "Seminal Questions," *The Guardian* January 17, 2006, http://www.guardian.co.uk (accessed January 14, 2009).

54. The Quranic translations are taken from the "Compendium of Muslim Texts" at the Muslim Student Association Web site of the University of Southern California. MSA-USC Quran Database, "Compendium of Muslim texts," *University of Southern California* http://www.usc.edu/dept/MSA/reference/searchquran.html (accessed January 14, 2009).

55. Paul Halsall, "Queers in History," http://users.cybercity.dk/~dko12530/queerhis.htm (accessed January 14, 2009).

56. Greg Reeder, "Same-Sex Desire, Conjugal Constructs, and the Tomb of Niankhkhnum and Khnumhotep" *World Archaeology,* 32, no. 2 (2000): 193–208.

57. Gordon Wenham, "The Old Testament Attitude to Homosexuality," *Expository Times* 102 (1991): 259–363 http://www.biblicalstudies.org.uk/article_attitude_wenham.html (accessed January 14, 2009).

58. "Even Common in Earliest Man," *Homosexuality and the Bible* http://www.lionking.org/~kovu/bible/section18.html#early_man (accessed January 14, 2009).

59. E. K. Rowson, "Homosexuality in Islamic Law."

60. Jennifer Robison, "What Percentage of the Population Is Gay," *Gallup* October 8, 2002, http://www.gallup.com/poll/6961/What-Percentage-Population-Gay.aspx (accessed January 14, 2009).

61. Abdul Majid Daryabadi, *Tafsir-Ul-Quran Translation and Commentary of the Holy Quran,* vol. 1 (Pakistan: Darul-Isha'at Urdu Bazar, 1991): 310; reference at http://www.answering-islam.org/Responses/Osama/lesbian.htm (accessed January 14, 2009).

62. Ibn Hazm, "Chapter 28: Of Vileness of Sinning," *The Ring of the Dove,* trans. A. J. Arberry (London: Luzac Oriental, 1997), http://www.muslimphilosophy.com/hazm/dove/chpt28.html (accessed January 14, 2009).

63. Barnard, "Homosexuality."

64. al-Tabari, *The History of al-Tabari: Prophets and Patriarchs,* trans. William Brinner (New York: State University of New York, 1986), 112–18.

65. Ibid.

66. Siraj Kugle, "Sexuality, Diversity and Ethics in the Agenda of Progressive Muslims," in *Progressive Muslims: On Justice, Gender, and Pluralism,* ed. Omid Safi (Oxford: Oneworld Publications, 2003), 190–234.

67. Khaled El Rouayheb, 126.

68. Khalid Zaheer, "The Prophet Lut (sws) and His Daughters," *Renaissance: A Monthly Islamic Journal* February (2006), http://www.monthly-renaissance.com/issue/query.aspx?id=4 (accessed January 14, 2009).

69. Barnard, "Homosexuality."

70. "Judges 19 tells of a very similar event in Gilbeah, except that the house guest was a man, not an angel, and the people accepted the concubine women in place of the man. The concubine was raped until she died and the city was destroyed for heterosexual rape and violation of the law of hospitality." in "Sodom and Gomorrah Had Nothing to Do About [sic] Homosexuality," *Homosexuality and the Bible* http://www.lionking.org/~kovu/bible/section06.html#Sodom (accessed January 14, 2009).

71. Ibid.

72. Kugle indicates that nobody prescribes the absurd capital punishment for killing camels on the basis of the story of Salih, thereby indicating the need for deriving reasonable conclusions based on the story of the people of Lot. See Siraj Kugle, "Sexuality, Diversity and Ethics in the Agenda of Progressive Muslims," in *Progressive Muslims: On Justice, Gender, and Pluralism,* ed. Omid Safi (Oxford: Oneworld Publications, 2003), 190–234.

73. Mission Islam, "Islam and Homosexuality," *Mission Islam*, http://www.missionislam.com/knowledge/homosexuality.htm (accessed January 14, 2009).

74. James Arlandson, "Islamic Law Is Not Gay," *American Thinker* June 25, 2005, http://www.americanthinker.com/2005/06/islamic_law_is_not_gay.html (accessed January 14, 2009).

75. Mohamed El-Shinqiti, "Threats to Behead Homosexuals: Sharia or Politics?" *Islam Online* June 9, 2008, http://www.islamonline.net/servlet/Satellite?cid=1212925140273&pagename=IslamOnline-English-Ask_Scholar%2FFatwaE%2FFatwaEAskTheScholar (accessed January 14, 2009).

76. Mission Islam, "Islam and Homosexuality."

77. Razi Allah, "What's the Classical Definition of Zina?" *Understanding Islam* May 31, 2003, http://www.understanding-islam.com/related/text.aspx?type=question&qid=2295&sscatid=245 (accessed January 14, 2009).

78. Arlandson, "Islamic Law Is Not Gay."

79. Abdurrahman, "Homosexuality: What Is the Real Sickness," *Abdurrahman*, http://abdurrahman.org/character/sodomy.html (accessed January 14, 2009).

80. Arlandson, "Islamic Law is Not Gay."

81. Abdurrahman, "Homosexuality."

82. Habib, 17–18.

83. Moiz Amjad, "Narratives on the Prohibition of Anal Sex," *Understanding Islam* June 15, 1999, http://www.understanding-islam.com/related/text.aspx?type=question&qid=262&sscatid=68 (accessed January 14, 2009).

84. Moiz Amjad, "Gays and Lesbians," *Understanding Islam* June 5, 1999, http://www.understanding-islam.com/related/text.aspx?type=question&qid=382&sscatid=415 (accessed January 14, 2009).

85. Lumumba S., comment on "Ibn Rushd and Al Ghazzali," *Understanding Islam* May 1, 2007, http://uiforum.uaeforum.org/showthread.php?t=6000 (accessed January 14, 2009).

86. Nation Master Encyclopedia, "Islam and Homosexuality," *Nation Master*, http://www.nationmaster.com/encyclopedia/Islam-and-homosexuality (accessed January 14, 2009).

87. This may be compared with the 40 or 80 lashes penalty for drinking. See James Arlandson, "No Drinking and Gambling in the Quran: Prohibition

in Islam," *American Thinker* July 10, 2005, http://www.americanthinker.com/
2005/07/no_drinking_and_gambling_in_th.html (accessed January 14, 2009).

88. Ibn Hazm, "Chapter 28: Of Vileness of Sinning."

89. Khaled El Rouayheb, 133 and 141.

90. Vardit Rispler-Chaim, *Disability in Islamic Law* (The Netherlands:
Springer, Dordrecht, 2006), 47.

91. "The prophet has also said, 'Marriage is my tradition who so ever keeps
away there from is not from amongst me.'" Jannah, "Marriage in Islam," *Jannah*,
http://www.jannah.org/sisters/marr.html (accessed January 14, 2009).

92. "(Wanting to avoid fornication) is a good reason for marriage[, it] is indeed
one of the most commendable and pious reasons for marriage." Moiz Amjad, "Is
Wanting to Avoid Fornication a Good Reason for Marriage?" *Understanding Islam*
May 20, 2002, http://www.understanding-islam.com/related/text.aspx?type=
question&qid=1568&sscatid=456 (accessed January 14, 2009).

93. See the explanation of the *hadith*: "When a husband calls his wife to bed,
and she refuses and [as a result] the husband spends the night in anger, then angels curse the wife all night till dawn." (Bukhari, No: 3065).

Shehzad Saleem, "'Refusing Sex to the Husband,' Islam and Women: Misconceptions and Misperceptions," *Renaissance: A Monthly Islamic Journal*
February (2005), http://www.monthly-renaissance.com/issue/content.aspx?id=
154 (accessed January 14, 2009).

94. Moiz Amjad, "Celibacy," *Understanding Islam* August 29, 1997, http://
www.understanding-islam.com/related/text.aspx?type=question&qid=529&sscat
id=456 (accessed January 14, 2009).

95. "So making decisions governed by such a taste cannot be primarily ob-
jected to . . . So if you think that in spite of all the good mannerisms found in your
fiancé, it is difficult for you to stand your fiance's physical appearance it is better
to take this seemingly harsh step of terminating your engagement than to psychologically suffer all your life."

Shehzad Saleem, "Separating from an Unattractive Fiancé," *Renaissance:
A Monthly Islamic Journal* September (2001), http://www.monthly-renaissance.
com/issue/query.aspx?id=491 (accessed January 14, 2009).

96. "Even if we were to imagine that a husband isn't quite as careful in his
conduct as Muslim men should be while dealing with the members of the opposite
sex and as a consequence he gets interested in another lady to the extent that he
wants to marry her, why should the first wife not be given the option to either live
with her husband, adjusting to the new reality, or leaving him?" Khalid Zaheer,
"Rationale behind polygamy and the consent of wife," *Khalid Zaheer*, http://www.
khalidzaheer.com/qa/154 (accessed January 14, 2009).

97. *Jabb* (being amputated of penis), *unna,* and *khisa* (castrated) have been
considered by Classical authorities as conditions that allow for the dissolution of
marriage." Vardit Rispler-Chaim, 56.

98. Ibid., 117–18.

99. Especially so since the word "*zawj*" in verses like 78:8 "And we created you in pairs," is gender neutral. See Samar Habib, *Arabo-Islamic Texts on Female Homosexuality 850–1780 A.D.* (New York: Teneo, 2009), 18.

100. Jakob Skovgaard Peterson, "Sex Change in Cairo: Gender and Islamic Law," *The Journal of the International Institute* 2, no. 3 (1995), http://quod.lib. umich.edu/cgi/t/text/text-idx?c=jii;view=text;rgn=main;idno=4750978.0002.302 (accessed January 14, 2009).

101. Sayyed Fadlallah, "Transsexuals: Sex Reassignment Surgery SRS," *Jurisprudence of Sex,* http://english.bayynat.org.lb/jurisprudence/sex.htm (accessed January 14, 2009.

102. Rispler-Chaim, 73–74.

103. Paula Sanders, "Gendering the Ungendered Body: Hermaphrodites in Medieval Islamic Law," in *Women in Middle Eastern History,* ed. Nikki Keddie and Beth Baron (New Haven, CT: Yale University Press, 1991), 87.

104. Islamic Medical Association of North America Ethics Committee, "Islamic Medical Ethics," *ISNA (Islamic Society of North America) Leadership Development Centre,* http://www.ildc.net/islamic-ethics (accessed January 14, 2009).

105. "God desireth for you ease; He desireth not hardship for you." (2:185) "He hath chosen you and hath not laid upon you in religion any hardship." (22:78)—Pickthal's translation MSA-USC Quran Database, "Compendium of Muslim Texts," *University of Southern California,* http://www.usc.edu/dept/ MSA/reference/searchquran.html (accessed January 14, 2009).

106. Mohammad Muslehuddin, *Islamic Jurisprudence and the Rule of Necessity and Need* (New Delhi: Kitab Bhavan, 1982), 31, 58–63.

107. Khaled Abou El Fadl, *The Great Theft: Wrestling Islam from the Extremists* (San Francisco: Harper San Fransisco, 2005), 187–89.

108. Tariq Mahmood Hashmi, "Paying Interest on Buying Apartments," *Studying Islam* March 9, 2005, http://www.studying-islam.org/querytext.aspx?id=283 (accessed January 14, 2009).

109. "The Sunna has been established keeping in view the fact that it is natural for right-handed people to eat with their right hand for the Sharia does not ignore the natural human build. Similarly when it is not natural and therefore not easy for a natural lefty to eat with right hand he is not bound to eat with his right hand." Tariq Mahmood Hashmi, "The Dilemma of Natural Left Handers," *Studying Islam,* October 31, 2005, http://www.studying-islam.org/showcounterqa. aspx?id=133 (accessed January 14, 2009).

110. "You as a Muslim man, or woman, deserve to seek a consensual monogamous relationship as would any Muslim, regardless of sexual orientation." Afdhere Jama, "Interview with Daayiee Abdullah," *Huriyah Magazine* (2004).

111. "To see a major change, it will take someone to cut the Gordian knot and say (for example), 'There can be *kiddushin* between two people of the same sex.' If

one rabbi says that, it is nonsense, but if hundreds of rabbis say that consistently over many years, it will be so." Barnard, "Homosexuality."

112. Rabbi Harold Schulweis, "A Second Look at Homosexuality," *Valley Beth Shalom*, http://www.vbs.org/rabbi/hshulw/homo.htm (accessed January 14, 2009).

14

---·•◦•·---

QUEER VISIONS OF ISLAM

Rusmir Musić

"Queer Muslims? Really?" People raise their eyebrows when I explain to them my academic work and my personal identity. "Is there such a thing? I thought Islam strictly condemns it." Some ask: "Why bother? Wouldn't it be easier to simply turn your back on the religion and live by Western standards?"

Queer Muslims[1] struggle daily to reconcile their sexuality and their faith. This struggle, positing *queer* and *Muslim* as two antagonizing concepts, originates in what Asma Barlas calls the "widespread tendency to blame Islam for oppressing Muslims rather than blaming Muslims for misreading Islam."[2] Though many choose to abandon either their faith or their sexuality, neither has to be discarded, only rearticulated. This chapter speaks to those queer Muslims questioning their faith, as an affirmation that God indeed accepts and celebrates their sexuality. The words here are principally a personal faith exploration and an activist's outcry against oppression; though academic in nature, this work is not from a detached or dispassionate point of view. Though I never believed God hated me for being queer, I have listened to countless individuals who were alienated from God under pressures of homophobic theology. I started this project while still in college as a way to investigate whether or not my love and desire for someone of the same gender disgusts God and whether it will propel me to hell. The answer, for me, is an unequivocal *no*. Furthermore, my research and reflection has helped me to imagine my sexuality as a gift from a loving, not a hateful, God.

I am inspired by John McNeill's maxim that "Good theology will result in good psychology and vice versa."[3] When speaking on panels on this topic, I inevitably have to field questions of relativism: if we are adjusting centuries of tradition for same-gender couples, what stops us from bending the interpretation in order to allow other forbidden moral transgressions? I answer in the form of *what if*. What if the Quran's text could be seen in a new light? What if this new interpretation seems more in line with the overall message of God's love toward humanity? What if this realignment with the overall message saves a young Muslim, struggling to reconcile faith and sexuality, from committing suicide? Why, then, are we so afraid to admit that a queer-friendly reading of the text could exist? The answers are complex, but they lie in human fears of change and liberation, not in divine pronouncements.

Behind Barlas's aforementioned statement that Muslims/humans, not Islam/God, are oppressive lies an idea that there may exist multiple Islams, as interpreted by and for different agents. Again, invoking multiple Islams does not invite moral relativism, but is an acknowledgment that times have changed and with them so must the law and theology. That I see Sharia as a human rather than a divine system should not belittle its colossal importance in the lives of many Muslims. Indeed, the oppressive rules may be a subconscious process in the minds of jurists and theologians who simply think they are performing God's will. Recognizing that they may have had the best of interests ought not to stop us from examining these inconsistencies within the (human) law. The sacred texts come to us layered with millennia of meaning piled upon a poetic and ambiguous language; this reading simply brings to the forefront inconsistencies with a bigger picture of a good theology producing a good psychology. In the following pages, I study the inconsistencies in exegesis discussing queer persons, arguing for egalitarian and sex-affirmative, instead of oppressive and homophobic, readings of Islam. Though Muslims and non-Muslims alike have emphasized Islam's latter, rather than its former qualities, I constantly return to Barlas's maxim that human interpreters, not God, should be found guilty of oppression.

My analysis starts with the four sources of any valid Islamic law: (1) the Quran, Islam's sacred text, (2) the *hadith*, sayings or deeds of the Prophet

Muhamad as reported by his contemporaries, (3) *qiyas,* analogies to similar cases, and (4) *ijma?,* or consensus of the Muslim community.[4] Many may find my analysis of Islam's sacred texts limited due to my lack of Arabic proficiency; however, many contemporary Muslims cannot speak Arabic apart from pronouncing prayers and must rely on translations for transforming Quranic verses into legal or social norms. The original Arabic of the sacred texts unlocks itself to multiple interpretations, accentuating the ambiguity at the core of multiple Islams responding to needs of its diverse constituents. For example, Ahmed Ali's translation of Surah al-A'râf, verse 81:

> for ye practice your lusts
>
> On men in preference
>
> To women[5]

in Behbudi and Turner's version, it becomes:

> In order to satisfy your lust, you sleep with men rather than women. Man's innate opposition is towards the opposite gender; by lying with those of the same sex [*sic*] you have corrupted your own souls and denied your women-folk their rights (to sexual satisfaction).[6]

Even a quick glance at the differences between these translations reveals the translators' ideological orientations, calling into question why scholars historically choose certain meanings when others, sometimes radically different ones, are also possible. It also underscores the importance of teaching hermeneutical tools to queer Muslims who do not speak Arabic, so that they can find a meaning for themselves.

Believers as far back and as authoritative as 'Ali ibn Ali Talib (Muhamad's cousin and son-in-law and one of his successors) confess that the Quran "does not speak with a tongue; it needs interpreters and interpreters are people."[7] Farid Esack offers that the Quran itself sanctions new theological expressions rooted in personal and group experiences:

> Dogma may precede praxis, but not in a case of theology that is committed to liberation . . . The qur'anic statement "and to those who struggle in Our way, to them We shall show Our ways" (29:29) affirms this view of "doing" theology.[8]

The queer hermeneutics, asking that the law reflect the needs of the people it governs, is organized here around Amina Wadud's proposal for a hermeneutics of *tawhid* (meaning unity) emphasizing "how the unity of the Quran permeates all its parts."[9] This hermeneutics sharply contrasts the "linear-atomistic approach" to the Quran that looks into the scriptures verse by verse, or even as parts of one verse. Even so, a close look at the origins of specific words and verses is indispensable. Though disassembling the law may suggest a destruction of the whole, I strive to reunite problematic parts with the overarching Quranic ethos of human liberation. Rather than destroying the whole, realigning its parts with the general message should, in fact, strengthen it.

The Prophet's *ahadith* offer a second clue to understanding God's intentions within the sometimes ambiguous Quranic text, but the *hadith* literature also incorporates a spectrum of attitudes and opinions. Barlas raises the problematic point that the medieval exegesis abandoned the Quran in favor of *hadith,* even if the latter clashed with the former. Here, we see society imposing oppressive meaning onto the sacred text. Amreen Jamal suggests:

> Rather than the Quran having influenced the *hadith,* the *hadith* literature has managed to connect Lot and same-sex sexuality exclusively, thus influencing various interpretations of the Quran, [and] perhaps also accounting for the later Islamic attitudes toward same-sex sexuality.[10]

Barbara Stowasser compellingly argues that the negative *hadith* may have been fabricated to fill in the blanks left by the metaphorical language of the Quran.[11] Nonetheless, rather than *a priori* dismissing the *hadith* due to possible contaminations, deeper analysis reveals that internal inconsistencies may be extremely valuable to queer-friendly rearticulations of the scripture.

Ijma?, or the consensus of the Muslim community, is a concept much harder to define, as Islam now spans virtually all continents. Though legal pronouncements remain historically harsh, expressions of same-gender sexualities or non-normative gender identities abound, particularly in the ʿAbbāsid period. Although the past 10 years have seen a growing movement of progressive Muslims willing to enter into a dialogue about a queer vision of Islam, articles and books on the subject remain far and few between. For example, few works on Islam parallel the meticulous tracings of paradigm shifts achieved by Biblical or Torah theologians.

I am interested in queering Islam by queering the claim on Islam. The concept is suggested by Barlas' interest in "querying the claim, implicit in confusing the Quran with its patriarchal exegesis, that only men, and conservative men at that, know what God *really* means."[12] Barlas is relentless in arguing "interpreters of sacred knowledge became its architects instead, reducing, by a series of mediations, Divine Discourse to their own interpretations of it."[13] I argue along with Barlas that Islamic scholars have *constructed their own* ontology of gender and sexuality, though they believe(d) themselves to be purely relating God's unchanging message. That the process may have crystallized subconsciously rather than maliciously still does not excuse the stubbornness of contemporary Islamic societies in working to preserve the status quo when so many are calling for change.

Even those with the best of intentions can yield to the confusion between divinity and its human interpreters. Amreen Jamal, for example, fears:

> [I]f Muslims are to continue to take the Quran as the unchangeable word of God, then queer Muslims have little choice. This then means that the reform movement within the Muslim homosexual community has to raise the question of the authority of the Quran and whether a text from the seventh century should indeed be allowed to legislate the twenty-first century.[14]

Jamal, like many others, seems to *a priori* dismiss that there can be a compatibility between the Quran and queerness. Nonetheless, regarding the Quran as the sacred word of God, or Sharia as divine law, we need not imply that *our* understanding of the message has not changed. Every reading of sacred texts, and especially the often ambiguous Quran, is always an interpretation, thus allowing and even calling for new meanings appropriate to each generation. The task at hand, then, is not abandoning or reanalyzing all religious codes, but maintaining a connection with God devoid of oppressive accounts brought about by biased humans. When approaching the Quran, Barlas asks whether the text is at all biased toward the male. I take her approach further and posit that the Quran (though not always its interpreters) is *unequivocally* committed to human liberation and erasing biases between people(s). Comprehended under this axiom, the sacred texts can indeed become a powerful moral tool, showing incredible freshness in providing hope and strength to the oppressed.

The chapter here builds on Abdelwahab Bouhdiba's articulations in *Sexuality in Islam,* on sexuality's prominent place within the religion.[15] Bouhdiba's version of Islam—one extremely affirmative of sexuality—is priceless to queer readings. The author places tremendous emphasis on reciprocity, a concept important in my exegesis of the story of Lot, historically the foundation for oppression of same-gender sexuality. He claims:

> If the unity of self passes through the two poles of sexuality and the love of God it is because they are ultimately one and the same thing. Moreover, in both cases there is reciprocity and reaction. Neither with the human partner, nor with God, does Islam accept one-way love. And reciprocity in one case implies reciprocity in the other.[16]

By extension, other Quranic requirements for egalitarianism imply that an oppression of a fellow human, including that of an unfair gender system, may show a profound disrespect toward God. Quran 49:13 reminds us that we are created different, "that / Ye may know each other / (Not that ye may despise / Each other)."[17] Here, differences do not imply hierarchy or incompatibility, but are rather a device that triggers human learning. The sexual act must be based on respect and reciprocity in order for the sexuality encountered in others to become a projection of God.[18] Sex, a union of two people in love regardless of their gender, opens the door to glimpses of God's own transcending unity and majesty.

The queer hermeneutics of *tawhid* begins with the Quranic story of humankind's origins, tracing all humans to one primordial soul. Wadud speculates that God created one human soul, *nafs*—grammatically feminine but conceptually genderless—dividing it into two equal male and female counterparts. She bases her discussion on verse 4:1:

> He created You (humankind) *min* [from, of same nature] a single *nafs,* and created *min* [from, of same nature] (that *nafs*) its *zawj* [mate, spouse], and from these two He spread (through the earth) countless men and women.[19]

Unlike the Platonic version of the story, I submit that the division of this primordial soul was not intended as a perfect separation: each pair carries a piece of the other. Consequently, two souls need not imply a binary tension, since they both trace back to one *nafs* and ultimately One

God. Bouhdiba's lens presents the creation of pairs as a gift of rejoicing at God's Oneness when uniting with significant others. Pains of love and desire are not simply longings to find our other half, but also to, once united in a sexual embrace, come closer to God.

Wadud suggests that each member of the created pair presupposes the other so that the pair's reality depends on a constitutive correlation. Such a relationship understands identity formation through *affirmation,* not *disavowal* of the other, allowing the other to lose its capital O and outsider status. Dominant ontology, on the other hand, views male and female as "natural" opposites, implying at once irreconcilable differences between genders and mutual incompatibility in same-gender relationships. Wadud declares "compatible mutually supportive functional relationships between men and women can be seen as part of the goal of the Quran with regard to society."[20] Bouhdiba likewise writes of the "profound complementarity of the masculine and the feminine."[21] But if, as Wadud alludes, the text nowhere establishes essentialist male and female descriptors, these compatible relationships can occur between any two individuals, regardless of their gender, as well as within one person.

The queer hermeneutics of *tawhid* then implies not only analyzing the text as a unified whole, but considering humankind as a whole rather than as split in two. Essentialist claims on male and female natures and the corresponding roles in society thereby disappear, leaving us free to imagine pairings based on complementary characteristics other than simply biological sex. Given the lack of requirement for sexual acts to result in procreation and given ways that sexuality can celebrate God, we can imagine same-gender couples who are as life-giving as their opposite-gender neighbors.

Unfortunately, traditional hermeneutics contends that God considers same-gender sexual acts abominable and a crime not just against morality but also against nature. Because most condemnations of same-gender sexuality start with the story of Lot, a close examination of references to Lot is indispensable to the new queer hermeneutics. I have already alluded that the translations of problematic verses vary widely, highlighting the need to trace the origins of such vehemently oppositional views and to find new meanings. English words such as *sodomy* or *sodomite* and Arabic *lūti* (from Lut), referring to same-gender sexual acts, take for granted that Sodom was punished exclusively for same-gender sex.[22] In contrast, I situate Lot in a much wider context of other messengers whose people rejected their call toward *Islam*—in its original form, meaning submission to God—and consequently paid the price, not for same-gender sex, but for their ignorance. I agree with McNeill's Biblical analysis that sees Lot's story as an illustration of wickedness in general, and pride and inhospitality in particular.[23] Starting with the assumption that, from a plethora of meanings, scholars have selected specific ones for specific goals, I aspire not to erase sexual connotations of some problematic words completely, but rather to place them in a larger context of warnings not to turn away from God. Tracing word appearances suggests a metonymical slide, inconsistent with the hermeneutics of *tawhid,* from a general injunction against indecency toward a very specific and modern application regarding (male) homosexuality.

Recall claims that the *hadith* literature, not the Quran, connects Lot and same-gender sexuality, as well as suspicions that some *hadith* may have been invented, possibly under the influence of negative *isra'iliyyat* (i.e., stories and ahadith emanating from Judeo-Christian sources). Immediately, a close analysis of challenging Quranic passages becomes a priority for a queer-affirmative theology and social movement. Jamal lists fourteen *surahs* that make references to Lot: 6:85–87, 7:78–82, 11:73 and 11:79–84, 15:58–77, 21:70–71 and 21:74–75, 22:43–44, 26:160–176, 27:55–59, 29:25 and 29:27–34, 37:133–138, 38:11–14, 50:12–13, 54:33–40 and 66:10, the last verse referring to Lot's wife rather than Lot himself.[24] Significantly addressed to men only, the passages contain a few noteworthy phrases, namely *approaching, lust, lewdness* or *indecency,* and *women/spouses.* The hermeneutics of *tawhid* dictates that, given the text's overarching themes of God's love and human love, and given that each problematic word in any other context has nonsexual connotations, interpretation should be shifted away from a narrow-minded condemnation of same-gender sex toward a broader understanding of ignoring God's call to *islam.*

According to *A Concordance of the Quran,* the phrase *ya'ti*—approaching someone, presumably in a sexual manner—generally denotes neutral actions such as "to approach, to commit, to perform, to come to or upon," out of which committing an "indecency" (again, assuming its sexual nature) is mentioned only 12 times. While the Quran warns both men and women against approaching indecency, thus constructing the phrase in gender and sexually neutral terms, if it refers to sexual acts at all, *ya'ti* in these verses now suspiciously signifies only male–male coitus. Throughout, *ya'ti* is qualified with the concept of *shahwah,* nonsexual lust akin to gluttony. While traditionally restricted to denoting a man's lust toward other males, *shahwah* generally depicts coveting the pleasures of this world that can turn a believer from prayer and God's path (e.g., 4:27 and 9:59, respectively). Likewise, the corresponding verb "to desire" usually appears in an environment of otherworldly rewards or punishments: while unbelievers long to suppress the truth (34:54), believers will be rewarded in heaven with all they desire (43:71, 52:22, 56:21, 77:42). Since sexual lust is denoted by *hamma, shahwah* is better understood as a human weakness used by idolaters to turn the believers away from God. Systematically embellishing earth's pleasures, pagans cause the believers to desire not God's eschatological promises but quick, though temporary, rewards.

In view of Stowasser's allegation that Bible-related traditions have influenced Quranic exegesis, findings by Biblical scholars help rid the interpretation of biased human assumptions. McNeill points out that Old Testament Hebrew consciousness connects same-gender sex with idolatry:

> It was a practice among some of Israel's neighbors to use both sexes as part of fertility rites in the temple services . . . Whenever homosexual activity is mentioned in the Old Testament, the author usually has in mind the use male worshippers made of male prostitutes provided by temple authorities.[25]

Here, the idolaters created a system of sacred prostitution in the temple, using sex in its basest form as a carnal exchange in order to worship false gods. The ban against lusting after members of the same gender pertains not to a reciprocal union, but to idolaters' rejection of God and disrespect of the integrity of the bodies used. The reasoning is underscored by Bouhdiba's discussion on reciprocity as central to Islamic values surrounding sexuality. Emphasizing orgasm as a shared pleasure, Bouhdiba finds "sexuality *encountered in others* . . . [as] a projection of God."[26] Sacred prostitution *uses* the body and exploits sex for pagan worship, disrespecting God in two ways. Being a one-sided pleasure, it denies the prostitute's humanity; through the theory of one *nafs,* it denies God's projection in either of the souls engaged in the practice. Desiring sexual acts, regardless of the partner's gender, does not necessarily contradict Islamic morality, but exploiting these acts in a nonreciprocal ritual does. In this worldview, God is not angered by same-gender sex, but by the use of bodies to worship false gods.

The term *fāhishah* (from the root FHSH), which the Quran applies to
Lot's people, likewise indicates general lewdness and indecency instead
of narrow connotations of same-gender coitus. Words from this root appear in three Lot-related passages, 7:78–82, 27:55–59 and 29:27–34, while
other terms from the same root can be found an additional 21 times in the
Quran.[27] The term *fāhishah* stands for a broad idea of sin, while in four
cases (4:15, 19, 25 and 17:34) it indicates adultery. Leaving implications of
adultery for a later analysis, consider that

> The term "indecency" (*fāhishah*) in Q.29/27 is used in reference to an in-
> discretion connected to those who "approach men, and cut the way" and
> who also commit "dishonour" (*munkar*) in the assembly.[28]

"Cutting the way" in Quran 29:27 indicates the sin of Lot's people as
highway robbery, a serious transgression in times when an attack on a
lonely traveler in the midst of the desert usually meant certain death. On
the other hand, author Richard Bell believes "there is no evidence that the
people of Lot were accused of that [i.e., highway robbery]. It [the phrase
in question] must mean 'cut off the way of offspring' or 'bar the ordinary
way.'"[29] Forcing a modification from a general injunction to an extremely
specific prohibition, Bell ignores the more or less straightforward interpretations analyzed above and stubbornly demands a reading that implicates and forbids same-gender sexuality. Bell disregards the Quranic text
itself and Islam's lack of requirement that each sexual act result in a procreative opportunity in his need to impose an ontological stigma on queer
individuals.

Conservative interpretations like Bell's attempt to entrap queer sexuality in unnatural, not just immoral terms. Essential qualities are assigned
to men and women in order to imply that the only naturally acceptable
pairing occurs between diametrically opposite individuals capable of producing offspring. This reading ignores the high value Bouhdiba's exegesis
places on love and sex as ends in themselves, without the need for procreation. Consider that Quranic passages on Lot always couple the concept of
"approaching men" with the idea of abandoning women/wives. Two words
appear in these verses: *nisā'* and *zawj*, the former denoting both "women"
and "wives," while the latter almost exclusively designating "spouse(s)."
While this warning has traditionally been read invoking men not to abandon *women* as their natural mates, the hermeneutics of *tawhid* insists that

the word in question be understood as *spouses*. Any natural, essentialist allusions are therefore erased, leaving the phrase located in moral terms concerning adultery. The immorality then arises not from the gender of one's sexual partner but rather from the moral choice to break a marital promise. Simultaneously, the verse becomes significantly liberating to women who have as much a need for sexual pleasure as their spouses.

Although *fāhishah* may denote a broader reading of sin, several of the verses call for a narrowing of the meaning to infidelity. Verse 17:34, for example, explicitly connects *fāhishah* with adultery: "And approach not fornication [*zina'*]; surely it is indecency [*fāhishah*], and it is evil [*sa'a*] as a way."[30] Infidelity parallels sacred prostitution in its perversion of a sexual act that disrespects, rather than celebrates, the body of another human being. Observing fertility rites inherently involves breaking a vow of faithfulness made to one's spouse—a moral crime the Quran explicitly mentions by name.[31] The discussion on the *immorality* of adultery lifts *unnatural* implications from two other verses discussing indecency between two men or two women. Jamal translates verse 4:19 as "Such of your women as commit indecency [*fāhishah*], call four of you to witness against them; and if they witness, then detain them in their houses until death takes them or God appoints for them a way."[32] Similarly, 4:20 instructs: "And when the two of you[33] commit indecency, punish them both; but if they repent and make amends, then suffer them to be; God turns and is all-compassionate."[34] Many arguments can repudiate that the above verses speak about sex between two members of the same gender: *fāhishah*'s linguistic ambiguity obscures what *indecency* signifies in the first place and whether the subjects are committing it together or with another party of a different gender. However, arguing that the verse indeed stands for adultery committed by a same-gender couple results in astonishing ontological implications for same-gender love and sexuality as discussed in the Quran. Assuming a same-gender couple, the Quran then acknowledges a possibility of same-gender *zina'*[35] and, by extension, same-gender desire, placing it on an entirely equal footing with its opposite-gender counterpart. This somewhat radical conclusion is supported by several *hadith* analyzed below. The precedent is also set in verses that explicitly name women's rights and responsibilities, ensuring their equal station with men.[36] Rather than rendering same-gender sex an unnatural and immoral abomination, this verse seems to recognize its possibility in everyday life, striving not to forbid it, but to regulate it in the same way as opposite-gender intercourse.

The last piece of the puzzle concerns Lot's offering of his daughters to the crowd assembled at his house. The townspeople want to punish Lot for his moral warnings, but instead of a direct attack on Lot, they choose vengeance on his guests, an approach more degrading considering the sacred status given to hospitality discussed above. The verses in question read:

> And when Our messengers came to Lot, he was troubled [si'a] on their account and distressed for them, and he said, "This is a fierce day." And his people came to him, running towards him; and erstwhile they had been doing evil deeds [sayyi'at]. He said, "O my people, these are my daughters; they are cleaner [athar] for you. So fear God, and do not degrade [tukhzu] me concerning my guests. What, is there not one man among you of a right mind?" They said, "Thou knowest we have no right to thy daughters, and thou well knowest what we desire [nuridu]."[37]

The passage implies the townspeople's desire for some sort of sexual contact with Lot's guests, making the key issue discernment of Lot's intentions in "giving away" his daughters and the crowd's corresponding answer that the daughters are not what they "desire." Jamal insists on the daughters' superior "cleanliness" as a direct symbol for the uncleanliness of same-gender sexual relations. On the other hand, she notes "the term 'clean' is used in an ironical fashion by those who were destroyed to refer to Lot. The city dwellers, in what seems to be a mocking fashion, jeer at Lot and his people for being 'clean.'"[38] Their previous mockery of Lot's cleanliness indicates that the crowd's desire lies in the symbolic rather than the physical plane. The term itself is situated similarly to shahwah, which speaks of turning away from God toward the passing pleasures of this world.[39] Jamal notes numerous uses of terms from the root RWD referring to nonsexual activities, as well as the moral-religious implications when used to denote sexuality. The latter passages, for example, refer to the Egyptian Governor's wife's desire for Joseph, who must remain faithful to God. Violating the host's sacred responsibility toward his guests, Lot's people choose the visitors rather than the family as the object of their intended defilement through rape, in order to bring out Lot's greater humiliation. The crowd's "desire" for the visitors cannot be farther from a reciprocal union, leaving rape, not consensual sex, as the abomination in question. A sexual act is implied, but only as a symbol of the townspeople's disrespect toward Lot's message to obey God, as well as his degradation.

Like the Quran, the *hadith,* read in a different light, appear to be validating rather than condemning same-gender sexuality. Though, as mentioned, the negative *hadith* may have been fabricated, their internal inconsistencies may be used to support a queer exegesis. On the one hand, authors like Jim Wafer believe that the Prophet took a lenient attitude toward same-gender sex, or that he viewed it with "philosophical indifference."[40] Wafer's comments on the aforesaid verse 4:20 note that punishment is not indicated, meaning that the Prophet was interested in *regulation,* not *prohibition.* Everett Rowson analyzes *hadith* about the Prophet's attitude toward cross-dressing men and uncovers surprising approval of their gender transgressions, which I take as a similar approval for non-normative sexual practices.[41] Rowson finds that the Prophet chastised these men not for their gender-crossing but for divulging secrets of his private life; this is very similar to the Quran asking for a punishment of adulterous indecency, not a blanket prohibition of same-gender sex. Paralleling Quranic understanding of indecency discussed above, some *hadith* are explicit in placing impulses toward either genders on the same level. Addressed to men, these *hadith* charge: "Keep not company with the sons of Kings, for verily souls desire them" or "Do not gaze at the beardless youths, for verily they have eyes more tempting than the houris."[42] Siraj Kugle points out that these *hadith* may have originated in the 'Abbasid period and then projected back upon the Prophet. If authoritative, the *hadith* radically acknowledge same-gender desire as an inherent inclination and attempt to regulate it, not completely restrict it. Even if fabricated, the *hadith* then speak of a current within a period in Islamic history when same-gender desire was acknowledged and at least tolerated, if not accepted.

Contrary to this tolerant or even affirmative attitude, Wafer cites several other intensely negative *hadith*, the most severe example testifying that

> Whenever a male mounts another male, the throne of God trembles; the angels look in loathing and say, Lord, why do you not command the earth to punish them and the heavens to rain stones on them?[43]

Though many medieval scholars have argued that the *hadith* is clearly fabricated, it remains one of the most cited examples of colloquial understanding of same-gender sexuality and the wrath it incurs with the Divine. Those eager to quote this *hadith* to justify oppression should recall that, though individuals have practiced same-gender sex for millennia, God has *not* commanded the heavens to rain stones on them. Even if we take the Quran as a historical rather than metaphorical account, Lot's story remains the only instance where God interfered with humanity for anything relating to same-gender sex. As'ad AbuKhalil records a *hadith* insisting, "He whom you find doing the deed of Lot's people, kill . . . the doer and the one being done unto."[44] According to Wafer, caliph Abu Bakr is supposed to have had a man engaged in same-gender sex burned alive, while Ibn 'Abbās argued that such men should be thrown from the highest building in town and then stoned.[45] Focusing exclusively on men, these *hadith* and punishments assume same-gender coitus as *the* cause for destruction of Lot's people, a claim this exegesis finds not so unambiguous. These assumptions operate either through linguistics—as mentioned, Arabic *lūti* derives from Lot[46]—or through the manner of the punishment—hurling a man from a tower replicates the method of Sodom's destruction. The lawmakers, eager to satisfy their own fears and prejudices, almost lay entitlement to punishments God has reserved for Himself. Wafer thus observes the dispute over authenticity due to a lack of Quranic sanction for the death penalty for any illicit sexual act,[47] as well as their unusual severity running counter to traditional Islamic punishments. The new Quranic exegesis offered here further jeopardizes the validity of such severely negative *hadith*, viewing them as products of human biases.

Overall, the passages concerning Lot may indeed speak of same-gender sex, but always as a nonreciprocal exploitation of bodies, whether as sacred prostitution, adultery, or rape. In the essay "Let Us Bless Our Angels,"[48] Robin Gorsline suggests a contemporary reinterpretation of the account of Sodom as a categorical imperative of liberation theologies that sacred texts should be living words offering hope and strength. Though I am not necessarily endorsing her interpretation, as the language assumes a contemporary understanding of same-gender sexuality originating in the West, Gorsline's narrative exemplifies how the same text can produce radically different meanings. In Gorsline's scenario, Lot's two visitors are a gay[49] couple to whom Lot immediately offers shelter. The crowd, recognizing the visitors' sexual orientation from their "effeminate" behavior (which Gorsline fails to discuss as an overgeneralization), demands that Lot gives his queer guests over so that they can be given "a taste of their own medicine" and realize "how disgusting they are."[50] The narrative reemphasizes the need to understand the Quran as prohibiting contempt for fellow human beings, not Bouhdiba's "loving fusion of bodies and spirits."[51]

Current interpretation, on the other hand, requests that queer people "see their deepest and sincere human love as cutting themselves and their loved ones off from God."[52] If words thought to be unambiguous are proved to be quite vague, and if someone like Gorsline could read Lot's story in a pro- rather than antiqueer light, we cannot turn a blind eye toward considering the *what if* scenarios outlined in the introduction to this chapter. If it is possible that human interpretation imposed specific meanings onto words that could be read radically differently in a new light, and if these new meanings allow for greater inclusion, then Muslims *must* consider them a viable option, rather than dismissing them *a priori* just because they imply a break with tradition. Queer hermeneutics of Islam imply doing theology and asking questions whose answers can create solace for the oppressed.

Though the theories presented here may seem radical to many readers, I do not introduce new concepts, but only explore inconsistencies already present in textual interpretations. I have argued that the sacred texts relent- lessly speak of equality and complementarity between men and women, which must, first and foremost, be reflected in sexual acts as a window into God's Unity. T. C. DeKruijf argues: "If one does not acknowledge the only true personal God, it follows unavoidably that one will also not acknowl- edge one's fellow man as a person who has a value of his own."[53] This dictum certainly rings true for Lot's people who "(ab)used human bodies, their own and others," in worship of false gods. Instead of an oppressive system, queer visions of Islam invite a fluid matrix that brings about the Quranic demand for human equality and sexual celebration.

Rather than violating the binary tension between male and female, the problem with this and similar projects is the violation of the tension be- tween public and private, and between Islam and the West. Rowson makes a key point distinguishing sexual behavior as a private matter, while gen- der is a public one:

> In a society where public power was a monopoly of those marked for gender as (adult) men, those not so marked were, as such, no threat, nor was their gender identity a focus of great concern . . . More problematic was the case of men who maintained a public image as men, yet in their private sexual behavior assumed a submissive [*sic*] role.[54]

Steven Oberhelman echoes this sentiment by claiming "a penetrated male citizen was a sexual but not a social possibility."[55] Joseph Massad resonates with these claims when speaking of the contemporary Cairo 52 case, where 52 men were arrested on a boat in Egypt for charges of unlawful sodomy.[56] Massad finds "that it is not same-sex sexual practices that are being repressed by the Egyptian police but rather the sociopolitical identification of these practices with the Western identity of gayness and publicness that these gay men seek."[57] The prosecution in the Cairo 52 case "pledged to defend the 'manhood' of Egypt against attempts to 'violate' it, and wondered what would become of a nation who [sic] sits by idly as its 'men become like its women' through 'deviance.'"[58] Upset at the public exposure of its secret "vices," branded as Western-led emasculation, the Egyptian state elects masculine virility, and its partner, feminine seclusion, as identifiers of national identity.

The overlap here of international politics, national history, spiritual connection, and sexual identity raises many problems for a queer Islamic hermeneutics. That modern-day queer liberation started in the West does not mean queer sexuality is a Western concept, as the preceding examples would have us believe. On the contrary, I have argued that non-normative gender and sexuality existed—tolerated, but perhaps even celebrated—throughout Muslim history. Similarly, Islam's sacred texts offer possibility for reinterpretations that inspire, rather than obstruct, thought, dialogue, and expression. Islam can be queried and queered—and I argue that indeed it has been—in a way that reaffirms faith, not negates it. Engaging the divine to find new answers to questions posed by modernity and allowing for a dialogue would require Muslims to be comfortable with multiple interpretations and multiple Islams (which, again, may already exist). I recognize that many would rather accept a single, monolithic interpretation rather than face the open-ended ambiguity of multiplicity of thought. If, however, we can find God through relationships with others in the space opened up by the exchange of human ideas, affection, and kindness toward one another, we must embrace the possibility of dialogue and construct a positive theology that would answer the needs of those who desperately need it.

Queer Muslims are alienated, attacked, and even executed simply because of expressing love and desire toward someone of the same gender. A liberation theology must embrace them too, especially when new readings of sacred texts suggest radical reinterpretations that are affirmative of sexuality. The hermeneutics of *tawhid*, whether applied to queer readings or everyday questions, can help in avoiding any kind of moral relativism, finding instead universal messages of God's love for humanity and an invitation to celebrate and wonder at all creation, not lessen it by small-mindedness and stubbornness against change. The road ahead is long, but I am optimistic; to borrow from Robert Frost, it is the road less traveled, and it will make all the difference.

NOTES

1. I avoid Western contemporary labels, which can both limit definitions and invite criticism of a Western agenda. *Same-gender sex* or *sexuality* will therefore be used—rather than more charged labels such as *homo-, hetero-,* or *bisexuality*—referring to acts between members of the same gender regardless of their professed or perceived sexual orientation. *Queer* remains the exception to the rule; sufficiently vague to avoid essentialist classification, it persists as the only term successfully encapsulating an intersection between non-normative sexualities and gender expressions.

2. Asma Barlas, *"Believing Women" in Islam: Unreading Patriarchal Interpretations of the Quran* (Austin: University of Texas Press, 2002), 2.

3. John J. McNeill, *Taking a Chance on God* (Boston: Beacon Press, 1996), 2.

4. See Joseph Schacht, *An Introduction to Islamic Law* (Oxford: Clarendon Press, 1964).

5. Ahmed Ali, *Al-Quran: A Contemporary Translation* (Princeton, NJ: Princeton University Press, 1988).

6. Muhammad Baqir Behbudi and Colin Turner, *The Quran: A New Interpretation* (Surrey: Curzon Press, 1993).

7. Farid Esack, *Quran, Liberation and Pluralism* (Oxford: Oneworld Publications, 1997), 50.

8. Esack, *Quran, Liberation and Pluralism,* 85.

9. Amina Wadud, *Quran and Woman: Rereading the Sacred Text from a Woman's Perspective* (New York: Oxford University Press, 1999), xii.

10. Amreen Jamal, "The Story of Lot and the Quran's Perception of the Morality of Same-Sex Sexuality," *Journal of Homosexuality* 41, no. 1 (2001): 1–88, 68.

11. Barbara Freyer Stowasser, *Women in the Quran, Traditions, and Interpretations* (New York: Oxford University Press, 1994).

12. Barlas, *"Believing Women" in Islam,* 19.

13. Ibid., 67.

14. Jamal, "The Story of Lot," 63.

15. Abdelwahab Bouhdiba, *Sexuality in Islam* (London: Saqi Books, 1998).

16. Ibid., 124.

17. Cited in Barlas, *"Believing Women" in Islam,* 145.

18. Bouhdiba, *Sexuality in Islam,* 92.

19. Cited in Wadud, *Quran and Woman,* 17.

20. Ibid., 8.

21. Bouhdiba, *Sexuality in Islam,* 30.

22. The Quran, significantly, never employs the names Sodom and Gomorrah—these proper names came into Quranic exegesis and social mentality through Bible-related traditions or *isra'iliyyat,* paralleling how negative views on women found their way into the Islamic canon (see Stowasser, *Women in the Quran,* for more detail).

23. John J. McNeill, *The Church and the Homosexual* (Boston: Beacon Press, 1993), 36–66.

24. Jamal, "The Story of Lot," 10. Jim Wafer offers a somewhat reduced list: 7:80–84, 11:77–83, 21:74, 22:43, 26:165–175, 27:56–59, 29:27–33. See Jim Wafer, "Muhammad and Male Homosexuality," in *Islamic Homosexualities: Culture, History, and Literature,* ed. Stephen O. Murray and Will Roscoe (New York: New York University Press, 1997), 87–96.

25. McNeill, *The Church and the Homosexual,* 57.

26. Bouhdiba, *Sexuality in Islam,* 92.

27. Jamal, "The Story of Lot," 25.

28. Ibid.

29. Cited in Jamal, "The Story of Lot," 75.

30. Ibid., 27.

31. Significantly, the Quran asks that final judgment be left to God; though it is a sin to disrespect the body of another human, God remains the ultimate judge.

32. Jamal, "The Story of Lot," 26.

33. Masculine dual, which could potentially be used for masculine *and* feminine plural.

34. Jamal, "The Story of Lot," 26.

35. In cases of *zina',* four witnesses who have seen the actual sexual act are needed to legally implicate the parties. Most other legal disputes require only two male witnesses.

36. According to Barlas, Umm Salama, one of Muhamad's wives, is said to have asked the Messenger why God was not addressing women directly in the Quran, instead grammatically lumping both men and women under the male plural form. As a result, numerous passages address men and women simultaneously. See Barlas,*"Believing Women" in Islam,* 20.

37. Cited in Jamal, "The Story of Lot," 13–14.

38. Jamal, "The Story of Lot," 37. I am grateful to Prof. Siraj Kugle for pointing out that the term in question is *mutattahirīn,* meaning "those who *think* themselves clean," making the irony even more profound.

39. The concept does not imply that Islam negates pleasure; on the contrary, Bouhdiba's analysis shows Islam as an extremely sex- and pleasure-affirmative religion. The problem arises when pleasure becomes the sole focus of one's life and causes one to abandon God.

40. Wafer, "Muhammad and Male Homosexuality," 89.

41. Everett K. Rowson, "The Effeminates of Early Medina," *Journal of the American Oriental Society* 111, no. 4 (1991): 671–93.

42. J.W. Wright Jr., "Masculine Allusion and the Structure of Satire in Early 'Abbāsid Poetry," in *Homoeroticism in Classical Arabic Literature*, ed. J. W. Wright, Jr. and Everett K. Rowson (New York: Columbia University Press, 1997), 7.

43. Wafer, "Muhammad and Male Homosexuality," 89.

44. As'ad AbuKhalil, "A Note on the Study of Homosexuality in the Arab/Islamic Civilization." *The Arab Studies Journal* (1993): 32–34, 48.

45. Wafer, "Muhammad and Male Homosexuality," 90.

46. Ironically, Lot is the messenger of God who remains pure in this story, and has himself no connection to same-gender sex.

47. Though the Quran suggests flogging for *zina'*, Sharia sometimes asks for the extreme punishment by death.

48. Robin Gorsline, "Let Us Bless Our Angels: A Feminist-Gay-Male-Liberation View of Sodom," in *Redefining Sexual Ethics: A Sourcebook of Essays, Stories, and Poems*, ed. Susan Davies and Eleanor H. Haney (Cleveland, OH: The Pilgrim Press, 1991), 45–56.

49. Her terminology assumes a self-identified same-gender couple in a reciprocal union.

50. Gorsline, "Let us Bless Our Angels," 54.

51. Bouhdiba, *Sexuality in Islam*, 97.

52. McNeill, *The Church and the Homosexual*, 33.

53. Cited in McNeill, *The Church and the Homosexual*, 62.

54. Rowson, "The Effeminates of Early Medina," 72.

55. Steven M. Oberhelman, "Hierarchies of Gender, Ideology, and Power in Medieval Greek and Arabic Dream Literature," in *Homoeroticism in Classical Arabic Literature*, ed. J. W. Wright, Jr. and Everett K. Rowson (New York: Columbia University Press, 1997), 55–93.

56. Joseph Massad, "Re-Orienting Desire: The Gay International and the Arab World," *Public Culture* 14, no. 2 (2002): 361–85.

57. Ibid., 382.

58. Ibid., 383.

15

QUEER, AMERICAN, AND MUSLIM: CULTIVATING IDENTITIES AND COMMUNITIES OF AFFIRMATION

Mahruq Fatima Khan

It is often noted that immigrant congregations use religion and religious organizational resources to cushion their experience as minorities in a host society, especially soon after arrival.[1] For Muslims living in the West, the fragile interplay between religious followers and the broader society manifests itself in remarkable ways. At times, it can entail a heightened, insular, and traditionalist religiosity among certain believers who struggle to maintain the social cohesion of their minority group during rapidly changing times. Other times, however, minorities struggle to have members of a dominant group perceive them as just as American as the next person, despite the pervasive, anti-Muslim hostility fomented in a post-9/11 United States.

Given the current political context within which American Muslims find themselves, strong ties to a faith community provide reassurance, solidarity, and emotional support for those facing prejudice and discrimination and enable resistance against larger structures of inequality. Simultaneously, the solidarity established by social networks bestows a particular legitimacy on the religious establishment. In this process of community members attaining social benefits and solidifying membership within the group, internal critiques against certain religious worldviews (e.g., homophobia) can be seen as threatening the solidarity of the group and are often met with resistance.

Much sociological research on Muslims in the United States focuses on studying formal congregations. Not all spiritual activity of a religious community occurs within institutions, however. By only focusing both on institutionalized forms of practice and on the relationship between religious institutions and their members, the lived experiences of many deinstitutionalized (and often marginalized) members, including queer Muslims, are often left out. Understanding the lived experiences of queer Muslims is critical since, as Nancy Ammerman notes, individuals who find themselves in both warring camps at the same time must engage in active identity work, especially where significant collective identities appear to stand in opposition to one another, as in the case of being gay and Muslim.[2]

Focusing on gay Muslims, especially second-generation immigrants, allows several arenas of marginality to converge at once: what does it mean to be queer in the diaspora? Similarly, what does it mean to be Muslim in broader queer American circles? How do heterosexual Muslims use religious discourse to discuss homosexuality? As a result, how are queer American Muslims reconciling their religious identity with their sexual orientation as members of both a traditional religious community and a civil society, where greater tolerance toward homosexuality exists? Here, I begin by highlighting the moral and social boundaries that queer American Muslims encounter within mosques, families, and communities as well as the consequences of such discourse and social interaction on their lives. I further elaborate on the strategies queer Muslims adopt to reformulate their social identities and foster supportive communities, allowing for a reconciliation of seemingly oppositional facets of their lives.

METHODOLOGY

This data emerges from my dissertation research, where I conducted approximately 55 in-depth interviews with both heterosexual and queer Muslims who primarily[3] live or have lived throughout the United States. By speaking with queer Muslims, I examined the types of beliefs and interactions they confronted with their families, Muslim friends, and religious communities. I solicited interviews through the queer Muslim e-mail groups and snowball sampling.[4]

Interviewing heterosexual Muslims who supported the normative religious practices of gender segregation, distinct gender roles, and who condemned homosexuality or alternative sexual behaviors and opposed women-led prayers allowed me to access to the plausibility structures, meaning the systems and rhetorical strategies that some Muslims employ to maintain particular beliefs and practices.

ENCOUNTERING HOMOPHOBIA

Since many queer Muslims are first- or second-generation Americans, they are embedded within immigrant faith communities that emphasize the importance of maintaining group solidarity and a distinct identity in their host society. One way they do this is by emphasizing specific family and gender roles.[5] Religious leaders uphold sexual taboos against conduct they see as threatening to the family structure, community stability, and even the survival of their faith itself. The maintenance of these established gender and sexual categories, however, relies in part on the continuous condemnation of any sexual behavior that contradicts these fixed roles.[6] This condemnation, often with the additional backing of scripture or divine law, results in queer Muslims being ostracized by their faith communities.

While many Muslims feel outcast for their religious beliefs in the United States, many also draw religious and social distinctions between themselves and those who challenge the traditional perspectives on the permissibility of particular sexual practices. For example, traditionalist Muslims attempt to distinguish sexual relations within the bounds of heterosexual marriage, which they believe upholds religious ideals, from those Muslims who engage in same-sex or bisexual relationships—viewed as lifestyles corrupted by Western hedonism and lax sexual morals.

In my ethnographic research of Muslims in the United Sates, some heterosexual Muslims expressed homophobia based both on Muslim religious rhetoric and on preexisting homophobia in American culture. All of the queer Muslims I interviewed heard Sunday school teachers, mosque Imams, family members, and Muslim friends describe homosexuality as "wrong," "sinful," and "unacceptable." The cultural (nonreligious) homophobia that heterosexual Muslims propagate includes ridiculing, rendering criminal, and fearing queer persons. Drawing from American culture, some heterosexual believers employ terms such as "sick," "faggots," and "disgusting" to describe queers in general and queer Muslims in particular.

CONSEQUENCES OF HOMOPHOBIA

As Donald Boisvert notes, marginality and exile have clearly emerged as two central images in gay believers' lives.[7] Likewise, feminist and queer Muslims live within a matrix of double, triple, or quadruple intersecting oppressions,[8] while non-Muslims discriminate against them on the basis of religion and often race, and some heterosexist Muslims marginalize them for challenging (or merely failing to comply with) prevailing gender and sexual roles and norms.

The rejection of homosexuality is another common family experience for queer Muslims. Many religious families refuse to accept their son or daughter's dual identity as both Muslim and gay. Especially after they come out, some queer Muslims' families and friends react with blame, guilt, denigration, and emotional disconnection. Some parents also threaten to rescind financial support for their children or try to cure their same-sex desire through psychological counseling or religious healing. As a result, many queer Muslims find their relationships with Muslim relatives and friends strained and they choose to avoid emotionally detrimental relationships. Others opt not to come out because they fear it would dishonor, disrespect, or emotionally burden their families, especially their parents. This distress that queer Muslims experience results in their dissociation from mainstream faith communities, self-loathing, suicide attempts, and efforts aimed at trying to cure themselves of their sexual orientation.

FOSTERING SUPPORTIVE COMMUNITIES AND IDENTITIES

Especially over the past 10 years, conversations regarding homosexuality in general and queer Muslims in particular have flourishing publicly among the growing community of second- and third-generation immigrant and convert Muslims. This is particularly the case for Muslims living in large cities in the United States and Canada and who encounter sexually open and diverse individuals at their universities, workplaces, and residential communities, which now extend far beyond the more isolated ethnic or religious enclaves that may have made up the worlds of their forefathers. In addition, queer Muslims cite heterosexual Muslims who are "college age" and "people in their early 20s and 30s" as among those who have had more exposure to, and demonstrate acceptance of, homosexuality and queer Muslims. Some queer Muslim respondents maintain connections to gay-friendly heterosexual Muslims (and vice versa) in a variety of ways: they are each other's neighbors; they babysit each other's children; they attend the same mosques, *halaqas,*[9] and Friday prayers and even volunteer to prepare *iftar*[10] dinners together; a few are coworkers.

While homophobic sentiments among many Muslims prevail, some 20- or 30-something American heterosexual Muslims are beginning to inject more nuanced concerns (i.e., beyond relegating it as a sin) regarding the way to "deal" with queer persons in general and queer Muslims in particular. More specifically, American-born Muslims are raising this matter formally during mosque board meetings and through religious discourse shaped by American-Muslim academics who have expanded the bounds of religious debate specifically on matters of gender and sexuality.[11]

COMMUNITY

As I alluded earlier, queer Muslims do not always attain social acceptance in the queer community at large due to their religious affiliation. When non-Muslim queers learn of queer Muslims' ties to Islam, they ask them questions about fasting, prayer, polygamy, and hate crimes. In addition, queer Muslims whom I interviewed between February and June 2006 recalled some of the more specific questions that non-Muslim queers ask them, such as: "Are you Muslim? How do you deal with that because Muslims act very aggressively toward the gay community?"; "Do you drink?"; "Do you know about Muslims and women—how they [Muslim men] treat women? Well, I can never be a part of something like that, you know, that treated women like that"; "Is Muhamad a god?"; "We [Christians] will go to heaven because of Jesus, what will you do?"

Many of these questions stem from the American mainstream media's propagation of negative stereotypes of and misconceptions about Muslims as patriarchal, homophobic terrorists. In turn, these anti-Muslim sentiments have exacerbated preexisting stereotypes about Muslims within the broader (non-Muslim) queer community. As a consequence, queer Muslims cannot always rely on these communities for unconditional support, especially as religious affiliation becomes a more divisive factor in determining in-group status. This alienation from their religious and other queer groups, nevertheless, has propelled queer Muslims in the United States to establish and join organizations and communities that uniquely address their ties to Islam and other queer Muslims.

The establishment of faith-based queer support groups underscores the need for queer believers across religious bodies to practice their faith (which can be as strong as those of nongay people) in ways that accurately reflect their concerns for experiencing connection, fellowship, and community with different kinds of people.[12] Most often, queer believers' ability to maintain religious beliefs in their formation of community requires a reexamination and reassessment of their faith. This often entails lesbian and bisexual women, especially, carving out new paths to "enlightenment" by including faith and sexuality in their lived experiences.[13] Furthermore, Maurine C. Waun argues that hegemonic heterosexual cultures either have not or have been reluctant to recognize the histories or existence of queer communities that have not historically been tied to traditional family reproduction and places of origin. As such, the struggle for community building becomes all the more necessary, especially outside of larger cities.[14] The section below details the role and formation of organizations and cyber groups, which are part and parcel of a nascent queer Muslim community.

One of the most prominent institutions established to support queer Muslims in the United States and abroad is Al-Fatiha.[15] Al-Fatiha currently serves and reaches over 3000 people around the world. Faisal Alam founded it in 1997 through an e-mail discussion group out of Boston, Massachusetts. In September 2005, Al-Fatiha held its fifth annual retreat in Atlanta, Georgia to discuss the theme "Sexism, Misogyny and Gender Oppression—Breaking Down the Systems of Patriarchy." This gathering enabled queer Muslims and their straight allies from across North America to convene physically in the same place on nearly an annual basis. For many closeted and openly gay Muslims, the conference(s) has become a site where they form their initial relationships and make contact with other queer Muslims within a safe public space. It also serves a wide range of other functions for queer Muslims, including: sharing conversations about sex, instructions for safe sex techniques, spiritual sex in Islam, instances and accounts of sexual abuse, joining supportive lesbian Muslim women's collectives, and writing erotica together.

First and foremost though, Al-Fatiha provides a space for queer Muslims to support one another morally and emotionally.[16] Often times, this occurs through the communal ritual of sharing coming out stories and learning how different families' reactions affected their queer children. Queer Muslims who attend the conference run the gamut of being completely closeted and growing up guilt-ridden about their sexuality to being among the most vocal and self-assured proponents of gay rights. The collective storytelling allows queer Muslims (especially those who are currently questioning their own sexual orientation(s)) to witness the wide range of queer Muslims' experiences, struggles, and the various techniques that queer Muslim youth employ when coming out to their heterosexual parents and friends.

The al-Fatiha and Salaam Canada[17] organizations have also enabled some non-Muslim queers to take the *shahada*[18] during conferences. The organizations have brought prominent heterosexual and gay national figures, such as Professor Amina Wadud, Imam Daaiyee Abdullah (an openly gay imam in the United States), and Scott Kugle, who published an academic piece in *Progressive Muslims*.[19] Kugle deconstructed religious verses, providing room for an acceptance of homosexuality in religious practice. Queer respondents cite these figures as being instrumental in their personal ability to continue to identify as Muslim despite their struggles with their sexuality. Here, Hina describes her sentiments regarding the first time she attended the al-Fatiha conference and how it shaped her sense of community, spirituality, and self:

> Life changing. I was so scared when I went, and I don't even know why I was scared, but I was. And, I was coming off of coming out of [an] entire month of being crammed into the closet with my family 'cause I was at home over the summer. I remember the very first day that I got there [the al-Fatiha conference]. It was so fucking amazing to look at somebody else and see myself and to see that person as beautiful, which was not how I was feeling about myself at all at the time . . . life changing and life-saving because it was a REALLY rough time. Just to know in theory that I was not the only one, but in [City], there aren't very many of us at all, and at the time, I didn't know anyone, and it's very isolating. It's very disempowering to feel that way and just that initial . . . "Holy shit! There are other people like me. There are other people like me who actually pray and remember how to read Arabic and sometimes pick up the Quran and actually fast. And Holy Shit! Wow! And we strap it on, too." Just having that connection made so much of a difference, and then it validated all of these other things I've been thinking about spirituality, about Islam, about Islam as being a very sexy religion, a very sex-positive religion, about what it means to submit oneself to the Divine, and give oneself over to the Divine, that means being out. It was incredibly empowering. It's still hard being one of the only people in [City] that I know of, and I still want to build a community here. I know I'm not the only one here, but it's SO under-the-rug . . . It's very closeted in [City], and there's tons of fear. I try to be authentic as I can . . . all the time. And I hope that that can act as a beacon to invite spirits around me at some point. —Hina[20]

Gary Comstock's work indicates that, within the gay (non-Muslim) faith communities of the United States, gay members left their gay-rejecting or unwelcoming established religious bodies by forming support groups and networks in addition to their own churches, synagogues, Zen centers, ecumenical groups, campus ministry programs, and *sanghas*—some of which have since become accepted within their mainstream religious bodies.[21] Within the more welcoming congregations that the diverse religious marketplace has to offer, queer believers have not only reclaimed their spiritual legacy,[22] but congregations of even the most hostile denominations have enabled queer persons to take their own (religious) lives and identities more seriously.[23]

While the abovementioned queer Muslim organizations do indeed make a deep impact on the lives of those who actively participate in them, the scope of their functions and activities has not yet led to much regular engagement or dialogue between them and the leadership of mainstream Muslim mosques in America. In other words, a vast disconnect still exists between these queer groups and mainstream Muslim organizations; this explains why mainstream mosques have not yet made explicit, official statements that denounce or accept the existence of these particular groups. Moreover, the primary focus of these organizations is to support the identities and lives of queer Muslims and not necessarily to debate the religious legitimacy of their sexuality with more conservative bodies nor direct their efforts toward gaining acceptance from without. However, this self-focus may be a result of the development stage that these organizations are in currently. As the queer Muslim community grows, the establishment of queer-friendly mosques and a wider engagement between queer groups and the established religious bodies may flourish.

For most queer Muslims across the United States or Canada, there is not always the option of being in close physical proximity to other queer Muslims on a regular basis, or outside of the annual al-Fatiha retreats, especially if they live in smaller cities or towns. However, the Internet is fulfilling queer Muslims' desire for contact and support from a Muslim-affiliated queer community. The widespread access to the internet and the subsequent emergence of LGBTQI Muslim online discussion groups such as Queer Jihad,[24] Trans Muslims,[25] and Muslim Gay Men[26] has fomented an increasingly interconnected, global queer Muslim community where common struggles can be conveniently raised, discussed, and debated in a safe space. Also, in their effort to learn more about their sexual orientation, questioning Muslims conduct Google word searches on "homosexuality and Islam," where a host of other Web sites, openly gay Muslims, organizations, and newsgroups emerge. The queer Muslims below describe how they use the Internet and the role their cyber communities play in their lives:

> Mostly though the group, Muslim gay men . . . that's really the only way to meet. There are not a lot of other places where you can go to. There are not a lot of other places you can go to. That's really the only place where you meet other people. I haven't met more than two other gay Muslim men who happen to be in the same area that I was. I wanted to know their perspectives, their struggles, what they were going through. Since they were in the same area, I was able to meet with them. —Mustafa[27]
>
> It keeps me connected with other queer Muslims—mostly gay men—but also women and transgender people. That's basically what keeps me in a community . . . that and the progressive Muslims, who are mostly heterosexual. It really means a lot to me to stay in touch with other queer Muslims, and it means a lot to be able to do so online—that I can connect with people that I've met at conferences and people that I've never met face-to-face. Sometimes, we'll chat through Yahoo Messenger, or we get to talk in the group, and I get to learn from people who are much more experienced or much more scholarly than I am, and I get to share my perspectives with others and find some comfort for other people, who are having a lot more trouble with these issues. —Michael[28]

More importantly, these forums enable access not only to a wide range of educational Web sites showcasing diverse literature, opinions, and experiences of queer Muslims around the world but also accord gay Muslims the space to form mutually supportive dialogues, relationships, and communities with one another online. Furthermore, when closeted Muslims are not yet out about their sexuality or orientation, the Internet provides a space where people can keep their identities anonymous as they explore further. In addition, the diversity of an online community's members allows queer Muslims more easily to find other Muslim friends or companions who, similar to themselves, are from a wider network of individuals than a (presumably smaller) physical community may typically provide.

IDENTITY

As mentioned earlier, some non-Muslim faith communities are witnessing the rise of religious organizations or splinter groups such as Dignity—a gay-friendly Catholic religious organization—that are accepting of queer members whose prior congregations may have cast them out due to their sexuality. Here, Buchanan, et al. note that those who participated in Dignity experienced lesser degrees of homophobia.[29] Also, their involvement was associated with the gay men's acceptance of their sexual orientation. More importantly, not only does their involvement in an organized religion allow them to remain close to their childhood tradition,[30] their continued affiliation with their religious establishment (i.e., the Catholic Church) reduced the anxiety that would usually be present around the challenge of being homosexual and religious.[31]

Similarly, with support from queer Muslim organizations, e-mail groups, and the increasing acceptance among some heterosexual Muslims, queer Muslims are ultimately accepting themselves as gay/lesbian/bisexual/transgender/queer/intersex Muslims and are coming out with these joint identities to their families and friends. Furthermore, some openly queer Muslims are working individually and within organizations like Al-Fatiha to provide emotional support to those queer Muslims who are facing greater struggles or obstacles with this reconciliation.

For instance, queer Muslims employ a few narratives that enable them to reconcile their religious and sexual identities. These narratives fall into three broad categories: (1) "God Is Merciful;" (2) "This Is Just Who I Am;" and (3) "It's Not Just Islam." The "God is Merciful" narrative consists of queer Muslims ascribing the qualities of mercy, forgiveness, compassion, and empathy to God, who they believe wills all creation, including those with alternative sexual orientations. Queer Muslims who employ this narrative believe that "God is not so petty" as to punish them for their sexual desire. Those who still believe acting on their same-sex or bisexual desire is a sin, though, posit God's mercy as superseding any other attribute, such as anger or wrath. Their belief in these qualities enables them to accept themselves, their sexual orientations, and their affiliation with Islam, despite their religious communities' condemnation of it. Here are two respondents' uses of the "God is Merciful" narrative:

> It's painful in a way because I'm very confident in my feeling of "Of course, God loves me! Why wouldn't He?" Actually, it really boils down to, with the day-to-day stuff, I can't believe that God's that petty, and that doesn't go over too well with the older community. I didn't lose my sense of humor either [upon conversion to Islam]. God gave me that, and I actually think God has a great sense of humor. He created us, and if that doesn't prove it,

nothing will. I have this belief in a compassionate deity. I really don't have any place in my life for a deity that is as vengeful as so many religious people like you to believe. I just can't believe that. If that turns out to be true, then I don't want to have anything to do with that. —Jill[32]

I am Muslim by God's grace. I am gay by God's grace—two facts. If there is any problem there, it is in the person who says this is irreconcilable. Islamic history is clear that this was and is a part of the human condition. Islam is 1,000 percent trusting in the all-powerful perfection of God's mercy. Even if I go to hell, that is God's mercy—that is what the companions said; that is what the companions did; that is what the companions believed; that is what they acted on. No harm to anyone by hand, tongue, or flesh. —Zakaria[33]

The second narrative, "This Is Just Who I Am," describes those queer Muslims who have come to accept themselves after realizing that their sexual orientation is a part of their everyday reality, which they have concluded they cannot will away and which has not passed with time. These Muslims view their sexuality as a truth or normal part of their lives and for which they do not need to seek confirmation or validation from third parties:

You cannot rationalize truth. If your hair is on fire, you don't have time to look it up in a dictionary to make sure you are right. —Zakaria[34]

It [the al-Fatiha conference] was amazing. It was a big relief for me because I realized I'm not deviant, and there's many other people on this planet that call themselves Muslims and they're gay, and they're fine with that. I felt that I was really struggling because I realized that if I come out, I'm going to lose my friends; I'm going to lose my relatives-everything in my life. And, just being in my (gay) Muslim community really, really helped me and supported me, and gave me strength to accept myself, and I even came out to my sister. So, it really gave me the strength to deal with things, to accept myself, and to have my normal life because I was so stressed in dealing with this pressure. I realized that being gay is not the only thing I have in my life, I have many other things, so I need to live my life . . . being a good person and not using my gayness to prevent me from doing that. —Azza[35]

The third narrative, "It's Not Just Islam," involves queer Muslims who compare the commonly held perspectives on homosexuality with other (monotheistic) religions' teachings on the subject. They find that similar homophobic sentiments exist within other faiths' discourses, and this enables them to view their particular religious communities as not uniquely homophobic, misogynist, or worthy of isolation. More interestingly, their efforts to explain the need for separating sexist or homophobic aspects of patriarchal *culture* from homophobic interpretations of *religious* doctrine or edicts to other non-Muslim queer believers also enables them to bolster their belief in Islam as a religion that is inclusive of members of their sexual orientation.

> I usually talk about that with people. I had a conversation because I realized it has nothing to do with Islam itself. It has something to do with Islamic culture. You can be an American Muslim, or you can be a Sudanese Muslim, or a Pakistani Muslim. I usually tell them that not only Islam, but all other religions, act same way towards gay people. —Azza[36]

Similar to the way queer Muslims' employ the narratives above, Andrew K. T. Yip notes that queer Christians' negotiation of spiritual/religious and sexual identities has become their dominant internalized discourse, which is a primary way for religious lesbian, gay, bisexual, transgender, intersex, and queer (LGBTIQ) persons to respond to the patriarchy and hierarchy of their religious institutions. It is the drawing upon different frameworks that enables queer believers, Christian and Muslim alike, to successfully negotiate an identity that incorporates both their sexuality and religious beliefs.[37] While some queer believers construct their identities in opposition to the institutional norms based on the Church's teachings,[38] most attempt to construct gay and lesbian identities within their faith that reflect the larger struggle for self-definition and a resistance to being defined by others.[39]

COMING OUT

In addition to their growing self-acceptance as both queer and Muslim, supportive heterosexual Muslims, queer Muslim organizations, Web sites, and e-mail groups are also providing space for some queer Muslims to begin coming out to their family and friends. Most of the queer Muslims who have come out to their family and friends are typically young Muslims born in the United States or Canada and/or are convert Muslims. Donald Boisvert, too, underscores the phenomenon of greater self-acceptance among younger gay men who "reinvent their identities" and "subvert the dominant power discourse of homophobia" by "abid[ing] by the rules of normality."[40] These young Muslims are also connected to more diverse social networks that extend beyond their religious communities, and are more likely to participate in queer (religious or secular) organizations than their immigrant counterparts. Moreover, after some queer Muslims come out to themselves and Muslim family members and friends, they usually individually support other queer Muslims in their struggle for self-acceptance.

Before queer Muslims come out to their Muslim family members, they often fear rejection and a loss of ties, especially with their parents. However, they are still risking these outcomes out of a desire to share these previously hidden aspects of their lives with those closest to them. Some people come out to their family members over the phone, even if they live in the same city. Others who live away from their families wait for the opportunity to come out in person. Finally, others assume their parents "already know" and do not feel a desire to formally come out to them.

Jennifer, a transgender woman, came out to her wife, daughters, mother, and a few friends. She sat her wife and her eldest daughter down and explained the term "transgender." Soon thereafter, Jennifer began wearing dresses more frequently in public. Initially, her wife did not accept her gender identity and referred to it as "not real," "mistaken," and called Jennifer "selfish." Her mother reminded her: "I raised you to be a man." However, over time and after many conversations, her wife stopped actively resisting it, too.

Danielle called her parents and came out to them over the phone. She claimed, "I'm coming out to you. Too much shit is going on, and this is one less thing [for me] to worry about." Her mother responded by presuming she was in a cult but acknowledged that she was aware of her daughter's attraction to both men and women. Her father simply said, "okay." According to Danielle, they did not say much beyond that. They did not actively resist her identification as bisexual, but did not attempt to engage in a deeper or lengthier conversation with her, either. Similarly, Fadila claims her mother "just knew" that she was a lesbian, but never addressed it until Fadila approached her directly. After Fadila came out to her, her mother claimed that "it's unnatural." She told Fadila that she was not going to support her and never raised the issue again with her.

As Hina began to see herself as "gay," she no longer censors herself around Muslims anymore. She describes her self-acceptance as "a layer of gauze that's been lifted." Hina also had a difficult time keeping her sexuality secret from her younger brother. They had been "best friends since he was born." She loved him, yet she feared losing him. She resolved to come out to her brother the next time she saw him in person, since they lived in different cities. When he came into town, he met Hina's partner who is a transgender man. They all went out to dinner and Hina declared, "I'm queer." According to her, he was relieved that her announcement was not that she was pregnant, that she was HIV positive, or that she had been raped again. For the next three days, he processed the news and revisited past incidents or events with a succession of "Oh, that's why . . . blah, blah, blah" Later, her brother excitedly asked Hina, "We can talk about girls [together] now?"

When queer Muslims decide they are ready to come out to their friends, they are deliberate in deciding to whom they will come out. Outside of the (online) queer Muslim community, respondents commonly choose to initially come out to their heterosexual and queer *non*-Muslim friends. The experiences of coming out to their non-Muslim friends is not always followed by supportive reactions, though. At times, patronizing reactions ensue. For instance, when Danielle came out as a bisexual Muslim to her friends, her heterosexual male friends described bisexuals as "sluts" and her non-Muslim lesbian friends were suspicious of both her bisexuality and her religious affiliation. They claimed she "hasn't sorted things out," and stated, "You can't be religious and queer," or remarked that she has chosen the "no fun religion." Also, Matthew came out to his non-Muslim friends by meeting with them on a one-on-basis and saying, "I am gay." He describes their comments, which included: "surprised," "shocked," "Gay?? Nahhh," and "Are you kidding? Is this a joke?"

Fearing their old friends' reactions, some queer respondents come out over e-mail, since it provides a forum to fully express their thoughts in one sitting and not directly or immediately receive the (expected negative) physical response of the person on the receiving end. Azza wanted to come out to an old best friend but was not sure how he would handle it. So, she chose to e-mail him and wrote:

> I was struggling with my sexual orientation since I was a kid and had those tendencies and couldn't control them. And, I tried a lot . . . I went to a counselor and did all I could do. It seems it's something I can't change or do anything for it.[41]

When she did not receive an immediate e-mail reply from her friend, she followed up with a second e-mail, stating:

> I know you must be shocked, but this is really important for me, and I want to know what you think about me because you are my close friend. And, I can measure your reaction and see how other people will react to it.[42]

Her friend eventually replied back, reassuring her that they were still friends, despite his not accepting her sexual orientation.

After he came out over e-mail, Mustafa received a similar delayed response from his friend, who quoted passages from *Surah Al An'am*[43] of the Quran to justify his religious disapproval. Despite these reactions, queer respondents are continuing to come out to others and reject assertions that they cannot claim both identities.

A few other respondents, though, describe their more supportive friends (and their reactions) as "accepting" of their sexuality. For instance, over a period of about six months, Jennifer, a transgender woman, began gradually showing up at social events, shifting from "male presentation" in her clothing to "gender queer" to "all the way full-femme." During this transformation, she asked her friends to begin referring to her as "Jennifer" and using the term "she" to describe her. Jennifer describes her friends' acceptance of her as she began to wear black eyeliner and dresses (without providing them with continuous explanations for her appearance) as a demonstration of their true friendship toward her.

Hina, Akram, and Jill have come out to various family members and friends, yet are, at varying levels, comfortable with their sexuality. While they are not necessarily afraid of being recognized as gay, lesbian, or bisexual, they also do not feel the need to "wear it on their chest." Moreover, their more successful experiences in coming out to their friends often do not require them to officially state their sexual orientation in their conversation. Instead, they talk about their encounters with members of the same gender and common responses from friends included: "Stay strong" "You can do it. If you need to talk, let us know," "We like you for who you are," "I knew all along," or "You're still my brother, and I love you no matter what." Again, these supportive individuals are under the age of 30, American-born, work on social justice issues, and have met other queer persons at their universities. All of these factors contribute to queer respondents' abilities to personally reconcile their queer and Muslim identities and come out to others as queer Muslims.

SUPPORT FROM WITHIN

In addition to coming out as queer Muslims to themselves, their family members, and their friends, some respondents have extended themselves to provide personal and direct support to other queer Muslims. Most often, this support takes place either during al-Fatiha local chapter meet-ups, on e-mail groups, or at queer Muslim conferences. Furthermore, queer Muslims are providing more ethnic, sexuality, and conversion-specific advice and counseling to one another, especially as the diversity of Muslims in general and queer Muslims in particular grows.

More interestingly, it is primarily the white converts to Islam who are the most morally secure about their ability to reconcile their sexuality with their faith as compared to their Muslim-born counterparts who were raised within immigrant households and religious communities. These converts and a few American-born Muslims are also the most vocal and prominent in providing support to other queer Muslims who are heavily entrenched within immigrant families and communities, a circumstance that can play a significant role in sustaining hostile religiocultural attitudes toward homosexuality. Here, a couple of gay and lesbian white Muslim converts describe their encounters with and attempts to support queer Muslims who come from immigrant Muslim families and face difficulties accepting themselves:

> Most of the conversations I had come up online mostly or sometimes in conversations with other Muslims. For me, it's mostly online in a gay Muslim context, and you get lots of mostly young men from the Middle East or South Asia who are terrified of God's wrath and struggle to reconcile their sexuality with their religion. Some of them say, "Oh, I'm gay, but I've never touched another man, *alhamdulillah.*" My own position is, "Oh, honey, relax!" (Laughs.) —Michael
>
> Most of it is just about them accepting themselves. A lot of the lesbians who were born Muslim have turned away from Islam, and it leaves this sort of emptiness. And, they don't really know how to reconcile that because everything they've ever been told, everything they've grown up with has said there's no greater evil than being gay or lesbian, and that just isn't true. So, basically, I'll give a wrap-up of what Scott [Kugle] had to say. —Jill

Jill also composed a journal on her experience as a lesbian Muslim and shared it with a heterosexual Somali Muslim woman who found commonality in their experiences as an "oppressed minority." In addition, on one lesbian Muslim e-mail group, Jill recognized that another Muslim lesbian who was a European immigrant was afraid that coming out would lead to further castigation in her religious community and initially remained anonymous on the e-mail group. Upon realizing this woman's fears, Jill deliberately made her sexuality known to the e-mail group by stating, "Yes, I'm lesbian, and I'm out." Soon thereafter, the previously closeted lesbian contacted Jill over the e-mail group, and the two have maintained contact over the phone. Through an established relationship with Jill and observing the dialogue over the e-mail group, this particular European Muslim woman came to understand that the other lesbian Muslims on the e-mail group could and did, indeed, accept her as both Muslim and lesbian. She also noted that her friendship with Jill and time spent on the e-mail group enabled her to accept her sexuality and the woman in her life as a part of her reality and not as a "condition" that she had.

Convert Muslims, in their efforts to provide support to other queer Muslims, often employ alternative understandings or interpretations of Quranic verses that conservative Muslims have traditionally used in order to justify condemnation of homosexuality. The recent articles by Scott Kugle, mentioned earlier, entail a religious deconstruction of the story of Lut in the Quran. These articles have been frequently cited by queer Muslims to add academic weight to their own religious arguments. Primarily through the Internet, convert Muslims persuade other queer Muslims to reject the notions that "God hates gay persons" or that "homosexuality is disgusting." Instead, they ask others to revisit the Quranic verses that extol the importance of diversity. Furthermore, they specifically tackle the Quranic story of Lut and claim that God's destruction of that society was a reaction to the rampant rape, murder, and caravan robberies, not "two people of the same sex who happen to love each other."[44] They also draw on the broader religious injunctions to "protect the weak and the vulnerable" in their rhetorical efforts for greater acceptance and space for queer persons within their faith communities.

This kind of reevaluation of religious interpretation has also been a strategic tool for acceptance within the Catholic queer community. In his research on gay and lesbian Catholics, Yip underscores the importance for these individuals to recognize the possibility of inaccuracy, subjectivity, or bias in prior common biblical exegesis within the Church's teachings. This recognition, according to Yip, not only enables queer Catholics to accept the full expression of same-sex love, but also the consideration of these relationships as entirely compatible with the Catholic faith. He further explains, "The management of faith and identity signifies their ability to not only survive, but thrive in a social environment despite the lack of acceptance and support."[45]

In addition, some queer Muslims rationalize their support of other queer Muslims by rooting their arguments in frequently employed religious rhetoric (i.e., they draw upon widespread Muslims' belief in God's complete control, will, and authority over all creation). More specifically, they claim that the prevalence of queer persons in societies, present and past, is a result of God's explicit will for their existence:

> The way I addressed his [friend's] concern is by telling him, 'Why would you think that out of 5 billion, what you think is the right thing to do? That's just plain arrogance and ignorance. How could you think that 5 billion people are made to think the exact same way? If God created humans and God created animals, and there are many examples of animals that are homosexual in behavior, and if God was to say that this behavior is not right, why would he ingrain that behavior in animals? So, God let it happen. —Mustafa
>
> A lot of them are still in the mindset that they're committing these horrible sins and God hates them. And, part of what I see as my job is to be there and say, "No, God doesn't hate you. God made you. God loves you. And you have as much right to exist as anyone else." —Jill

Outside of the support queer Muslims provide one another online, a few individuals started local chapters of the national al-Fatiha organization in various cities throughout the United States. Organizers post announcements on their respective queer Muslim e-mail groups for their monthly in person meet-ups, which usually entail informal socializing over dinner at a restaurant. In their announcement postings and during the meet-ups, queer (convert) Muslims remind their Muslim-born counterparts of their availability to discuss matters of faith and sexuality and answer questions or concerns. They view themselves as playing a vital "bridge-building" role for the heterosexual Muslim, queer Muslim, and queer non-Muslim communities' relations with one another and within the broader (predominantly heterosexual) American culture.

Some of the support groups' local chapters that have recently emerged are also focused on the sexual, gender, or ethnicity-specific identities of their members. For instance, Fadila, who is bisexual, began a chapter in the Northeast that was specific to lesbian and bisexual women's concerns. Jennifer, who is a transgender woman, began managing the Trans Muslims Yahoo e-mail group and volunteers by answering e-mails and other administrative tasks, after initially subscribing to the aforementioned e-mail groups. Jill, a lesbian, has formed a committee for lesbian Muslims and provides spiritual counseling online and over the telephone. Also, Azza created a Sudanese-American queer group in her city and has reached out to other Sudanese-Americans who talk about their combined cultural/ethnic experiences and their sexualities. On this e-mail group, coming out is the salient issue, and members air their ongoing struggles with that. After collecting stories and experiences from these local chapter discussions and meet-ups, most of which are focused on the varying social locations of their members, organizations then share this information (i.e., being lesbian, a convert, coming from an Indian family, etc.) with other queer Muslims by conducting workshops at the national Al-Fatiha conference with the hope of supporting others in their struggle with their identities and communities.

Indeed, the queer Muslims of this chapter reject the notion that being a queer Muslim is a paradox. While Yip notes that, as a consequence to the patriarchy and lack of affirmation from religious communities,[46] many religious gays and lesbians have the tendency to reject organized religion and embrace individualized spirituality,[47] these queer Muslims have not entirely rejected organized religion, either. The emergence of queer organizations and cyber communities have enabled queer Muslims not only to claim a joint queer Muslim identity for themselves but also to come out to their families and friends and mutually support each other. As Boisvert argues, gay spirituality is transformative and situates itself in opposition to the orthodox religious norm.[48]

CONCLUSION

For most contemporary religious groups, the development and maintenance of their social identities remains critical to their survival. As Peter L. Berger notes, the identity work involved in religious community building is socially constructed and rests on solidifying ties among the community's members.[49] It is the shared meanings that construct group identities and solidify group membership in a moral community.

One particular way in which some Muslims, as minorities in the United States, work together to strengthen their collective identity involves maintaining rigid boundaries around the sexuality of its religious adherents. For instance, traditional Muslims often promote conceptions of sexuality that rely on the belief in an essential difference between the sexual desires of women and those of men. This phenomenon underscores the more public measures taken by traditional Muslims to segregate and condemn fellow believers for blurring or transgressing social distinctions. The hostility religious communities exhibit toward men and women challenging constrictive gender bounds and toward the acceptance of queer Muslims is, in essence, a fear of alteration, modification, or resistance to divinely prescribed or clearly delineated gender or sexual roles that secure the privileged status of heterosexual Muslim men as heads of households and financial caretakers of their families, as Imams in their religious spheres, and as primary decision makers and leaders in the broader public sphere.

Both queer and straight Muslims who have clashed with their religious communities on points of gender roles or sexuality, on the whole, express a continued commitment to their religion. However, the combination of rampant homophobia and the pressure for gender and sexual-role conformity have resulted not only in emotional distress but also a waning of queer and nonheteronormative Muslims' participation in formal, mainstream congregations. Moreover, heterosexual Muslims encounter discrimination across the United States for their faith (Islam), their race (as mostly non-whites), and their gender (for women), while queer Muslims experience yet another layer of oppression, based upon their sexual orientation. Furthermore, the stereotyping of Muslims in mainstream American media, the U.S. invasion of Iraq and Afghanistan, and the U.S. government's racial-religious profiling of immigrant Muslims in the United States have engendered or exacerbated negative sentiments held by some non-Muslim queers toward their Muslim counterparts, intensifying the spiritual and social isolation they face. Those who maintain some connection to many of these aforementioned communities have led or continue to lead "refracted lives." In other words, queer Muslims find difficulty in sharing all aspects of their life (e.g., sexual orientation and religious affiliation) with members of each of their social circles. This compartmentalization of their lives has led to self-loathing, suicide attempts, alienation, and searching for cures for their sexuality.[50]

Despite their individual and community-level experiences of hostility, rejection, and isolation, queer Muslims are interrogating the bounds that mainstream institutions place around religious identity and practice.

There are several social factors that, in recent years, have enabled Muslims to reconstruct a Muslim identity that reconciles these multiple intersections (i.e., gender, sexuality, and faith). For instance, the events of September 11, 2001, and the history of the civil rights movements in the United States play a significant role in this broader reexamination of community boundaries. As well, the language of civil and human rights and an emphasis on scriptural passages that focus on God's love and mercy enable Muslims, especially in the West, to question the constraints on religious acceptance. Such contextual circumstances enable queer Muslims to slowly accept themselves, gain acceptance among more tolerant heterosexual Muslims, and provide emotional support to other queer Muslims.

The multiple intersecting oppressions that queer Muslims face produce alternative stories that lead to respondents making sense of their lives and provide narratives and explanations for how the world works in ways that conflict with the traditional metanarratives. The alternative meaning systems combined with the ever-increasing ideological, religious, and cultural pluralism of the United States allows my interviewees not only to merge identities such as feminist, queer, American, and Muslim but also underscore the heterogeneity within and disrupt any inherent quality to each of these categories.

If current trends are any indication, this religious diversity will increase as the community's gender, sexual, and racial differences become more variant and as believers find their social or spiritual needs unmet by existing institutions. Though the religious marketplace of the United States evidently facilitates pluralism and competition, the queer Muslims of this study have not chosen to leave their faith to join Protestant, Catholic, or Jewish congregations. Instead, they have remained committed to their faith and have injected critical doubt and the discourse of civil, sexual, and human rights in order to create space for themselves within Islam. Indeed, the establishment of openly queer Muslim identities and communities is shifting interpretations and practices of Islam that place respect, dignity, and justice at the core of belief.

NOTES

1. Richard Alba and Victor Nee, "Rethinking Assimilation Theory for a New Era of Immigration," in *Handbook of International Migration: The American Experience,* ed. Charles Hirschman, Philip Kasinitz, and Josh DeWind (New York: Russell Sage Foundation, 1999) 137–60; Helen Rose Ebaugh and Janet Chafetz,

Religion and the New Immigrants (Walnut Creek, CA: Alta Mira Press, 2000); Lawrence H. Fuchs, "Race, Religion, Ethnicity and the Civic Culture in the United States," in *The Accommodation of Cultural Diversity,* ed. Crawford Young (New York: St. Martin's Press, 1999), 176–211.

2. Nancy T. Ammerman, "Religious Identities and Religious Institutions," in *Handbook of Sociology of Religion,* ed. Michelle Dillon (Cambridge: Cambridge University Press, 2003), 207–24.

3. All subjects live in the United States, with the exception of two who reside in Canada and two who live in Turkey; they recounted experiences while living in the United States.

4. I put out my call for research interviewees primarily over the Internet. As such, this medium allowed me to reach a relatively large number (55) of respondents in various states throughout the United States within a particularly short period of time (from January 2006 through July 2006). Methodologically, though, it limited the participation of those who did not have access to or familiarity with particular email groups, listservs, or the Internet at large. This significantly impacted the scope of the research study. Nevertheless, I was able to interview 55 respondents, 20 of whom were men and 35 were women. Nineteen of them were in their 20s; 19 were in their 30s; five were in their 40s; nine were in their 50s; and fewer than five did not disclose. I also asked respondents about their formal educational backgrounds. Out of 55 total interviewees, between five and 10 had less than a Bachelors degree; between 10 and 15 had attained a Bachelors degree; 20 respondents had attained their Master's degree; 10 had some sort of professional degree or a Ph.D., and fewer than five did not disclose their educational backgrounds. When I asked about their race and ethnicity, 10 respondents indicated that they were white; 11 indicated they were black; 25 were South Asian (Indian, Pakistani, or Bangladeshi); five were of Arab descent; and fewer than five were either East Asian or Hispanic. Finally, when I asked what sexual orientation with which they identified, 35 said "heterosexual," 10 said "gay," three said "bisexual," two said "lesbian," three said "queer," and fewer than five did not disclose their sexual orientation.

5. Jack Nichols, *The Gay Agenda: Talking Back to the Fundamentalists* (Amherst, NY: Prometheus Books, 1996); Melinda L. Denton, "Gender and Marital Decision Making: Negotiating Religious Ideology and Practice," *Social Forces* 82, no. 3 (2004): 1151–80.

6. Christie Davies, "Sexual Taboos and Social Boundaries," *American Journal of Sociology* 87, no. 5 (1982): 1032–63.

7. Donald Boisvert, *Out on Holy Ground: Meditations on Gay Men's Spirituality* (Cleveland, OH: Pilgrim Press, 2000).

8. Patricia Hill Collins, *Black Feminist Thought: Knowledge, Consciousness, and the Politics of Empowerment* (New York: Routledge, 1991), 66.

9. A meeting or gathering of Muslims for the purpose of learning about Islam.

10. The sunset meal with which Muslims break their fast during the month of Ramadan.

11. Omid Safi, ed., *Progressive Muslims: On Justice, Gender, and Pluralism* (Oxford: Oneworld Publications, 2003); Amina Wadud, *Quran and Woman: Re-reading the Sacred Text from a Woman's Perspective* (Oxford: Oxford University Press, 1993); Asma Barlas, *"Believing Women" in Islam: Unreading Patriarchal Interpretations of the Quran* (Austin: University of Texas Press, 2002); Kecia Ali, *Sexual Ethics and Islam: Feminist Reflections on Quran, Hadith and Jurisprudence* (Oxford: Oneworld Publications, 2003); Leila Ahmed, *Women and Gender in Islam: Historical Roots of a Modern Debate* (New Haven, CT: Yale University Press, 1993).

12. Maurine C. Waun, *More Than Welcome: Learning to Embrace Gay, Lesbian, Bisexual, and Transgendered Persons in the Church* (St. Louis, MO: Chalice Press, 1999).

13. Darren Sherkat, "Religious Socialization: Sources of Influence and Influences of Agency," in *Handbook of Sociology of Religion,* ed. Michelle Dillon (Cambridge: Cambridge University Press, 2003), 151–63.

14. Waun, *More Than Welcome.*

15. Arabic for "The Opening," referring to the opening prayer and the first chapter of the Quran.

16. Al-Fatiha's goals include: (1) Support Muslims who self-identify as lesbian, gay, bisexual, transgender, and those who are questioning their sexual orientation or gender identity; (2) Provide a supportive and understanding environment for LGBTQ Muslims who are trying to reconcile their sexuality or gender identity with Islam; (3) Empower LGBTQ Muslims by creating safe spaces to share individual experiences, advocating on their behalf in national and international forums, and providing information about institutional resources; (4) Foster spirituality among LGBTQ Muslims, and; (5) Encourage dialogue with the larger Muslim community around issues of sexuality and gender. From http://www.tegenwicht. org/16_imams/al_fatiha_en.htm (accessed January 30, 2009).

17. El-Farouk Khaki founded Salaam Canada in 1991 as a support group for LGBTQI Muslims in Canada. Its Web site was formerly found at http://www. salaamcanada.org.

18. Declaration of faith.

19. Scott Siraj al-Haqq Kugle, "Sexuality, Diversity, and Ethics in the Agenda of Progressive Muslims," in *Progressive Muslims: On Justice, Gender, and Pluralism,* ed. Omid Safi (Oxford: Oneworld Publications, 2003), 190–234; "Sexual Diversity in Islam," in *Voices of Islam,* vol. 5, *Voices of Change,* ed. Vincent J. Cornell and Omid Safi (London: Praeger, 2007), 131–67.

20. This is an excerpt of a recorded phone interview conducted in March 2006.

21. Gary Comstock, *Unrepentant, Self-Affirming, Practicing: Lesbian/Bisexual/Gay People Within Organized Religion* (New York: Continuum, 1996).

22. Dugan McGinley, *Acts of Faith, Acts of Love: Gay Catholic Autobiographies as Sacred Texts* (New York: Continuum, 2004).

23. Comstock, *Unrepentant, Self-Affirming, Practicing.*

24. *About Queer Jihad,* January 10, 2003, http://www.well.com/user/queerjhd/aboutqj.htm (accessed June 7, 2009).

25. TransMuslims@yahoogroups.com is "An e-mail support group for Muslims who are transgender, and for those who consider themselves gender variant. This includes anyone who is MTF (male to female), FTM (female to male), or any identity outside of the conventional gender binary. Issues of relevance to the trans Muslim community are welcome on this list, including gender identity, issues of gender socialization in Islam, hormone replacement therapy and genital reassignment surgery, Islam's views towards transgender people, and spiritual aspects of being trans. This group is intended as safe space for Muslim trans people to talk about issues of religion and transgender." See "Message from Group Moderator" *Yahoo Groups,* http://groups.yahoo.com/group/TransMuslims/summary (accessed June 7, 2009)

26. MuslimGayMen@yahoogroups.com "is a discussion, information, and support resource for believing Muslim gay men who wish to maintain their faith and continue to serve Allah SWT while they are at various stages of dealing with and accepting their homosexuality. The aim of this group is to promote knowledge, brotherhood, and a positive self-image among Muslim gay men throughout the world. It promotes seeking a healthy balance between our identities as Muslims and our identities as gay men. This group focuses primarily, but not exclusively, on Islamic issues, including the Quran, Sunna, Hadith, culture, and family, and how to reconcile faith with social and religious rejection. It is international in nature and does not seek to promote any one nationality, culture, or point-of-view." See "Description" *Yahoo Groups,* http://groups.yahoo.com/group/MuslimGayMen/ (accessed June 7, 2009).

27. This is an excerpt of a recorded phone interview from March 2006.

28. Ibid.

29. Melinda Buchanan, Kristina Dzelme, Dale Harris, and Lorna Hecker, "Challenges of Being Simultaneously Gay or Lesbian and Spiritual and/or Religious: A Narrative Perspective," *The American Journal of Family Therapy* 29 (2001): 435–49.

30. David Shallenberger, *Reclaiming the Spirit: Gay Men and Lesbians Come to Terms with Religion* (New Brunswick, NJ: Rutgers University Press, 1998).

31. Buchanan, et al., "Challenges of Being Simultaneously Gay or Lesbian and Spiritual and/or Religious."

32. This is an excerpt of a recorded phone interview from March 2006.

33. Ibid.

34. Ibid.

35. Ibid.

36. Ibid.

37. Andrew K. T. Yip, "Dare to Differ: Gay and Lesbian Catholics' Assessment of Official Catholic Positions on Sexuality," *Sociology of Religion* 58, no. 2 (1997): 165–80.

38. David F. Greenberg, *The Construction of Homosexuality* (Chicago: University of Chicago Press, 1988).

39. Jeffrey Weeks, *Invented Moralities* (Cambridge: Polity Press, 1995).

40. Boisvert, *Out on Holy Ground,* 33.

41. This is an excerpt of a recorded phone interview from March 2006.

42. Ibid.

43. Arabic for "cattle; livestock."

44. This is an excerpt from a phone interview with an interviewee who was paraphrasing what his friend relayed to him.

45. Yip, "Dare to Differ," 165–80.

46. Ibid.

47. Mary Mendola, *The Mendola Report: A New Look at Gay Couples* (New York: Crown, 1980).

48. Boisvert, *Out on Holy Ground.*

49. Peter L. Berger, *The Sacred Canopy: Elements of a Sociological Theory of Religion* (New York: Anchor Books, 1967), 1–28.

50. These were common sentiments expressed by the interviewees of this chapter and further discussed by Waun and Boisvert.

16

⦁⟶⦁

"YOU'RE WHAT?": ENGAGING NARRATIVES FROM DIASPORIC MUSLIM WOMEN ON IDENTITY AND GAY LIBERATION

Ayisha A. Al-Sayyad

I equated all things Iranian and Muslim with being anti-gay, and therefore anti-me, and those messages were reinforced by the mainstream LGBTQ movement.

—*Khalida Saed*

Khalida Saed's story was the first narrative I found when I began the task of locating and identifying queer Muslim women's experiences in diaspora.[1] Like many other Muslim women who are queer and living in diaspora, pressure to conform was aimed at Saed from multiple directions: tradition, family, and religion competed with assimilation and individualism.[2] While I had personally felt Islam was in opposition to my own queer identification as a young adult, I had never had the opportunity to discuss the shocked looks I received from the small lesbian, gay, bisexual, transgender, and queer (LGBTQ)[3] community in my hometown. Saed's life story highlighted my own discomfort with integrating my Muslim and lesbian selves, but more importantly, she articulated clearly what I had only sensed for a short time. The most contested site of her identity was marked by the *perceived* incompatibility of her Muslim and lesbian selves, and this negotiation was even more fraught because of her complex relationship with an LGBTQ movement that did not account for her culture, her religion, or even her presence. From this narrative, my own life experience, and the existing literature on the subject, I came to ask many questions. First, because Islam and sexuality are understood in the Orientalist imagination (and, perhaps by some Muslims as well, although the origin of this religious exclusivity will be discussed further) in the West as mutually exclusive, how do Muslim women who identify as queer in diaspora negotiate the tensions of an identity constructed as always in conflict? Second, how do Muslim queer women in diaspora relate to the mainstream LGBTQ movement, given that the movement is helpful for some, but is also a site where Islam is constructed in opposition to (homo)sexuality?

For the current chapter, I relied on a set of life stories I collected in the summer of 2007, as well as a few existing published narratives written by queer Muslim women, and a small body of related scholarly literature. As preliminary research to aid in developing interview questions, I analyzed four published narratives by Muslim women who identified as queer or lesbian. Two were from a Web site called *Bint el Nas* (translated as *Daughter of the People*), while the other two were from published anthologies.[4] Overall, locating willing interview participants was one of the major difficulties of this research. After a failed attempt to make enough contacts in one major city in North America to conduct most of the interviews there, I decided to try another method. I realized that the women I aimed to interview were mostly isolated, so I decided to travel North America by car to collect their stories. Searching online profile sites like MySpace and Facebook proved to be productive, and I was able to post my solicitation for participants on a few group pages for LGBTQ Muslims. After two months of searching for (mostly Arab) Muslim women who love/fuck/desire other women, I realized that the "out and proud" model propagated by Western LGBTQ activists meant I had lost several interviews because many women who contacted me were afraid of being outed. Despite this setback, I was able to collect 12 narratives from Muslim queer women living in North America. By asking these women to relate their feelings and experiences surrounding culture, religion, ethnicity, and sexuality, my research questions shifted throughout the process, and I continue to discover angles, ideas, and nuances unexplored in this rich and interesting set of data.

In this chapter, I investigate the role of the mainstream, Western LGBTQ movement in the formation of identity and personal politics for Muslim queer[5] women living in diaspora as well as the negotiation of a supposed contrary identification that is ascribed to them. The queer Muslim women's stories I collected through interviews as part of my fieldwork helped to problematize a formulation that Islam is in opposition to West-ern identifications of queer, lesbian, or gay because the participants I in-terviewed had varying relationships to mainstream movements for sexual liberation and strategies for negotiating the contradictions. In the follow-ing pages, I work to identify a few of the forces that place Islam and Arab culture in opposition to (homo)sexuality. I hope that demonstrating the wide range of relationships to sexual liberation that there are, as well as the similar experiences of conflicted and reconciled identities, will lead to a more complicated representation of queer Muslim women living in diaspora.

YOU'RE WHAT?: THE CONTRADICTION

Reformulating monolithic Western views of queer identity or practices in relation to Islam first requires an understanding of the constructed contradiction. Constructing Islam in opposition to homosexuality serves many functions. Namely, it normalizes and reifies the belonging and na-tionalism of upstanding hetero and homo American citizens while mark-ing the sexualized, racialized, and dehumanized bodies of Arab (terrorists) Muslims as other.[6] As Jasbir Puar has argued in her book *Terrorist Assem-blages: Homonationalism in Queer Times,* the constructed opposition of homosexuality and Islam are Orientalist in nature and historically specific to post–September 11, 2001 attacks on New York City.[7] Puar closely ana-lyzes a photograph of a South Asian queer man published in a collection in London. The man, Poulomi Desai, wears terrorist drag and holds a sign that reads "I am a homosexual also."[8] About this image, Puar writes:

> Queer Arabs and Muslims, doubly indicted for the fundamentalist religion they adhere to or escape from and for the terrorist bodies that religion pro-duces, are either liberated (and the United States or Europe are often the scene of this liberation) or can only have an irrational, pathological sexual-ity or queerness. These entanglements, debatably avoidable to an extent for queers from other traditions such as Judeo-Christian, plague Muslim queers because of the widespread conflation of Muslim with Islamic and Arab: Muslim = Islam = Arab. Religion, in particular Islam, has now supplanted race as one side of the irreconcilable binary between queer and something else. For queer Arabs and Muslims the either/or plot thickens: queer secu-larity understands observance of religious creed, participation in religious public spaces and rituals, devotion to faith-based or spiritual practices, as

marks of subjugated and repressed sexuality void of agency. But regardless of complex affinities with Islam, Arab nation-states, and Muslim identity, the agency of all queer Muslims is invariably evaluated through the regulatory apparatus of queer liberal secularity.[9]

This formulation of an Orientalist view of Muslim and Arab subjects as sexually repressed is necessary for the viability of a normative homo-subject at home, according to Puar. As she argues, queer Arabs or Muslims are either liberated by the West or occupy a conflicted space where their queerness is deemed pathological. While feeling that their sexuality is pathological or conflicted is not easily avoided, some queer Muslims or Arabs are still able to assimilate into the homo-national (that is, the "good citizen, good American") role by being neither religious nor overtly "cultural." Of course, the presentation of Islam (and Arab culture) *or* same-sex sexuality as a forced choice is, ultimately, the problem here and this contrary formulation has many consequences.

For example, one only has to look as far as Abu Ghraib to access how "Americans" view Arab and Muslim people sexually (both discursively and materially) in this time of war and occupation in the Arab world. Despite the history of rampant Orientalism that cast Arab men as always open to homosex, and that named colonialized brown women as hypersexual,[10] the rise of fundamentalism in the Middle East has caused some minor shifts in this very complex formulation. As noted by journalist Seymour Hersh, military intelligence considers *The Arab Mind*, a text written in 1973, to be "the bible" for prowar conservatives.[11] In this book, Raphael Patai argues that, while shame and sex are driving forces in the minds of Arabs, sexuality is overall very repressed and deemed taboo among Arabs. Drawing from this text, military strategy, led by neocons in Washington, according to Hersh, perpetuated a model of Arab sexual behavior that was extremely pious and thus properly heterosexual, always chaste, and deeply afraid of shame and humiliation.[12] By leaning on this view of Arabs and Arab culture as sexually repressed, torture such as what took place in Abu Ghraib illustrates the dominant view of what must be the most harsh and psychologically damaging to Middle Easterners in the minds of Westerners: sodomy performed on Arabs by white men, forced anal penetration, and many other sexually motivated same-sex positions and poses. Pictures of prisoners in compromising sexual positions (often homosexual in nature) were often taken and used as bargaining chips because it was believed that Arabs would do anything to avoid the shame of having these pictures shown to friends and family.[13]

It is not only the intelligence agencies linked to the military that hold the view of Muslim men and women as sexually repressed and thus necessarily heteronormative; in fact, LGBTQ liberationists also reproduce discourses that reify the impossibility of a Muslim queer. Even the founder of "Al-Fatiha," an LGBTQ organization for Muslims, Faisal Alam, called the torture "perverse and sadistic in the eyes of many Muslims" because the homosexual sex they were forced into threatened traditional notions of masculinity and sexuality in the Arab world.[14] When we consider the discourses employed by Alam and governmental agencies when it comes to (homo)sexual torture at Abu Ghraib, it seems a shift has occurred in the postcolonialist constructions of the Arab world. On this issue, Puar argues "the Orient, once conceived in Foucult's *ars erotica* and Said's deconstructive work as the place of original release, unfettered sin, and acts with no attendant identity or consequences, now symbolizes the space of repression *and* perversion, and the site of freedom has been relocated to western identity."[15] Instead of seeing the "Orient" or the exotic Middle East as the home of sexual lasciviousness, the West now constructs Europe and America as cultures of liberation, places to migrate to for otherwise persecuted queers, while the Arab world becomes increasingly dangerous for gays, who, according to this modified Western gaze, threaten fundamentalist religious[16] and cultural laws. It is in part this binary model of West = liberation, Middle East = persecution, that allows for the current discourses placing Islam and Arab culture in opposition to (homo)sexuality.

RECONCILING SEXUALITY, RELIGION, AND CULTURE IN THE DIASPORA

Why would God condemn anyone for loving someone else? At least it's not hate. I pray every day, but I feel like it's my personal relationship. So I say yes, I am a Muslim. I am a lesbian.

—Luna, July 2007.

Despite contemporary Orientalist constructions of Islam and homosexuality as incompatible, many of the interview participants in my study who shared their stories felt comfortable being Muslim and queer. Although many felt they had reconciled their religion, culture, and sexuality, this

Western formulation of Arabs as sexually repressed and heteronormative still has many effects on Muslim queer women in the diaspora. For example, Luna is a first-generation American and 38 years old. Her parents emigrated from Palestine to the east coast of the United States in the 1950s. As she explains above, she is often asked about the compatibility between her religious and cultural background and her sexuality. Luna must explain over and over again that yes, she is queer, yes she is Muslim, yes she is Palestinian. Another participant, Mena, relates her story of negotiation and reconciliation:

> I used to feel like I had to pick one or the other (Islam or having relationships with women). Growing up I would go to the mosque and learn the Quran and Hadith and that's been drilled into you. It's not something that anyone talks about, but you just know same-sex attractions and relationships are not allowed. You just know this. After high school I remember being depressed and feeling like I can't live with this. I needed to be content with myself. After talking to my friends and other queer youth, I found that these identities can exist in harmony. They are not contradictions. I used to be like that, you know, those people who pray and pray and pray that they will be straight, but not anymore. Only God can judge me, right. And all these people handing down fatawa (religious decrees) about homosexuality, I just don't listen to them. They should worry about their own practice. Allah would not have made me to have to go through all of this. I know God loves me.

Mena is South Asian and lives in a large city in Canada where she regularly attends the Mosque and participates in her religious and culturally based community. Her declaration that "these identities can exist in harmony" represents the majority of participants' opinions in this chapter. That is, many of the queer Muslim women who are interviewed here felt some difficulty reconciling their lesbian and Muslim selves, yet they also recognized this difficulty as something they can, and mostly have, overcome. Just as Saed describes feeling pressure to choose her sexuality or her religion and culture, many participants felt a similar message coming from mainstream Western culture, their own Muslim families, and the LGBTQ movement: to be a queer woman and an (Arab) Muslim was nearly impossible. Because of this formulation, this double pressure and ideal Muslim daughter image that is expected from many of these participants, they do not fully belong to either white American (and thus, the "sexually liberated") culture, or to their ("sexually repressed") homeland. The forces that construct Islam as in opposition to (homo)sexuality are pervasive and effect both the LGBTQ and diasporic communities.

Another participant, Dedra, immigrated to the United States from Algeria when she was 19. She describes how she first came to a queer women's space:

> I was dating a Moroccan guy . . . growing up in Algeria the culture is you can date but nothing happens . . . his reaction [to being rejected sexually] was "this is America!" and "oh maybe you're gay." I said, "what the heck! What are you talking about? There is no such thing. We don't exist." ' So he took me to my first lesbian bar.

As Dedra once told her boyfriend, queerness is not intelligible to many within the Arab cultural framework or mainstream Islamic ideology. Without a cultural point of reference for lesbians or woman–woman love and desire, many participants explained that they had no way of describing their sexuality in Arabic. Dedra's first encounter with other women who loved women gave her the (Western) language to name her desire. In the bar scene, she saw an opportunity to define her sexuality on her own terms, and, as she says, "a way to understand my difference." While it may seem logical to argue that the lack of commonly used terminology in Arabic for a homosexual identity means none exists, or that it is so taboo there is no word for it, but this is an oversimplification.[17] Perhaps this demonstrates nothing more than those sexualities are culturally and historically specific, and not universal givens.

Dedra pushed aside Islam for a short period of time because she believed she had to in order to maintain her deeply felt identification as a lesbian. When I asked her why she did this, she explained that the source of her conflicted feelings about Islam and (homo)sexuality were not clear, but that she knew her family would not accept her choice of sexual partners. She also linked her conflicted feelings to the mainstream movement in the West for LGBTQ rights (which Dedra works for in her own state), which rarely takes the time to consider a more culturally sensitive approach for anyone, particularly Arab or Muslim people in this time of rampant, unchecked anti-Muslim/Middle Eastern sentiments. She explained her struggle to reconcile her culture, Islam, and her sexuality:

I still kept my religion. I was raped when I was 12 years old and I hated God for it then. Some people say this is why I am a lesbian, so I hate to talk about it. But then, as a teenager, when I came here, I joined the Muslim student association. I still believed. Then I realized the men ran this organization. I learned there that I did not need an Imam; I did not need an organization. I practiced on my own. Then I realized I was a lesbian and I put Islam aside. I felt conflicted about it, but the religion was always in my mind. I am not a praying person anymore, but I still believe in God. I would never betray my religion and I would never betray God. What brought me back to religion was when I was making out with this girl in my bed, and you know, I sleep with the Quran under my pillow and I realized something was under us. And I saw the Quran and I said, "this is it— I am a Muslim lesbian." And I knew I could be both.

Instead of Dedra feeling constrained by her religion, she found it comforting to be confronted with the Quran at precisely the moment she was supposed to be violating her cultural codes, her family, and her religion.

While family rejection may be used to demonstrate the incompatibility of Arab culture and Islam with homosexuality, many complex factors are left out in this oversimplification. It is true that many participants discussed their families' and parents' negative reactions to or rejections of their sexual identification, but it is also important to consider that all of the participants interviewed maintained close relationships with their families. The strength of familial ties was overwhelmingly evident for the group of women I interviewed and whose narratives I analyzed. Despite this, many queer Muslim women living in the diaspora did feel pressure from their families to adhere to normative gender roles and, most notably, to marry a suitable man, as most of them are not "out" in the mainstream American sense.

Several of the participants who lent their voices to this study described themselves as the "black sheep" of their families, communities, and culture on both sides: North American and "Other." Mena said, "My family is very conservadox, meaning that they are very traditional and conservative in terms of their beliefs about Islam and how each gender role is supposed to play out. I am not like that at all . . . so there is no way I could invite my family to my [queer] wedding." While Mena plans to maintain a queer household complete with Muslim children and a religious wife, she does not expect to share this with her very traditional family. She feels this way because of her family's staunch antiassimilationist attitude whereby they intend to preserve their Muslim and South Asian identities in diaspora, which they see as standing in stark opposition to Western homosexuality. When Mena's younger brother came out to her mother as gay, Mena witnessed the difficulties he had—her brother is, in fact, now reformed and has renounced his homosexuality. Because of this, she feels confident that her family's position on her choice in sexual partners would never change and she does not wish to further complicate her situation at home, where she lives with her parents. Mena already describes the environment at home as "walking on eggshells" because her views are so different from her parents' traditional, "reactionary" cultural convictions.

Nur, another participant who is a recent immigrant to Canada, explained her position in her family as an outcast. She said, "I am the black sheep of the family because I insist on living here and doing what I want to do. All my family, they don't like [my independence]." Nur's story is very complex and at times violent, as she described her familial obligations as the only unmarried daughter and the humiliation her father put her through when he found out about an affair she was having with another girl as a teenager. Because of her insistence on living in the West, and her sexuality (which her family members know about although it is never, ever discussed) she is often berated by her brother because she refuses to conform to his ideas about what a good Muslim and Arab woman acts like.

The point here is that diasporic, traditional Muslims see their own culture threatened by Western and American influences. This reproduction of the binary between tradition and modernity, heterosexuality and homosexuality, serves to strengthen the hegemonic view of the West as liberated/liberator and the Other as repressed/repressor. In the formulation, the deviant, racialized, and queer Muslim subject becomes doubly outcast, pressured by all sides to choose one side or the other. As I argue above in relation to Mena's family, many diasporic Muslims or Arabs feel unbearable pressure to assimilate in North America, threatening their cultural ties and traditions, and thus potentially providing evidence for the construction of Islam and Arab culture in opposition to homosexuality. This is just one reason why some participants had a difficult time negotiating their families' negative views of their sexuality.

It may also be possible that some diasporic families in North America react to "deviant" sexualities like many of their neighbors do. Take, for example, Farsa, a 20-something first-generation Arab queer woman living in the American southwest. Here, she describes the aftermath of coming out:

[My father] wrote me some really painful letters and we stopped talking for six months at a time. And we both decided it was ridiculous and we both needed to make an effort, but it was difficult. It took a while, but at this point he is one of my biggest supporters and he came to the wedding and walked me down the aisle. It wasn't an easy process.

Farsa's father's transformation from not speaking to his daughter to walking her down the aisle during her commitment ceremony to her partner is a big one. Farsa describes her relationship with her father as something that took a lot of work for many years before he could come to terms with her lesbian identification. Her twin sister's story of coming out was partially Farsa's as well, since her (previously lesbian-identified) sister was the first to discuss her sexuality with their parents. Despite her sister's coming out being very difficult in Farsa's eyes, she still wanted to share her preferences with her parents and felt it a necessary step in living her life and maintaining a close relationship with her family. Some might argue that her Americanization made her identification as a lesbian more readily available or accessible, or even that her father's negative reaction to her sexuality demonstrated a heightened taboo against homosexuality in Arab culture. This argument too easily makes the West, or America, a sexually liberated, accepting place while setting up Arab culture and Islam in opposition to freedom and personal expression. In actuality, Farsa's father did not object to his daughter's sexuality on religious or cultural grounds. Instead, he felt that her life would be hard (even though she plans to live in the United States) and feared that people would treat her differently. Overall, she explained, her father just did not "get it" (meaning her sexuality), despite his being a naturalized American citizen.

The queer Muslim women here intervene in the oppositional construction of "traditional" (read: Orientalist, Islamic) versus "progressive" (read: Western, secular) by complicating the divisions between tradition and modernity, between "us" and "them." While many of the participants struggled with fitting into their own culture and religion, they also found it difficult to belong in white Western (and even queer) communities. Perhaps this is because these women not only represent culturally "conservative," religious, brown, and Arab peoples in the "liberated" West, but also because they serve as symbols of tradition and cultural preservation in the diaspora. Surina Khan, a Muslim South Asian woman, in her personal narrative called *Sexual Exiles,* explains: "I was constantly reminded I was different by my accent, my brown skin color, and my mother's traditional clothing."[18] Perhaps these queer Muslim women are unexpectedly queer because of the discourses in the West that construct their identities as impossible and because they occupy a sort of "doubled diaspora"—they are outcasts from white American culture, outcasts from "traditional" cultural and religious roles, and ultimately responsible for their own proper assimilation into both.

Amir, an Arab Muslim woman living on the American west coast who immigrated less than five years ago, explains her relationship to her homeland: "Most Lebanese people have a different mentality than I do . . . the whole culture and tradition thing . . . I am more open-minded and liberal than they are." Just as Jasbir Puar contends in her introduction to *Terrorist Assemblages,* "liberal" politics, based on acceptance and resistance to norms, is in opposition to tradition, culture, and religion for Amir. She sees herself as markedly different from most Lebanese people since she is openminded and therefore they are closed-minded. The question still remains, however: is Amir's formulation influenced by a Western view of Islam and Arabs as socially conservative, pious, oppressive, and, ultimately, in opposition to sexual freedom? And, what is the role of the LGBTQ movements and their visibility politics in this narrow, Western gaze?

LGBTQ HUMAN RIGHTS AND THE OTHER

Constructing (homo)sexuality and Islam as mutually exclusive is intrinsically connected to international human rights and gay liberation abroad. This "us" versus "them" formulation has been challenged by many theorists, including Chandra Talpade Mohanty in her critiques of Western feminists in the late 1980s and in her revisions that addressed the increasingly compelling use of a "human rights" agenda in the 1990s.[19] Mohanty's foundational essay "Under Western Eyes: Feminist Scholarship and Colonial Discourses," argues that Western feminists create a homogenized "third world woman" who is always a victim of male violence, always undereducated and poor, and always limited by tradition, family, and culture.[20] Western feminists use this "third world woman" to mark themselves as free with choices, agency, and modes of resistance unavailable to the "third world woman" who would use them if she could.[21] Similar to the feminists Mohanty criticizes, and the Orientalism that attempts to save Muslim women from Muslim men, the international gay liberation movement also works to "save" LGBTQ people from their backward culture, their hateful countries, and their unjust nation-states. According to this problematic model, human rights initiatives in the Arab world create stability at home, in the West. If "those" LGBTQ folks in the Middle East need Westerners' help to secure equality, then perhaps queers at home are already liberated and adequately visible, have choices and freedoms, and are, at the very least, better off than the monolithic, oppressed, Other in the Arab world.

Western movements abroad also universalize sexuality and the categories of gay, straight, and so on in the campaigns for international gay liberation; this creates singular victims and serves to mark deviancy where it may not have existed in the Middle East. As Joseph Massad explains in his book *Desiring Arabs,* the current international LGBTQ movement participates in an "*incitement to discourse* on sexual rights outside the United States and Western Europe [that necessitates] that human rights organizations and advocates incorporate existing anthropological knowledge of the non-Western world. This is central for the purpose of constructing the human subjects—or, more precisely, objects—of human rights discourse."[22] Massad claims that these types of colonialist human rights campaigns create two victims of injustice: women and homosexuals.[23] By creating a minority, a helpless victim in the "Arab homosexual," international gay liberation has many results with varying degrees of success. First, this can create the category of heterosexual where one may not have been before. Second, Massad argues, this is a modern form of colonialism; international human rights is just one more way for the West to invade, investigate, and persecute Arab people. Massad writes: "the goal can also be and often is one of ethical epistemic normalization" when it comes to this form of colonial, global rights-seeking.[24] As Jasbir Puar has argued, another consequence of international gay liberation is to create and reify a homonormative subject at home, one who is invested in the nation, liberated, and without traditional ties that limit their erotic possibilities.

Wile Puar and Massad's arguments are compelling and mostly very useful, the notion that Western liberationists can create homosexuals in the Arab World, or that they have the power to limit erotic possibilities is not totally unproblematic. This is especially true given that some participants in this study believed they had the agency and determinism to choose their own identifications, and that they did so without Western influence. It seems, however, impossible that any of these participants, living in diaspora as they do, might be free from all discourses surrounding sexual liberation and the binary sexual system that supports lesbian, gay, bisexual, and queer identifications.

Agency is a key distinction here between homonormative nationalists and the "others." The question becomes: where do queer Muslim or Arab women living in the diaspora fit into this binary that divides agential, resistant subjects from "complacent" ones? As Puar argues, "the queer agential subject can only ever be fathomed outside the norming constrictions of religion, conflating agency, and resistance."[25] Puar is arguing here, like the transnational feminists before her, that in the West adhering to religious doctrine, especially Islam, is not seen as resistant, and so those who are religious must not have agency and are in need of outside rescue. Just as Saba Mahmood advocates rethinking the meaning of agency for Muslim women in the Egyptian Mosque Movement in *The Subject of Freedom*,[26] Puar argues that the agency of intelligible, nationalist, queer (properly American) subjects depends on their subscription to homonormative ideologies. While properly assimilated, Western subjects can resist inequality or be apathetic, Muslim queers *must* use their agency to resist "homophobic" religious tyranny by adopting mainstream secular LGBTQ politics or they are marked as complacent to homophobia. Mahmood's challenge to a singular understanding of resistance can be linked to Puar's because both work to reformulate notions of agency, freedom, and secular liberalist views of Arab and Muslim subjects. Orientalism and American Exceptionialism construct queer Muslims and Arabs, and especially women, as conspirators in their own oppression who do not resist and therefore do not have agency. Because the women in this study are diasporic subjects, their relationship to these discussions of agency become muddled. Are queer Muslim women living in North America agential simply because of location, or must they renounce Islam and Arab culture to be liberated? By refusing this question, and others like it, I hope to show here that the relationships held by diasporic queer Muslim women to human rights' movements, especially for sexual liberation, are complex and widely heterogeneous.

ON INTERNATIONAL GAY LIBERATION:
CONTESTED TERRAIN

Gay liberation is the site of much tension about homonormative, liberal identification and citizenship on the one hand and traditional, religious, racialized queer subjectivities on the other. Joseph Massad briefly argues that diasporic Muslims (or, more specifically, Arabs) are mostly responsible for leading the local charges for sexual equality in the Middle East and furthering the Western LGBTQ agenda.[27] While their relationships to mainstream politics in the West were varied, in stark opposition to Massad's claim, many of the queer Muslim women living in the diaspora who shared their stories with me had very complex and mostly oppositional relationships to the international movement for LGBTQ equality. Reasons for distrust of the larger movement include feelings of exclusion, cultural insensitivity, essentialist and universalizing sexual constructs, and male-dominated meetings and activities. The women interviewed here did not, in general, feel responsibility toward liberating their "brothers and sisters" in the Middle East, or toward other LGBTQ people (with only one exception). We might also ask what choices are there for diasporic queer Muslim women other than silence (which can be powerful, if it is a viable choice) or assimilation into liberationist politics?

Generally speaking, however, each participant's relationship to gay liberation was not only complex but also in constant flux. For example, Mena explains:

> The whole coming out process I feel . . . well the whole notion of coming out is very Eurocentric and Westernized. I don't think that coming out is the same for everyone depending on your ethno-racial background. Even though I was raised here I still have some of my back home values . . . I don't need to come out as long as I am happy with myself. So I don't need to go out there and tell the world "I'm queer, look at me." I just don't need to do that. I just don't think the coming out model can be readily applied to anyone.

Mena's frustration with the LGBTQ movement in the West initially stems from coming out and the high valuation of visibility politics. The individualism fueling mainstream movements for equality are in stark opposition to Mena's familial obligations and cultural sensibilities. She feels her loyalty to South Asian Muslims is contested by both local and global LGBTQ politics. Mena says: "I have mixed feelings about (international gay liberation) because when you have large movements it's hard to represent everyone's interests. I mean it is good that they are raising awareness and things but my question to them is always who's getting heard and who's not."

While Mena questions the representation of interests and politics going on in the mainstream movement at home, she is even more scathing about Western movements invading the Muslim world:

> It is usually people from the West going in and saying "we're going to civilize you and help you." They want to help the "others." It should be local women . . . it can't be outsiders coming to liberate us. I do think support is important for queer people. You may not have your family of origin to back you up anymore as a queer Muslim.

Despite Mena's insistence that local women must lead the move for equality around sexual politics, she does subscribe to a biological model of sexual identification popular in international and domestic LGBTQ movements. At the same time, her account does, however, take into account cultural meanings. She says:

> If I was in India or Pakistan I would be queer. But I don't know if I would have the independence or the strength to say "Mom, I can't marry so and so." Here, if the shit goes down really bad I could leave. But there I would probably be married off and having affairs with women. I believe that I can't change my sexuality. Although I do believe it is a fluid concept in general. In South Asia, you don't have to label yourself like here. Or I am homosexual, or straight or whatever.

Mena's assertion that she "would be queer" no matter where she was living complicates her understanding of South Asian sexualities and her relationship to mainstream rights-based movements for sexual equality in the West. While on the one hand she believes her sexuality to be fairly static, she also acknowledges that the sexual systems imposed in the West that clearly divide hetero and homo are not always present in the rest of the world. Mena argues that indentifying as "heterosexual" is not available to most South Asians, just as calling oneself "homosexual" would not be required, encouraged, or even necessarily understood.

Dedra, who is the only participant involved in mainstream LGBTQ rights organizing, serves on the board of her state's equality activist group. About coming out and visibility she says, "I am very close to my family. I left when I was 28. But we've kept in touch. That's the only part of me that we don't discuss. I can't say 'my girlfriend and I went . . . ' I have to say I went with my friends." While Dedra wants to come out to her family, other participants saw this as a purely Western phenomenon that is not sensitive to cultural differences. For Dedra, however, this was not true. Her work for equality and LGBTQ visibility is an important part of her life. On the other hand, Dedra does use discretion when it comes to her community of other Arabs and Berbers:

> When I go to gatherings of North Africans, I am living a double life. I cannot be myself in these groups. But I still go. I am used to this. It is the same when I go back to Algiers. They are still my people. It's not easy for me. It's already a different world for me because all the other women I know here, in my culture, they are at home all day and I am a professional woman. So here is already a big difference in our lives.

While Dedra values the work of her American LGBTQ organization, she also understands that some strategies leave her out and make her feel as though she is leading a double life. Despite her continued efforts to choose who knows about her sexual identification, Dedra does not feel her identity is in conflict or that she cannot live a happy and successful life as a "half-closeted" Muslim lesbian. On the contrary, her strategic use of Western sexual politics and ideologies provides her with more options and available discourses without her identity being constrained or scripted.

Another participant, Sarah, grew up in Yemen and later relocated to the Deep South with her American mother and Arab father. When I asked about her politics and identification she said, "I love to tell people I'm Middle Eastern, especially because of politics right now." Sarah's consciousness of her place in politics, Arab communities, and the mainstream LGBTQ movement is quite varied. On the one hand, as she explains above, she uses her race and background to challenge others' views in a climate particularly hostile to Arabs and ignorant of the possibilities of queer–Middle Eastern identification. On the other hand, Sarah also subscribes to a model that constructs the West as already liberated and progressive while she sees her country of birth, Yemen, to be overly traditional and hostile toward homosexuals. Of the small communities of Arab LGBTQ people forming in large cities around North America, she says:

> I found a gay and lesbian Middle Eastern group in the city and they were very cliquey and political. It was like group therapy. Really angry people getting together to vent . . . and there were some divisions among people from different countries. I just wanted to hang out with other Middle Eastern

people. I didn't really enjoy the experience because of that. In the end, I feel more of a community with people who enjoy photography or dogs or other things I'm interested in, and not my nationality.

Sarah's feeling that she could be more connected to dog lovers illustrates how varied her experience has been both in Yemen and in the American South. Despite Sarah's ambivalence about her Middle Eastern gay and lesbian brothers and sisters and LGBTQ politics in general, she continues to maintain a close connection to her family and hopes to return to Yemen soon to carry out her own dream of helping liberate queer "children" there. While Sarah uncritically categorizes "little gay and lesbian" kids in Yemen, her intention demonstrates her acknowledged social status in relation to those she grew up around. Sarah feels that she must use her privilege to give back:

I really would like to give something back to the little gay and lesbian Yemeni boys and girls living there. I feel like I had it easy because my mom is American. How could I make it better for them? If we hadn't moved here, I could be married to a man with three kids in Yemen. I feel like it's the next move in human rights.

Just as Joseph Massad argues, Sarah believes she can return to the Arab world and make changes that mark progress for international gay liberationists. She sees her relationship to the movement at home as unnecessary, but her obligation to return to help LGBTQ children in Yemen is important to her. In keeping with Puar and with Mahmood's formulation, Sara sees herself as already liberated, with agency, and obligated to help those in her country of birth without the power to resist. While Sarah was the only participant who embraced visibility politics and a Western formulation of sexuality abroad, her position demonstrated the varying relationships to LGBTQ movements held by queer Muslim women. While on the surface Sarah's dream to return to the Middle East may partially prove Massad's point that diasporic activists are the people leading the movements for sexual freedom in the Arab world rather than grassroots locals, I am arguing that the majority of queer Muslim women living in the diaspora have very complex views of sexual equality at home and abroad. At least for the 12 women I interviewed, Sarah is not the rule, rather, her view of the Arab world and sexual politics is the exception in this group.

FINAL THOUGHTS

*Our challenge in claiming our cultural and political identity as Arab
lesbians is to know ourselves as Arabs and lesbians.*

—*Leila Makoul*[28]

These queer Muslim women tell an amazing story of resistance. They
negotiate an impossible construction every day that renders them almost
invisible, unintelligible, and without agency. While I argue here that the
oppositional nature of (homo)sexuality and Islam (and/or Arab culture)
is a Western construction and an extension of Orientalism revised, it is
not a stereotype that will be easy to dismiss. It is clear that almost all the
women here found this to be no easy task, with much time spent explaining and (re)explaining that "yes, I am a lesbian," and "yes, I am an active
Muslim."[29]

Overall I found, both in published narratives and the oral histories
I collected, that many of these queer Muslim women were not invested
in the Western human rights rhetoric of loud and proud, and were even
less excited by, or involved in, any type of international movement. Some
of them saw the imperialism present in the internationalization of Western sexualities and human rights. For example, Mena described a negative human rights strategy for LGBTQ people in the Middle East as one
where liberators from the West try to save the brown people. Instead, most
participants favored a local, grassroots effort in their countries of origin
(or no action at all) that can only be led by those living and working in
the communities they may try to change. While Massad partially blamed
those living in the diaspora for many of the problems of the international
work on gay rights, the women I interviewed, as well as the published narratives, seem to be skeptical of this movement and are clear about the dif-
fering sexual systems in their cultures and their relation to the diaspora.

This is not to imply, however, that the movement is wholly dismissed
by the women interviewed here. In fact, their relationships to the Western
LGBTQ rights movement were varied and wide ranging, including Dedra
who serves on the board of a state-wide equality initiative. Because they
are living in diaspora, and many of the interviewees saw the potential for
political action, yet their relationship to the movement was complicated.
Every participant was influenced, to some degree, by the human rights discourses used in Western movements for equality, although they recognized

that this does not translate internationally. I hope this chapter has aided in complicating this fraught relationship even more by recognizing the tactics used by queer Muslim women as both resistant and conforming at times.

In relation to this international movement for LGBTQ liberation, queer Muslim women continue to challenge and reformulate questions of agency and resistance. They use those parts of the movement that work for them in the moment and reject those that are not suitable. While tactics employed by the movement, such as visibility politics, continue to pose problems for queer Muslim women among others, they are constantly working to renegotiate the terms of their identities and their relationships to this movement. As Saed explains in her narratives, the mainstream movement told her she could not be both Muslim *and* a lesbian. These queer and Muslim women need the freedom to sit "on the edge of belonging," as Saed so rightly named her narrative. Detailed attention must be paid to how the larger movement organizes its efforts against Muslim countries and communities. As Massad reminds us, in some cases these efforts only marginalize even further people who engage in same-sex sex but may not identify with Western binary sexualities.

NOTES

1. It is important to distinguish my understanding of "diaspora" from others. When I call these women "diasporic subjects," I mean to highlight not the place in which they live, North America, but instead the *state* they live in. Being displaced and persecuted is still a part of this configuration. After all, in these times of war, terrorism, and a national Arab enemy, Muslim Arab women living in North America have a unique social position that is influenced heavily by images in the media and imperialist Western ideas about Islam and gender. Even more central to my use of "diasporic" is situating these women as always already removed from their homelands (even if first generation) and in some state of isolation. Despite this, the women whose stories are told here should not be read as inauthentic or foreign to their own families and culture. Diaspora, in the way I evoke it, serves to describe precisely the state of being within a displaced home where one simultaneously conforms and rejects, preserves and discards, and builds communities while challenging them.

2. See, for example, Khalida Saed, "On the Edge of Belonging," in *Living Islam out Loud: American Muslim Women Speak,* ed. Saleemah Abdul-Ghafur (Boston: Beacon Press, 2005), 86–94; Surina Kahn, "Sexual Exiles," in *Women and Sexuality in Muslim Societies,* ed. Pinar Ilkkaracan (n.c: Women for Women's Human

Rights, 2000); Yafa, "The Daughter of The People," http://www.bintelnas.
org/02distance/introl.html; and Leila Makoul, "A Coming Out Story," *Bint El Nas*
2, no. 1 (2000), http://www.bintelnas.org/02distance/journey.html (accessed September 11, 2006), see page 7.

3. After careful consideration, I chose the acronym LGBTQ (lesbian, gay, bisexual, trans, and queer) to describe the participants in this research and the larger
community of same-sex-identified/gender-transgressing folks. Intersex identity
is not included in this acronym since this is a hotly contested issue among many
different intersex organizations, scholars, and individuals. I tend to agree with the
Intersex Initiative (in particular, Emi Koyama's arguments), which argues that
intersex people should not be included in LGBTQ issues by default. My work specifically addresses lesbian, gay, queer people, and less so, it applies to some trans
identities as well.

4. Yafa and Makoul, Saed and Khan.

5. I use "queer" here after much deliberation. Of the 12 women I interviewed
from various parts of the Middle East, Canada, the United States, North and West
Africa, and Europe, each used "queer" to describe her identity, although one preferred "lesbian," and another preferred "dyke." While Joseph Masad has argued
(and I generally agree) that universalizing sexual systems (such as the hetero/homo
binary) do not work, including ascribing sexual categories to non-Westerners,
I have honored the participants' wishes by choosing a label they all used at times.
I also choose queer because of the fluidity it invokes that may possibly represent Arab sexualities more closely than strict Western divisions such as "gay" and
"straight."

6. Jasbir K. Puar, *Terrorist Assemblages: Homonationalism in Queer Times*
(Durham, NC: Duke University Press, 2007), 11–15.

7. Ibid., 40.

8. Ibid., 12.

9. Ibid., 13.

10. Edward Said, *Orientalism* (London: Routledge & Kegan Paul, 1978); Jasbir Puar *Terrorist Assemblages*; and Ania Loomba, *Colonialism/Postcolonialism*
(London: Routledge, 1998).

11. Joseph Massad, *Desiring Arabs* (Chicago: University of Chicago Press,
2007). See Massad for a more complete discussion of *The Arab Mind* and Orientalism. Also see Seymour Hersh, "The Gray Zone," *New Yorker,* May 24, 2004.

12. Seymour Hersh, "The Gray Zone."

13. Ibid.

14. Joe Crea, "Gay Sex Used to Humiliate Iraqis," *Blade,* http://www.wash
ingtonblade.com/2004/5-7/news/national/iraq.cfm (accessed February 11, 2009).
Also see Puar, "Abu Ghraib," in *Terrorist Assemblages,* 79–113.

15. Puar, *Terrorist Assemblages*, 94.

16. Of course, some governments do prosecute people for crimes resembling "homosexual acts." While this threat is very real for some people living in oppressive regimes, I am mostly concerned here with how the Arab world becomes characterized by Western movements and discourses surrounding sexuality.

17. While all of the participants in this study, most of whom were fluent in Arabic and many of whom were recent immigrants from Arab countries, believed there were no terms in Arabic to describe same-sex love, particularly in the way "homosexual" or "lesbian" do in the West (that is, they carry a lot of political meaning and assign identities to behaviors, practices, or desires), there have been some developments on the terminology in Arabic. See "Glossary of Terms" *Aswat*, http://www.aswatgroup.org/FileServer/7021eeed18d9f369ab95220d60add 483.pdf(accessed February 2009). Additionally, Samar Habib's work reveals that women used a code word to refer to themselves and each other as same-sex-identified dating back to the 12th century. See Samar Habib, *Female Homosexuality in the Middle East: Histories and Representations* (New York: Routledge, 2007). The scope of my argument here is that, according to the participants interviewed for this study and published narratives on the issue, there is no commonly used term in mainstream Arab homes to describe homosexuality, especially in its Western conception of a central, fixed, political identity.

18. Surina Khan, "Sexual Exiles," in *Women and Sexuality in Muslim Societies* (Istanbul: Women for Women's Human Rights, 2000), 289–98.

19. Chandra T. Mohanty, "Under Western Eyes: Feminist Scholarship and Colonial Discourses," in *Third World Women and the Politics of Feminism*, ed. C. T. Mohanty, A. Russo, and L. Torres (Bloomington: Indiana University Press, 1991).

20. Ibid., 64–65.

21. Ibid., 78–79.

22. Massad, *Desiring Arabs*, 37.

23. Ibid., 37–38.

24. Ibid., 39.

25. Puar, *Terrorist Assemblages*, 13.

26. Saba Mahmood, "The Subject of Freedom," in *Politics of Piety: The Islamic Revival and the Feminist Subject* (Princeton, NJ: Princeton University Press, 2005).

27. Massad, *Desiring Arabs*, 46–48.

28. Leila Makoul, "A Coming Out Story."

29. Khan, "Sexual Exiles," 298.

17

"EVERYWHERE YOU TURN YOU HAVE TO JUMP INTO ANOTHER CLOSET": HEGEMONY, HYBRIDITY, AND QUEER AUSTRALIAN MUSLIMS

Ibrahim Abraham

This chapter emerges out of a qualitative sociological study of gay, lesbian, and bisexual Muslims in Australia. Cognizant of the plurality of issues that queer Muslim subjectivity touches upon, and the diverse approaches that one could take to the subject, in this chapter I will be focusing on two key issues. First, I will explore the maintenance of hegemonic Muslim and queer identities within Muslim and queer communities in Australia, each of which exclude the viability of queer Muslim identity. My second concern will be with analyzing Australian queer Muslims' strategies for resisting queer Islamophobia and Muslim homophobia. I will argue that two types of strategy emerge: a private, spiritual, and politically liberal approach, contrasted with a public, explicitly religious, and politically radical approach that constitutes the beginnings of a critical queer Muslim hybridity that moves beyond mere tolerance. I will argue that, although largely theoretical, the latter approach offers a preferable strategy for countering the insularity and prejudice of the Muslim and queer communities, as well as the broader hegemonic tendencies of late capitalist Australian society that offers limited private diversity in exchange for public conformity.

Since this chapter presents a sociological case study of the limits of Australian liberal multiculturalism, wherein the rhetoric of tolerance meets with the right-shifting political reality, a little recent history is in order. Australia adopted a policy of multiculturalism in the mid-1970s after the arrival of successive waves of immigrants from Europe, the Middle East, and Asia after World War II. Despite its ongoing oppression of its indigenous peoples, Australia is usually viewed around the world as a multicultural success story, not least for its thriving "pink economy," epitomized by the annual Sydney Gay & Lesbian Mardi Gras. In the past decade, however, under the center-right Liberal-led coalition government and its similarly conservative successors in the Labor Party, the word "multiculturalism" has been banished from official documents, moves toward same-sex equality stalled, and the movement to reconcile white Australia with its black history was largely abandoned, albeit momentarily resurrected in 2008 in a carefully worded apology to the Stolen Generation, cautiously stripped of any legal implications—a little like digging up the corpse of history to bury it deeper and silence a haunting specter.

Most dramatically, immigrants and minority communities—particularly Muslims—have come under increasing suspicion. Afghan refugees were privateered at sea by the Australian army in 2001, to the overwhelming applause of the nation;[1] tabloid fears of Lebanese rape gangs in Sydney combined with broader Islamophobia and xenophobia to culminate in an anti-Muslim riot in Sydney in 2005;[2] and reports of nests of Muslim terrorists in neighboring countries and at home have competed for headlines alongside fears of sexual deviants undermining the nuclear family. In Australia, then, like much of the West, a culture of fear has developed amidst the national and civilizational identity crises called the "clash of civilizations."[3]

It is within this context that I locate this chapter on Australian queer Muslims. Such identities are constitutive of the tensions and contradictions within contemporary Australia. This is often the case with hybrid identities that muddy notions of neat political or cultural belonging, particularly in tightly managed multicultural societies where community identities are often questions of bureaucratic convenience. As Pieterse suggests, "take any exercise in social mapping, and the hybrids are missing. Take most models of multiculturalism and hybrids are not counted."[4] Crucially, the same is usually true in sociological studies of religion that rarely move far from hegemonic Christian capitalism[5] and remain preoccupied with quantitatively mapping the deviation of minority groups from the bourgeois, white, male, Christian, heterosexual norm. When sociology escapes this hegemonic approach, such as in qualitative ethnographies, what emerges are often banal and essentially interchangeable portraits of religious and ethnic minorities in large metropolises—Sikhs in New York, Turks in Berlin, Lebanese in Sydney, and so on.[6]

RESEARCH METHODS

Departing from normative sociology, my approach is explicitly Marxist, in line with what Steve Seidman calls "post-disciplinary sociology," which sees the question of the generalizability of sociological findings as more a question of praxis than of laying down immutable social laws.[7] My data comes from interviews with 12 self-identifying gay, lesbian, or bisexual Muslims living in Australia conducted between 2006 and 2007. I use "queer" here as an imperfect catch-all, for whilst the label was used only intermittently by participants, it is in line with general trends and the now quite apparent inability of a "queer" political identity to replace existing sexual and political identities,[8] I find the term preferable to "non-heterosexual," a term that has been used in previous studies. I refer to my participants by letters of the alphabet (A. to L.), which gives more anonymity than pseudonyms, and avoids the tendency of researchers to choose the most common Muslim names, thereby making many qualitative male-dominated Muslim datasets appear like a roll call of the Shiites' 12 orthodox Imams. I interviewed 11 men, but, problematically, only one woman. This is not an uncommon problem for male researchers of sexuality, and the situation was compounded by the fact that Australia lacks the queer Muslim groups that previous studies, such as those by Yip[9] and Siraj[10] in the United Kingdom and Minwalla, et al.[11] in the United States relied upon for participants. Accordingly, my main vehicle of recruitment was the queer press; readily available in the affluent inner suburbs of large cities where queer life predominates, the publications are far less available in the working class suburbs where most Muslims live. Most also have a distinct male bias.

It is therefore not surprising that only two of the participants were Australian-born, and only four were raised in Australia. Only L., an Egyptian Australian gay man from Melbourne and I., a Lebanese Australian lesbian from Sydney resemble the normative image of Australian Muslims: first or second generation immigrant, Arab, from a working class background, living in Sydney or Melbourne. Australian-born F. converted to Islam as an adult, and, like most of the other participants, lives in an Inner West suburb of Sydney, where queer Australian life is centered. The remaining participants are foreign born and raised, and are either young professionals or students. All are highly educated—or want to be—and affluent. They belong to the voguish liberal sociological categories of "transnationals" or "cosmopolitans." As B. told me in a Melbourne café, when an iconic tram rumbled past, "tomorrow I could go and live in New York and be quite comfortable." However, transnational capitalism—not transnational people—provides the most appropriate frame of reference here. We are dealing with the sons of the developing world's bourgeoisie. Having the financial capital to transcend *political* borders, the need is then for the social capital to transcend *cultural* borders.

My research participants are:

- A., a male in his early 20s, born and raised in Pakistan, studying in Melbourne.
- B., a male in his early 30s, born and raised in India, working in Melbourne.
- C., a male in his late 20s, born and raised in Lebanon, studying and working in Sydney.
- D., a male in his late 20s, born and raised in Indonesia, studying and working in Melbourne.
- E., a male in his early 20s, born and raised in Bangladesh, working in Melbourne.
- F., a male in his early 50s, born and raised in Australia, of Anglo/Celtic background, an adult convert to Islam, living and working in Sydney and Egypt.
- G., a male in his early 20s, born and raised in Malaysia, studying in Sydney.
- H., a male in his early 30s, born and raised in Bangladesh, educated in the United States, working in Sydney.
- I., a female in her early 30s, born in Lebanon, raised from an early age in Australia, working in Sydney.
- J., a male in his late 20s, born and raised in Mauritius, studying in Sydney.
- K., a male in his early 20s, born in India, raised in Australia, studying in Adelaide.
- L., a male in his early 20s, born and raised in Australia, of Egyptian background, working in Melbourne.

Now I will turn to an analysis of the participants' experiences, beliefs, and hopes, as narrated to me in the interviews. I will begin with the issues of hegemonic Muslim homophobia and hegemonic queer Islamophobia before turning to issues of resistance, the limits of liberal, private resistance, and the creative possibilities of a public resistance and its development of hybrid identities.

HEGEMONIC MUSLIM HOMOPHOBIA

Although all participants except I. and K. had Muslim friends or family with whom they were open about their sexuality, all but F. closeted their sexuality around most other Muslims. Only H. and K. specifically cited Islamic beliefs and teachings as the primary source of their Muslim communities' condemnation of homosexuality. "What the religion says, the culture practically says the same thing," K. said. Other participants who discussed the matter saw scripture and religious practices as secondary means used to reinforce pre-existing social and cultural attitudes. "It's not the religion, it's the culture," said C., noting that Lebanese Christians faced similar problems. Regardless of the initial source of conservative Muslim attitudes toward sexuality, whether there is a single source or whether sexuality, like most other social phenomena, is an overdetermined one, we see attitudes toward sexuality and identity operating in a hegemonic fashion within Muslim communities. Drawing on Gramsci,[12] we see hegemonic relationships of power working far more subtlety than brute domination. Indeed, Gramsci's concern was with how to create a revolutionary counterhegemonic force in Western Europe where the ruling class governs not by brutality alone but through a veneer of culture, coercion, and consent. Thus, in Muslim and queer communities, hegemonic identities establish and reproduce themselves by articulating a universality that masks their particularity. Within conservative Muslim communities, the universal norm that is projected as valid for all Muslims is heterosexual marriage and the adherence to broader gender roles. As D. said, "there's only one expectation at the moment, if you're Muslim, you're expected to be married and have a son."

Indeed, if there is a single issue that renders queer Muslim identities problematic from within Muslim communities, it is the expectation that Muslims will enter into heterosexual marriages and raise families. This expectation was present in Minwalla, et al.'s study in the United States,[13]

and Siraj and Yip's studies in the United Kingdom.[14] Most of my participants spoke at length about the pressure to marry. K. had broken off an
arranged marriage, noting that "everyone in the community asks me so
many times, 'when are you going to get married?'" The same was true for
L., who told me "once I start hitting very close to thirty there'll be massive
alarm bells if I'm not married. People always talk to me about marriage
and just *assume* . . . I don't know how I'll deal with it." It is in this assumption L. alludes to where we can see hegemonic forces at work. L. recounted
a discussion with a young Muslim woman from his community who:

> told me, "there's this other girl and she really likes you," and I'm like, "how
> do I respond?" And she's like, "tell me which girls you're attracted to and I'll
> tell you if it's her," and I'm thinking, "well, I'm actually not attracted to any
> of them." But it was just so *normal*.

This "normal" is, of course, the "norm" in heteronormativity, showing very clearly the working of a hegemonic identity. What seemed like
harmless gossip proved profoundly confronting for L. because of its predi-
cation in the hegemonic discourses of herteronormativity. These norms
become hegemonic by taking on an air of naturalness, such that one of the
most-cited texts on Muslims in Australia, Saeed's *Islam in Australia* can
place heterosexual marriage and family in what he calls "the life-cycle of a
Muslim,"[15] as if he were discussing a type of female spider that has evolved
to eat its mate after sex.

D. tied these hegemonic gender expectations of marriage back to the question of queer Muslims, arguing that "a lot of queer Muslims feel they have
to follow that expectation of what it means to be a Muslim man or a Muslim
woman. That has to be challenged before the issue of homosexuality can be
discussed." Indeed, implicated within the hegemonic Muslim view of marriage is a particular ideology of gender that also renders a public homosexual
identity problematic. A. explained that, amongst his Pakistani-Australian
Muslim friends, a lesbian Muslim was as unimaginable as a Muslim woman
who did not wear *hijab*. "They are not aware of patriarchy," he shrugged.
Equally, the typical way to insult a man in I.'s Arab Muslim community in
Sydney was to "call him a 'poof' . . . if a woman is a bit masculine, then she's
a 'dyke.'" In either case, the insult is not necessarily about one's sexual activity or orientation, but denotes a failure to properly perform one's hegemonic
gender identity. However, it is through such language that certain sexualities

and certain hegemonic forms of gender performance are reproduced and certain behavior and identities rendered beyond the accepted boundaries of the community. As Connell notes, the proximity to homosexuality has long been a measure of one's status in the broader hegemonic masculine hierarchy.[16] Thus, in contrast to the figure of the "poof," L.'s Arab Muslim community in Melbourne told him that a man "should be strong and masculine and married." According to I., in her community a man is expected to be "the provider or being [sic] the leader of the pack. The woman is just in a 'yes, Sir, no, Sir, here are your kids, Sir' kind of position."

This expectation of heterosexual marriage, related to the strong expectations for other forms of gendered behavior, is also related to homophobic attitudes amongst Muslims that emerge from stereotyped media depictions of queer life—such as the popular depictions of the Sydney Mardi Gras—which are then fed back into Muslim communities' national-cultural and religious discourse that has become tinged with fear since the instigation of the War on Terror. As L. said of these hegemonic depictions of queer life, "I thought I wouldn't be accepted because I don't act like that. That's what I thought all gay people were like and I realized later on that that was far from the case." A. also referred to the Mardi Gras imagery as being the basis for his friends' claims that "queer people are non-religious," and their viewing homosexuality as "'mere hedonism.'"

What we see as a result of this heteronormativity is a pattern of "closeting," such that queer Muslims are not comfortable in disclosing their sexuality in Muslim, and sometimes all other, spaces. Given the ubiquity of the closet on studies of homosexuality, from theorizing the normative status of life and (sub)cultures developed in the closet from Sedgwick[17] to Seidman's[18] extrapolation of a postcloset world, it is worth exploring the reality of the "closet" in the Australian Muslim context. As we will see in the remainder of this chapter, the lives of Australian queer Muslims are lived in multiple closets.

Life in the queer closet—as (partially) distinct from life in the Muslim closet, which I shall come to—also requires changes in behavior, constant self-censoring and self-doubt. Living life in the closet(s) requires "deception and duplicity" as the norm.[19] When interviewed, L., for example, was very concerned with whether I thought he appeared "stereotypically gay." Equally, E. described how he had to act "very straight" around his Muslim friends. "We just talk about girls, I say 'yeah, she was looking good, good boobs.'" As K. concurred, "in my culture, all guys talk about is girls." For

K., complying with hegemonic community norms was important—"you grow up with all that in mind and with the thought that if you ever rebelled what the consequences will be." Similar sentiments were current in Yip's study, with a Muslim lesbian explaining the reason she didn't come out was because it would upset her family who "support one another when things get sticky, like racism."[20] What we see, then, is the operation of rather unexceptional diasporic communities where a support network is in place providing social and economic assistance,[21] but only in return for conformity with cultural hegemony.

As Seidman argues, living in the closet damages "the psychological and social core of an individual's life."[22] Or, as I. put it, "it really screws up your head." In fact, I. was the most eloquent participant in discussing the effects of the closet:

> It's frustrating when [I] have to hide because who I am is a very confident, very extroverted, very, kind of . . . it's very hard to put me down and no matter how hard you put me down, I always bounce back very well. I'm very good at taking a lot of heat, but you can only take so much before you just say, "you know what, I'm just gonna pretend that I'm this or that just so I don't have to deal with the crap that comes with being that or this." You fill up, and as confident and as strong as you are, there's always that bit inside you, saying, "just hide who you are, otherwise it will be your downfall." The most frustrating thing is that you have to be so many different personalities and you have to remember which is which and to pull back and you become so good at it that it's almost like waking up in the morning. You meet your gay friends and, well, there you are, you're gay, then you run into someone in the street who knows you and you're a good Muslim so it's like this absolute rollercoaster that never ends.

HEGEMONIC QUEER ISLAMOPHOBIA

As I. later added, "everywhere you turn you have to jump into a different closet. You never can be just you, you always have to be me as either gay, or me as a Muslim." Just as we've seen hegemonic heteronormative Muslim identities impede the articulation of a queer Muslim identity, so too do hegemonic *homonormative*[23] queer identities. As Mauritian-born J. states:

> [B]eing gay in Sydney . . . you are seen to have to live your gay life as a Western's gay way of living, which I'm not part of. If you're not part of that

Western gay lifestyle you have to choose; you can't be Muslim and gay, to put it bluntly.

Just as they were reticent about coming out as queer amongst fellow Muslims, most of the participants were also concerned about revealing their religion and sometimes nationality or ethnicity to other queers. For those who are open about their religion in queer spaces, they are expected to be representatives and explicators of the religion itself and apologists for the actions of other Muslims. "Sometimes people are surprised that I'm a Muslim and I'm gay," B. said. "And then all the questions! 'How can you reconcile being Muslim and gay?' and things like that." D. was constantly called up to explain and justify his religion as well. "Sometimes you think that you're wasting your time," he said.

> Sometimes you think that you have changed their perception. Other times you just say, "well that's it; that's all I'm gonna tell you, I'm a Muslim and *that's it* and whatever questions you're gonna throw at me I'm just gonna ignore it!" You do get tired after a while.

All participants felt that it was the fear of Muslim terrorism that had hardened non-Muslims' views of Muslims and Islam. Malaysian-born G. learnt that in Australia "it's very rude to ask if someone's a Muslim because of the whole terrorism thing." He continued:

> 9/11 has had so much impact not only on the Islamic world but on the gay world as well because people didn't know anything about Islam, and now they just know Muslims are all terrorists!

The same point was made by the founder of the British queer Muslim organization *Al Fatiha*: "to them"—meaning the mainstream queer community—"everyone is like the Taliban."[24] As a result of this prejudice, G. said, "I only tell my religion to gay men if I *really* know them [and] if I know it's safe to tell them." Those who could pass as non-Muslims felt a great deal of relief. Bangladeshi-born E. said, "when people look at me, they don't see me as a Muslim, they don't know about religion—they just see an Indian." G. felt fortunate that "[gay men] don't think I look Muslim, they think of Arabic guys . . . they'll be racist to them." One person unable to pass as non-Muslim was Egyptian-Australian L. "The first time I went out to an openly gay place," he told me, "there were a few people who made comments about my beard making me look like a terrorist."

The conflation of Islam with terrorism is a political trope that has developed within a queer context alongside the rise of what Lisa Duggan calls "homonormativity;"[25] the emergence of affluent liberal gay men and lesbians asserting nationalist, ruling class political identities. "Homonormativity" has had a lot to say during this War on Terror with Muslims a convenient Other against which liberal capitalism can be defined. Significant here are high-profile figures like Irshad Manji, the lesbian writer, self-promoter, and self-declared "Muslim refusenik" who picks up various neoconservative tropes in her book *The Trouble with Islam*. As well as deploying the wisdom of TV pop psychologist Dr. Phil to contemporary religion and politics, Manji fuses neoconservative and homonormative tropes together into cheerful reactionary bile. The welfare system, she writes, simply allows immigrant "extremists" to "buy the time to organize and execute their plans."[26] Equally, one of Manji's various troubles with Islam is Muslims who are "stuck in self-pity." For her, this makes Muslims as contemptible as African Americans who fail to acknowledge all the good that American capitalism in general, and George W. Bush in particular, has brought them.[27]

As well as further evidence of the dearth of intellectual talent on the right, Manji's ramblings are evidence of what Gramsci called an "organic crisis"—rapid social and economic change dissolving existing political alliances and the possibility of a new order emerging.[28] Thus, homonormativity hints at the broader "disaggregation of a civilization and the construction of another one,"[29] with conservatives beginning to see queer communities as natural allies. In other words, this is an act of redrawing the boundaries of belonging akin to George W. Bush declaring that "you're with us, or you're with the terrorists." Having said this, a number of queer scholars and activists are rejecting the rhetoric of the Clash of Civilizations and seeking to draw attention to the common struggles for recognition and justice of Muslim and queer communities, including scholars such as Anjali Arondekar and particularly Jasbir Puar[30] and groups such as the outrageous pro-Palestinian activists Q.U.I.T.—Queers Undermining Israeli Terrorism.[31]

It is not simply contemporary debates about Islam that inform hegemonic queer Islamophobia, however. There are two pre-existing hegemonic tendencies within Australia's queer community that have proved a fertile ground for Islamophobia. The first is hegemonic secularism. In a 2005 survey, 72 percent of Australian nonheterosexuals claimed "no religion"[32] and said that faith is an aspect of queer life that is rarely discussed. D. argued that all religion is seen as incompatible with hegemonic queer identity:

> We still haven't found a place to put religion in our community, mainly because we've been excluded from a lot of religious institutions. Even [the Metropolitan Christian Church] still feel that they're not part of the community.[33] They still feel like they are a separate group, so that tells you a lot about the way the community accepts religion.

The other issue is racism, particularly toward Asians in the queer community. In Australia, gay Asian men have taken a semiseparatist approach in response to white Australian prejudice.[34] Racism was also present in Yip's study of South Asian participants in the United Kingdom,[35] as well as in Minwalla, et al.'s study in the United States.[36] Most of the participants in my study have experienced racism, including those who alluded to anti-Muslim attitudes in the queer community but had not encountered them directly, such as B., D., G., and H. For his part, G. was greatly amused to be asked if he had experienced racism in Sydney's gay community. "This is such a common thing amongst gay men!" he laughed. "For gay Asian men and the gay Asian community, I know it's an issue," D. said, referring to racism in the broader gay community. "We talk a lot about exclusion; we talk a lot about alienation." As Chong-Suk Han argues in the American context, the focus on mainstream acceptance by the gay rights movement has lead to the construction of an affluent white group identity that marginalizes non-Europeans.[37] The maintenance of the "illusion of normalcy," he argues, requires the constant reinforcement of racial borders, hence the exclusion that D. finds so common amongst gay Asian men.

We need to put these issues of ethnicity, religion, and exclusion within the broader problematic of hegemonic queer identity. As B. said, "Most certainly, there is racism in the gay community; anyone who is not stereotypical is viewed with some apprehension." To drive home this point about hegemonic queer identity in Australia, B. used the absurd situation that a gay Muslim received a similar reaction to a gay heavy metal fan: "you're *Muslim* and you're gay!?" Or, "you like *heavy metal* and you're gay?" In fact, other hegemonic aspects of Australian queer identity beyond religion and ethnicity alienated my participants. F., notably, argued that age was a significant issue. "When I reached 35 or 40 I thought I'd passed my use-by date," he said:

> But I didn't; I found a whole different world . . . In Egypt the older I get the more attractive I seem to get, which is the opposite here . . . There's a prejudice against people who are old as much as there is a prejudice against people who are Muslim.

Age was part of the hegemonic image of queer Sydney that F. said was characterized by its "superficial" values: "suntans, body shape, age." Body shape was also an issue that L. raised. "If it's not about conforming to their culture," L. said, alluding to hegemonic gay culture that he disliked, "it's about religion and race and all that, and then weight . . . I'm weight-conscious, I'm [also] a lot of other, you know, things that are barriers."

It is not just physical traits that construct the hegemonic norms of the queer community, of course. It is also patterns of consumption—too often depoliticized and reduced to the term *lifestyle*.[38] J., in particular, was critical of the way gay identity had come to be epitomized by broader mass consumption and hedonism. "Being a gay Muslim, I won't drink," he said:

> Being a gay Muslim I won't take drugs. I might not gamble, I might not like partying a lot . . . but that doesn't mean I'm not enjoying myself. If being gay means to be so open and accepting too much of everything, I'm not part of it. I'm quite a conservative person in my lifestyle but I assume my gayness fully.

Or, as F. described Sydney's gay scene, "it's party, party, party!" He was critical of the bourgeois ambition he saw in the gay community, with the focus on "having a home and a nice car." E. noted a similar attitude, and he likened it to the materialism he encountered in the Bangladeshi-Australian community. "Having a boyfriend is treated like having a nice car," he said. "That's really bad, but it's a fact." L. saw the hegemonic gay scene in Melbourne exemplified by certain patterns of consumption. "I think everyone's pretty, um, selfish and, um, callous and superficial," he said, before adding as an afterthought, "I wouldn't be able to generalize, mind you." Of course, these criticisms are not *Islamic* criticisms as such, nor are they criticisms unique to Muslims. Moreover it is difficult to know precisely how these more general concerns about, or perceptions of, normal life in the queer community affect or interact with specific concerns about religious or racial discrimination, or religious prescriptions.

Nevertheless, what is being signaled here is a broader insularity and hegemonic identity in queer communities not dissimilar in logic and function of hegemonic identities in Australia's Muslim communities. Whilst the content differs, of course, the processes are similar, predicated not on brute force to maintain social norms, but on more subtle forms of consent-seeking, universalizing coercion. Participants noted the insularity of the queer community served to perpetuate these hegemonic norms, just as it did with Australia's Muslim communities. "I think there is a lot of prejudice, a lot of 'us and them' mentality in the queer community," I said. "They're also not as open minded as you think they would be," she said.

Having explored the construction, maintenance, and effect of hegemonic Muslim identities and hegemonic queer identities in Australia, showing how each prevents the viable articulation of a queer Muslim identity, I now want to turn to the issue of the resistance that Australian queer Muslims are enacting and theorizing in response to these hegemonic identities.

PRIVATE RESISTANCE AND THE LIMITS OF LIBERALISM

Research participants advanced strategies that fall within two broad, imperfect, heuristic categories that I am calling public and private. We could also characterize them as spiritual and religious, or liberal and radical. In what follows, I will explore how participants articulated—that is, enacted, theorized. or imagined—the responses to prejudice and exclusion, and offer a deeper political analysis of the ideologies underpinning each of the approaches. My concern is not with criticizing any particular approach, but rather with analyzing the limits and effects that each approach frames, arguing that only a public, explicitly religious, and politically radical approach can achieve the viability of queer Muslim subjectivity.

First, in relation to reducing Muslim homophobia, the *private* strategy for resistance is to embrace a self-guided Islamic "spirituality" that must be considered separate from public or communal expressions of faith and identity. J., for example, insisted that that "there's a socio-political way of things and then the spiritual way. I am most richly closer to God than really being into the social-political aspects of Islam." Similarly, D. argued that:

> [I]ndividuals who can combine religious and sexual identity together are those who believe in the spirituality, not the religious practice that defines the connection between the self and God. I believe those who cannot combine the two together are those who are stuck between the religious institutions and sexuality, because the institutions are telling them what to do and what not to do. But once you get to that higher understanding of spirituality you'll be fine, because then you realize that every decision you make is your own.

D.'s religious approach here was heavily oriented toward the individual, in line with his insistence that the decision to disclose one's sexuality or not is a purely individual choice—"it always has to be individual . . . anything that you do in your life, it's always an individual choice."

Of course, as the experiences and attitudes of the participants show, the decision to disclose or closet one's religion cannot be seen in purely liberal, individualistic terms unless, of course, one sees this as a utopian or existential liberalism undermined by what we might call actual-existing liberalism. Thus, I am tempted to adapt Slavoj Žižek's take on the old Polish antisocialist joke, "True, we don't have enough food, electricity, flats, books, freedom, but what does that matter in the end, since we do have Socialism!"[39] In this context, we see the reality is closer to, "True, individuals don't have the freedom to choose, but what does that matter in the end, since we do have liberalism!" In the case of both Polish socialism and Australian liberal multiculturalism, the signifier becomes stripped of its constitutive content to become a self-referential cause all its own, forever delaying its realization—a little like the famous scene in *The Life of Brian* when a male freedom fighter is placated by his comrades telling him that, whilst he cannot *have* a baby, he nevertheless has the *right* to have a baby.

Now, this private and spiritual strategy would not concern itself with directly challenging hegemonic Australian Muslim attitudes to sexuality, gender, or other matters, which in keeping with the broadly liberal-individualist approach, would be relegated to the private sphere. Only challenges to the sacrosanct nature of this private sphere would be directly challenged. For example, B. was not particularly concerned about the hegemonic attitudes of his Muslim community toward sexuality, saying "I don't see that as a big issue, because I consider [sexuality] as something private." This strategy is described by Yip as "compartmentalisation," a strategy which "a majority" of his research participants employed, and which he described as involving "sexuality or religion tak[ing] prominence in a particular context, without leading to the relinquishing of the other, which takes on prominence in a different context."[40]

In terms of reducing anti-Muslim queer prejudice, such an approach would see the formation of Muslim or ethnically specific queer groups that would have a semiseparatist approach, similar to the development of Asian queer groups in Australia.[41] After his first date with a non-Muslim in Australia ended in a tirade of anti-Muslim abuse from his date, E. explained that, "now I'm just trying to focus on Indian, Pakistani, and Muslim guys—mostly Muslim guys." This could certainly be described as a "private" solution to Islamophobia—to retreat from the perceived source of the prejudice into a context or situation where one feels more comfortable. L. discussed a similar strategy, saying, "for those that whine about not being accepted because they're Muslim, well, good for them if we can have a community where we are accepted with people they feel comfortable around." He then added his concerns about being involved in a queer Arab group that might be dominated by Maronite Christians—"I'm open-minded as a Muslim," he said, "but there'll be lots of Arab Christians who don't like Muslims."

If queer Muslims were to develop any sort of public-political face, such an approach would be housed in the liberal language of tolerance and decency. Hence F.'s argument that "what you need to do is humanize homosexuals [so] Muslims can see gay people as not having a choice in the matter and just being human beings." Similarly, A. spoke of the need to "show queers are also human" and I. insisted that heterosexual Muslims need to be able to see the queer other "as a person." Here, one hears talk of increasing knowledge and tolerance of queers by Muslims and Muslims by queers, and both groups by mainstream Australians. This is the ballad of liberal tolerance—"boutique multiculturalism," in other words;[42] the acceptance of minor cultural tics, paid for by prior cultural homogenization and public conformity. However, as liberal multiculturalism readjusts to the logic of the "clash of civilizations," the tolerance for banal difference is becoming explicitly coupled with an equally celebrated *in*tolerance of differences that the hegemon cannot assimilate.

This is one of the many problems with such an approach, for despite the efforts of people like Irshad Manji and a new generation of very well behaved, middle class "model minority" Muslims in Australia, Islam is proving rather hard for hegemonic liberal capitalism to assimilate. This is most evidently in the recent debates on headscarves in Europe and its colonies.[43] The holy liberal grail, freedom of choice, ran aground with young Muslim women making the *wrong* choices. The answer was to rhetorically curtail this through the insistence that those who acted in an unpopular fashion were *obviously* coerced; but one day they may be liberated, when they can have their freedoms back. The sign of this liberation will, of course, be their choice to conform to social norms. This is Adorno and Horkheimer's old argument—we are free to chose a religion if it has been politically neutralized. The freedom to choose *ideology,* however, is freedom "to choose what is always the same."[44]

In the queer Muslim question, tolerant approaches are typically accompanied by calls for liberalization, Westernization, or the reformation of Islam, seen as the troublesome party—Yip does this in his study of the United Kingdom.[45] Here, liberalization, Westernization, and reformation largely work as code words for rendering Islam harmless within a broader liberal capitalist hegemony. The reduction, in other words, of Islam down to the level of a harmless conglomeration of consumer choices to be played out in the free market that, in fine liberal tradition, makes no claims to exclusivity or superiority to any other individual choices. The result of this liberal approach would leave each constituent group unmolested, but ease movement between them, not least because sexual and religious identities would lose their significance. The *other* approach is more radical, however, rejecting the notion that each parent culture is a wholly contained entity, as in the chauvinist logic of Islamic homophobia or queer Islamophobia, whilst resisting the notion that these identities are irrelevant or ironic, as in the liberal formula. What I am signaling here is a process of *hybridity* that actively seeks to disprove notions of stable cultural borders against isolationist tendencies, whilst maintaining that significant social worlds can still be constructed through the maintenance and dialectical transformation of traditions and beliefs, rather than through their mere liberal negation or disavowal.

PUBLIC RESISTANCE AND CRITICAL HYBRIDITY

Hybridity emerged as a critical concept within social theory around the same time as queer theory, the early 1990s. Whilst queer theory reached its apogee in the United States, it has been the United Kingdom and the nations more recently released from Her Majesty's protection where the concept has proved most popular, as a part of the shift from Commonwealth studies to postcolonial studies. Adapting Fredric Jameson's notion of a third space,[46] a key elucidator (and occasional obfuscator) of hybridity theory, Homi Bhabha speaks of a *hybrid* third space emerging when what is produced by the fusion of parent cultures becomes sufficiently ambivalent that one cannot say where one culture begins and the other ends.[47] We get a sense of this with B.'s statement, "I'm a very complex mix. I'm Muslim, Indian, Gay, and Australian." His subjectivity becomes incomprehensible without an understanding of the mutually dependent nature of this mix. That is, absent the other cultures, and the transformative effect of their hybridization, at a certain point his identity breaks down into contradiction and incomprehension.

Hybridity theories have attracted much criticism for the unduly optimistic approach to questions of identity and the assumption that we are all free to break and remake our identities as we like. What is missing, according to Marxist critics of hybridity and allied trends in postcolonial theory (such as the work of Ahmad,[48] Dirlik,[49] and Papastergiadis[50]), is an appreciation of the materiality underscoring cultural change and continuity, but what the process or concept of hybridity can provide us with is a critical methodology to examine the limits of multiculturalism. As Papastergiadis argues, "[t]he critical challenge of hybridity theory is not an unending celebration and display of difference but rather a critique of the conditions that constrain the complexities and exclude the totality of cultural exchange."[51] In other words, if we posit the hybridization of identities as a heuristic end point—with the question of whether it is desirable or not set aside for now—we see the social and political realities that inhibit that hybridization. This is why, for example, I. says of her Muslim and queer identities, "it's very *hard* to mix the two; it's very *uncomfortable* to mix the two; it's very *frustrating* to mix the two."

I am positing a critical hybridity as the end point of what I am calling public strategies of resistance to Muslim homophobia and queer Islamophobia, that also manifests itself as explicitly religious, not merely spiritual, and politically radical, not merely liberal, regardless of whether this is the intention or not. In relation to reducing Muslim homophobia, a *public* approach challenges hegemonic Australian Muslim attitudes on sexuality, gender, and other issues from within the framework of Islamic ethics and history. This is not, as in the private approach, the retreat into a personal

spirituality that does not seek to make its claim for validity in the broader
Muslim marketplace of ideas, (to employ a thoroughly repugnant capitalist analogy). As A. said:

> Islam talks about social justice. It talks about human rights. Islam has al-
> ways been attractive for the marginalized—look at the early converts, most
> of them were women or slaves. The wider message of Islam gives queer
> people a voice.

K. said:

> It's repeatedly stressed in the Quran and the sayings of the Holy Prophet
> that no one is better than anyone except if they have done good deeds. If
> you're from a different race, speak a different language, are a different skin
> color or man or woman or child, you're all equal. I guess gay people would
> be equal to straight people, too. We could stress that we should be following
> that example and not discriminate against anyone.

What was also suggested was a public queer presence in Muslim communities, but this was hampered by those who were most involved in Muslim communities typically being the most reticent about revealing their
sexuality. "I'm the sort of person who wants to be out there," I. said. "I'd
love to run around and help set up this and that, but I also want to hide in
the background at the same time." Given that rigid gender expectations, as
we have seen, are a source of homophobia, advocates of public approaches
to changing hegemonic attitudes also spoke of the necessity of linking issues, including patriarchy and broader issues of sexuality, particularly A.
who was deeply concerned by the lack of awareness his fellow Muslim men
showed in relation to "patriarchy."

It was in relation to addressing hegemonic queer Islamophobia that the
most public and thoroughly subversive approaches to questions of identity
emerged, however. This is also where a critical hybridity emerges most
clearly. Similarly to public approaches to changing Muslim homophobia,
public approaches to changing queer Islamophobia would see an increased
and visible presence of Muslims in queer communities, just as it would see a
visible public queer presence in Muslim communities. This would lead to a
process of cultural hybridity whereby the integral grounds of each seemingly distinct identity group are challenged and blurred, creating Jameson

and Bhabha's third space. Here, I look to the ruminations of D., who sees a very public hybridity as an answer to Islamophobia and homophobia. "Islam," he said:

> can influence the perception of what being queer is all about. It will change how we see ourselves as a community, letting more people in and redefining it so that it's not just about same-sex attraction, it's about the different things, including family, religion and cultural background that create an individual.

Not content with changing what being queer is all about, D. also wants to change what being Australian is all about. "I reject assimilation," he said. "I always argue that assimilation is only a one-way process. The minority is always expected to assimilate into the majority; this is not right. This is why I like the word hybridity—then we can start blending in different aspects of our personality." D. argued that same-sex desire has become part of the heterosexual imagining of mainstream Australia, in recent years. "We're a part of the heterosexual system," he announced. What is now needed, he continued, is "to incorporate Islam into the wider Australian culture, so it's not just one way assimilation which is what they're doing now." There could hardly be a more controversial notion in present day Australia than that the nation needs to incorporate Islam, when mainstream Australian multicultural discourse limits itself to liberal tolerance for private spirituality and agreeable cultural tics, or the emergence of a national security state predicated on a hostile alien Islamic threat.

A rather similar approach was taken by F., an Anglo-Australian convert, who said, "friends and people that I meet are always totally shocked to find out that I'm a Muslim. I hear them going on about 'fucking Muslims' and all that and I ask, 'Oh, really? You think so? Well, *I'm* a Muslim,' and they go, '*nooo!*'" F. linked this witty and subversive approach to revealing and asserting his religious identity to his revealing and asserting of his sexual identity. "It used to be like that years ago with being queer," he said. "It's the same thing. Friends would be telling gay jokes and not realize that I was gay, and I'd say, '*I'm* gay.'" Similarly, I. used playful humor to assert her Islamic identity within the context of the queer community. "I make some remarks," she said of discussing Islam with her queer friends. "I put *fatwas* on people and call them infidels, and all that kind of stuff." At a time when politicians from both the dominant sides of Australian politics (the right and the center-right, that is) are accusing Muslims of being unassimilable and the embodiment of something called "unAustralianness," it is interesting that the primary targets of I.'s *fatwas*—the popular misunderstanding that it is a death sentence being something she toys with—are right-wing politicians and media commentators. All of which is to say that she has an iconically Australian sense of humor about these matters, whilst at the same time her humor masks a deeper political truth: that most Muslims and queers suffer similar experiences of marginalization and oppression within the hegemonic Australian political culture, and both share a common cause in building a diverse counterhegemonic force to change it; creating a society wherein "oppressions of race, class, and gender can be transformed into social forms in which diversity and difference are not only possible, but celebrated."[52]

This is where it gets even more interesting from a political point of view, for in contrast to the tolerant liberal approach that talks of reformation as a code for assimilation, many of the participants' solutions to homophobia and other prejudices can only be called Islam*ist*. "The conflict becomes the solution," said J. "You're conflicting with your religion while the solution is *in it*." Others spoke of the political problem of Muslim homophobia being a lack of appreciation of core Muslim values. "We should follow the example of the Prophet and not discriminate," said Indian-born K. Against the assumption that queer rights go hand in hand with liberal secularism, many participants felt the solution to homophobia was not less Islam, but more Islam—if *only* everyone was as good a Muslim as they were, there would be no homophobia. The same thing goes for Islamophobia the solution is not *less* Islam in public or to assimilate Islam into non-Muslim liberal capitalist culture (such as it is), but a truly hybrid approach engendering precisely the opposite: "we need to incorporate Islam *into* the Australian culture," said D. "So it's not just one way assimilation which is what they're doing now ... *They* have to negotiate *themselves*, otherwise it won't work. What a lot of people don't understand is the spirituality of Islam is not fixed." What D. points to at this final point is a very thorough project for a queer Australian Muslim hybridity that goes far beyond tolerance and its own apparent struggles to incorporate the struggles of others.

IN PLACE OF A CONCLUSION

There are a variety of approaches one could take to conclude this chapter. My approach has been to work through a Marxist analysis of the empirical data, building up a picture of the multiple sites of alienation affecting queer Muslims in Australia and pointing to the political logic underlying it. The final salient political point to be drawn from all this is not particularly clear, however. Certainly the limits of a liberal approach to tolerance are evident, but I am reticent to criticize such approaches in the Australian context, given the dearth of realistic alternatives. Indeed, as was clear, the public solutions to addressing queer Islamophobia remain rather theoretical or are subtly contained within the sort of everyday resistance loved only by Foucauldians. Being unable to point to a realistic resolution to the queer Muslim question, I wish to conclude with a small vignette that points toward what a reconciled and transformed queer Australian Muslim subjectivity may look like, if it materializes. As B. told me as another one of those Melbourne trams rumbled past, "When I'm invited to dinner at a gay friend's place during Ramadan, I take my prayer mat with me, so after I break my fast with them, I can say my prayers. I don't conceal that I'm a practicing Muslim, nor do I conceal that I'm gay."

NOTES

1. David Marr and Marian Wilkinson, *Dark Victory* (Sydney: Allen & Unwin, 2004).

2. Scott Poynting, "What Caused the Cronulla Riot?" *Race & Class* 48, no. 1 (2006): 85–92.

3. Samuel Huntington, *The Clash of Civilizations and the Remaking of World Order* (New York: Simon & Schuster, 1996).

4. Jan Nederveen Pieterse, "Hybridity, So What? The Anti-Hybridity Backlash and the Riddles of Recognition," *Theory, Culture & Society* 18, nos. 2–3 (2001): 219–45, 220.

5. T. R. Young, "Marxism and Social Movements: Theory and Practice for Social Justice," *Contemporary Sociology* 28, no. 3 (1999): 268–70.

6. Gerd Bauman, *The Multicultural Riddle* (New York: Routledge, 1999).

7. Steven Seidman, "The Political Unconscious of the Human Sciences," *Sociological Quarterly* 37, no. 4 (1996): 699–719.

8. Matthew Waites, "The Fixity of Sexual Identities in the Public Sphere," *Sexualities* 8, no. 5 (2005): 539–69; Ibrahim Abraham, "'On the Doorstep of the Work': Ricoeurian Hermeneutics, Queer Hermeneutics and Scripture" *Bible & Critical Theory* 3, no. 1 (2007): 04.1–04.12, 04.1–04.2.

9. Andrew K. T. Yip, "A Minority within a Minority: British Non-Heterosexual Muslims. Report of Research Activities and Results." 10 May 2003, *Economic and Social Research Council,* http://www.esrcsocietytoday.ac.uk/ESRCInfoCentre/Plain

_English_Summaries/governance_and_citizenship/identity/index190.aspx (accessed June 7, 2009); also see Yip's "Negotiating Space with Family and Kin in Identity Construction: The Narratives of British Non-Heterosexual Muslims," *Sociological Review* 52, no. 3 (2004): 336–50; also see his "Queering Religious Texts: An Exploration of British Non-Heterosexual Christians' and Muslims' Strategies of Constructing Sexually-Affirming Hermeneutics," *Sociology* 39, no. 1 (2005): 47–65; and "Uniquely Positioned?: Lived Experiences of Lesbian, Gay, and Bisexual Asian Muslims in Britain," First International Conference of Asian Queer Studies, Ambassador Hotel, Bangkok, July 7–9, 2005. http://bangkok2005.anu.edu.au/papers/Yip.pdf.

10. Asifa Siraj, "On Being Homosexual and Muslim: Conflicts and Challenges," in *Islamic Masculinities,* ed. Lahoucine Ouzgane (London: Zed Books, 2006), 202–16.

11. Omar Minwalla, et al., "Identity Experience Amongst Progressive Gay Muslims in North America: A Qualitative Study within *Al-Fatiha,*" *Culture, Health & Sexuality* 7, no. 2 (2005): 113–28.

12. Antonio Gramsci, *Selections from the Prison Notebooks,* trans. and ed. Quentin Hoare and Geoffrey Nowell-Smith (London: Lawrence & Wishart, 1971).

13. Minwalla, et al., "Identity Experience Amongst Progressive Gay Muslims" *Culture, Health and Sexuality* 7, no. 2 (2005): 120–21.

14. Siraj, "On Being Homosexual and Muslim," 210–11; Yip, "Negotiating Space with Family and Kin," 342–45.

15. Abdullah Saeed, *Islam in Australia* (Sydney: Allen & Unwin, 2003), 83–88.

16. R. W. Connell, *Gender and Power* (Palo Alto, CA: Stanford University Press, 1987); also see Connell's *Masculinities,* Second Edition (Sydney: Allen & Unwin, 2005).

17. Eve Kosofsky Sedgwick, *Epistemology of the Closet* (Berkeley: University of California Press, 1990).

18. Steven Seidman, *Beyond the Closet: The Transformation of Gay and Lesbian Life* (New York: Routledge, 2002).

19. Ibid., 7–8.

20. Yip, "Negotiating Space with Family and Kin," 346.

21. Saeed, *Islam in Australia,* 90; Robin Cohen, *Global Diasporas: An Introduction* (Seattle: University of Washington Press, 1997).

22. Seidman, *Beyond the Closet,* 7–8.

23. Lisa Duggan, "The New Homonormativity: The Sexual Politics of Neo-Liberalism," in *Materializing Democracy,* ed. Russ Castronovo and Dana D. Nelson (Durham, NC: Duke University Press, 2002).

24. Cited in Anjali Arondekar, "Border/line Sex: Queer Postcolonialities, Or how Race Matters outside the United States," *Interventions* 7, no. 2 (2005): 236–50, 243–44.

25. Duggan, "The New Homonormativity."

26. Irshad Manji, *The Trouble with Islam* (Sydney: Random House, 2004), 196.

27. Ibid., 220.

28. Gramsci, *Selections from the Prison Notebooks,* 210–18.

29. Ernesto Laclau and Chantal Mouffe, *Hegemony and Socialist Strategy, Second Edition* (London: Verso, 2000), 70.

30. Arondekar, "Border/line Sex"; Jasbir Puar and Amit Rai, "Monster, Terrorist, Fag: The War on Terrorism and the Production of Docile Patriots," *Social Text* 72 (2002): 117–48; Jasbir Puar, "On Torture: Abu Ghraib," *Radical History Review* 93 (2005): 15–38; Jasbir Puar, "Mapping U.S. Homonormativities," *Gender, Place & Culture* 13, no. 1 (2006): 67–88.

31. See Abraham, " 'On the Doorstep of the Work,'" 04.8–04.9.

32. Marian Pitts, et al., *Private Lives: A Report on the Health and Wellbeing of GLBTI Australia* (Melbourne: La Trobe University, 2006).

33. The MCC is a 40-year old queer-focused church founded in the United States with congregations in major Australian cities.

34. Damien Ridge, et al., "Queer Connections: Community, 'The Scene' and an Epidemic," *Journal of Contemporary Ethnography* 26, no. 2 (1997): 146–81; Damien Ridge, et al., " 'Asian' Men on the Scene: Challenges to 'Gay' Communities," in *Multicultural Queer: Australian Narratives,* ed. Peter A. Jackson and Gerard Sullivan (New York: Haworth Press, 1999).

35. Yip, "Negotiating Space with Family and Kin"; Yip, "Queering Religious Texts"; and Yip, "Uniquely Positioned?"

36. Minwalla, et al., "Identity Experience amongst Progressive Gay Muslims."

37. Chong-Suk Han, "They Don't Want to Cruise Your Type: Gay Men of Color and the Racial Politics of Exclusion," *Social Identities* 13, no.1 (2007): 51–67.

38. Neil Maycroft, "Cultural Consumption and the Myth of Life-Style," *Capital & Class* 84 (2004): 61–75.

39. Slavoj Žižek, *The Metastases of Enjoyment* (London: Verso, 1994), 49.

40. Yip, "A Minority Within a Minority," 6.

41. Ridge, et al., "Queer Connections"; Ridge, et al., "'Asian' men on the scene."

42. Stanley Fish, *The Trouble with Principle* (Cambridge, MA: Harvard University Press, 2001).

43. Ibrahim Abraham, "Hijab in an Age of Fear: Security, Secularism and Human Rights," *Australian Religion Studies Review* 19, no. 2 (2006): 169–88.

44. Theodor Adorno and Max Horkheimer, "The Culture Industry: Enlightenment as Mass Deception." http://marxists.org/reference/archive/adorno/1944/culture-industry.htm. (accessed January 10, 2009).

45. Yip, "Uniquely Positioned?," 10–11.

46. Fredric Jameson, *The Political Unconscious: Narrative as a Socially Symbolic Act* (Ithaca, NY: Cornell University Press, 1981).

47. Homi Bhabha, *The Location of Culture* (London: Routledge Classics, 2004), 314–19.

48. Aijaz Ahmad, *In Theory: Classes, Nations, Literatures* (London: Verso, 1992); Ahmad, "The Politics of Literary Postcoloniality," *Race & Class* 36, no. 3 (1995): 1–20.

49. Arif Dirlik, "The Postcolonial Aura: Third World Criticism in the Age of Global Capitalism," *Critical Inquiry* 20, no. 2, (1994): 328–56.

50. Nikos Papastergiadis, "Hybridity and Ambivalence: Places and Flows in Contemporary Art and Culture," *Theory, Culture & Society* 22, no. 4 (2005): 39–64.

51. Ibid., 58.

52. Young, "Marxism and Social Movements," 270.

- • — • — • -

18

MARKETING DIVERSITY: HOMONORMATIVITY AND THE QUEER TURKISH ORGANIZATIONS IN BERLIN

Ilgin Yorukoglu

Over the last two decades, problems that are assumed to be related to the "integration of immigrants" (read here as Turkish Muslims), regardless of what one understands from the former, have increasingly appeared in the forefront of political discussions in Germany. Besides the fact that these discussions usually refer to an ideal conception of full citizenship and ignore the structural violence resulting in ongoing sociopolitical inequalities, the idea of a presupposed "cultural difference" is given as an explanation for the problems supposedly produced by these nonintegrated immigrant groups. Even when the conditions of inequality are not actually ignored, cultural and religious differences are used as explanations for the underprivileged status, or lack of political participation of immigrants. The immigrant resistance to assimilation, resistance to adopt what are usually dubbed as "core European values" is given as the overriding explanation for the socioeconomic disparity between Turkish citizens and their European counterparts. What is more, the latter are almost always instantly associated with the abstract domains of democracy, separation of church and state, tolerance, and, increasingly, gender and sexual equality.

Using Berlin as a social context, I briefly discuss the ways in which resistance against one type of oppression, that is, intolerance of gay and lesbian people, is transferred and transformed into essentializing statements about the "differences" of certain ethnic and national communities.

NEOLIBERALISM'S HOMONORMATIVITY

Europe's soul is tolerance. Europe is the continent of tolerance.

—*Angela Merkel*[1]

Berlin is in a delicate financial situation: between 1998 and 2004, for instance, while Munich and other big cities have grown, Berlin has experienced a financial loss (along, to some extent, with Dusseldorf). The sectors of finance and insurance have declined and architecture and engineering have long taken a downward direction. Welfare dependence increased considerably during these same years, with a majority of dependents coming from a non-German background.[2] After the unification of the east and the west, similar to what has been experienced in many spaces of post-Fordism,[3] Berlin has experienced a polarization with a relative increase in service sector employment and financial improvement in the advertisement, software, and business consulting industries. In this context, and especially since the economic support received from the federal government is mostly for cultural issues,[4] it is not surprising that the city government is advertising its (cultural) diversity.

Starting with the city mayor, Klaus Wowereit, power holders do not think Berlin will ever be able to regain the investments of its glory days between the World Wars. "The banks," the mayor said in 2006, "aren't coming from Frankfurt. They're going to London. Volkswagen is not going to build a factory here. They're building new factories in Eastern Europe or Asia."[5] The only solution seemed to be to play Berlin as a swinging town, a magnet for culture and tourism. "This is the place to be at the moment, even more than London," the mayor says.[6] In the spring of 2008, Mayor Wowereit went even further, asking his citizens not only to be *in* Berlin, but also to *be* Berlin, by announcing the new campaign called "Be Berlin," modeled on earlier "I Love New York" and "I amSTERDAM" campaigns. He said the 11 million euro ($17.02 million) image makeover would be a catalyst for economic reforms for the city that is already an attractive spot for "creative people."[7]

Indeed, a 2007 study undertaken by the Berlin Institute for Population and Development and financed by the nonprofit Robert Bosch Foundation suggests that, through its investment in the so-called creative class "Berlin possesses a lot of development potential."[8] The study titled "Talent, Technology, and Tolerance: Where Germany Has a Future" is based on the theory of growth potential developed by American scholar Richard Florida who, to put it simply, suggests that importing the creative class (a category including scientists and engineers, university professors, poets and novelists, artists, entertainers, actors, designers, and architects) would be a determining factor in the population's prosperity. What is more, the theory emphasizes the role of diversity, openness, and tolerance in attracting the mentioned class of people. One of the indexes Florida uses to measure tolerance in a city is the "gay index," which focuses on the presence of gay residents as an indicator of "an area's openness to different kinds of people and ideas."[9]

A more recent study of Berlin's potential for economic prosperity that was also based on Florida's theory suggests that, while Munich appears to be the strongest among German cities in both the technology and tolerance categories, Berlin still outranked its competitors in the tolerance category. According to the study, this suggests that "the inclusion of a gay population in the urban fabric is an important part of the 'Creative Class' approach used to determine the ranking for German cities."[10] In line with this measure, Berlin indeed has been investing in consumers of diverse sexual orientations and marketing itself as one of the most tolerant cities in the world. From building the first full-service nursing home in Europe for gays and lesbians[11] to launching (at the recent International Tourism Fair) a new lesbian and gay hotel brand,[12] the city not only targets local gay residents, but also tries to attract gay and lesbian tourists from around the world. Some official buildings of the municipality of Berlin even display the rainbow flag.[13] In the legal realm, too, there has been major progress made: since August 2001, lesbian and gay couples in Germany have been legally allowed to enter into civil unions. This new institution of family law is not a marriage, although there are many areas in which partners living in civil union have the same rights and obligations as married partners.[14] Foreign nationals also have the right to enter into a civil union, which acts as a stronger protection from deportation.[15] Apparently, even the "extreme right-wing" could not ignore these major changes: twenty years ago, when Michael Kühnen, one of the main figures in the neo-Nazi movement, had his "coming-out" in 1986, a scandal split his movement into the pro-Kühnen and the homophobic wings. Although current gay-friendly, neo-Nazi activists in Germany are still ideologically rejected by their political friends, they are, according to Henning Fischer, "more or less *tolerated*."[16]

WHAT LIES BENEATH

In spite of this progress, though, not all bodies are tolerated. Especially after the September 11, 2001, attacks on New York City and the subsequent echoes of the old discourse of colonialism, "the burqa-clad body of the Afghan woman became the visible sign of an invisible enemy that threatens not only 'us,' citizens of the West, but our entire civilization."[17] Indeed, gender and, as we have seen, sexuality have become major factors in shaping dominant Western attitudes toward racialized and ethnicized cultural differences. In turn, it is these differences presented as opposites in a hierarchical order and reinforcing the stereotypical assumptions that result in the justification and exacerbation of the criminalization and surveillance of certain populations. As a matter of fact, even before September 11, 2001, one could find on both sides of the political spectrum in Germany a discourse on security coming together with antiforeigner and particularly anti-immigrant rhetorics. The Interior Minister in Helmut Kohl's government at the time, Manfred Kanther, for instance, declared 1998 to be "the year of security," promising stern measures to curb immigration.[18] Kohl's opponents, the Social Democrats, "neither are nor wish to be seen lagging far behind. And so Gerhard Glogowski, the Social Democratic interior minister of Lower Saxony, loudly demanded the restoration of German border controls."[19]

After the U.S.-led invasion of Iraq, more than 18,000 Iraqi refugees lost their legal status as asylum seekers in Germany. In 2006, the Federal Office sent letters of revocation to 8,600 refugees, 4,400 of them Iraqis. Only 411 of the 8,600 refugees were able to maintain their status. The United Nations High Commissioner for Refugees "calls Germany's practice of revoking the status of Iraqi refugees unique in Europe a violation of the 1951 Geneva Convention Relating to the Status of Refugees, of which Germany is a signatory."[20] However, German authorities justify this practice through Paragraph 73 of the German Asylum Procedure Act, which states "the granting of refugee status must be revoked when the preconditions for granting asylum have ceased to exist and no new reasons of persecution, which prevent the refugee to return to his or her country of origin, have emerged."[21] The Federal Office is also required to review the asylum status of each refugee at least every three years.

A report prepared by Thomas Hammarberg, the United Nations Commissioner for Human Rights, during his visit to Germany in October 2006, recommended that Germany add "religion as well as sexual orientation"[22] to the grounds on which Germany offers protection from persecution to refugees. The German interpretation of international asylum law, according to the report, has been particularly restrictive as regards the grounds for granting asylum status. For example, in the past, persecution emanating from nonstate actors as well as persecution for gender-specific reasons was not considered a relevant protection ground in German asylum law. In response, the Federal Government of Germany stated that "asylum law already grants protection in cases of persecution on grounds of sexual orientation (i.e., also in the case of persecution of homosexuals). In the case of persons who left their country without having been persecuted, however, it must always be examined whether persecution is highly probable if they return to the country of origin. This may be answered in the negative if a person has in the past been able to practice his [sic] sexuality without incurring persecution."[23]

It is indeed true that German asylum law now grants protection on grounds of sexual orientation. Although Germany was among the last major receiving countries to revise its asylum policies to recognize gender-based persecution, the new Immigration Act came into force on January 1, 2005. This new act embraces as refugees those individuals who have survived persecution by a nonstate party whom the state is unable or unwilling to control, and/or persecution "solely on account of sex."[24] In spite of this, many still criticize Germany's asylum policy as being racist and homophobic. Indeed, in order to be granted asylum, it is usually necessary to bring incontrovertible proof of "irreversible homosexuality."[25] These cases are devastating indications of multiple discrimination; especially in women's cases, based on gender, migration, and lesbian status. The requirement necessitating outing oneself in order to prove sexual orientation is clearly improper, degrading, and, in many cases, life-threatening. In 2007, observers and activists spoke out to prevent the deportation of an Iranian lesbian who had applied for asylum in Germany. Apparently, "officials had telephoned the mother of the woman in Iran to ask her if her daughter was indeed a lesbian, which the mother of course denied. Naturally, the negative reply from a parent was not at all surprising, considering that the penalty for homosexuality in Iran is death."[26] However, the answer was used as an official reason for the decision to deport, claiming that clear proof of homosexuality was nonexistent.[27]

Not only refugees, but also citizens, are affected by this unequal legal treatment. The "registered lifetime partnership" that gays and lesbians can enter into does not bestow the same privileges as marriage, which remains an option available only to heterosexual couples. For instance, people living in such partnerships are not entitled to receive part of their partner's pension when he or she dies.[28] It was not until late 1960s that homosexual acts between males were decriminalized in the country; the Nazi-era law persecuting homosexuals, the infamous Paragraph 175, remained on Germany's books until then. "[B]etween 1953 and 1965 the police reported 98,700 violators of Paragraph 175; nearly 38,000 of these were found guilty and sentenced."[29] Only in 1968 did the German Democratic Republic (GDR) decriminalize consensual sexual acts between members of the same sex. The Federal Republic of Germany decriminalized sex between adult men one year after the GDR, although the age of consent remained higher for male–male activities than it was for heterosexual acts; this was not changed until 1994.

Finally, as might be expected, in both mainstream and right-wing newspapers homosexuality is condemned.[30] The *Nationalzeitung* (*National Newspaper*) and others reject the idea of gay marriage and a homosexual or queer identity. A spokesperson for the National-democratic Party of Germany (*Nationaldemokratische Partei Deutschlands*, also known as the NPD), which is a pan-German nationalist and white nationalist political party commonly viewed as a neo-Nazi organization, called the Christopher Street Day in Leipzig in 2005 a "mistake of human evolution" and called for a campaign against homosexuality.[31] However, some other groups within the extreme right wing will ignore sexual orientation for the sake of "German struggle," so long as (homo)sexuality is kept in private[32] and since "[t]he homosexual race fighter has other values: free from family duties, he fights the war and shapes the culture of his people."[33]

In this context, what we see is the recreation of an "other" through the utilization of discourse on tolerance and diversity. An article dated June 2008 suggests that "Berlin, Germany is one of the world's most tolerant cities, but homophobic attacks are on the rise—partially due to illiberal immigrants." The article continues, "[m]igration to Germany from countries including Turkey and Russia, where homosexuality is taboo, has led to a rise in crime against gays. Gay-bashing hip hop music isn't helping, either. So how should liberal-minded Germans deal with less-tolerant immigrants?"[34]

Confining the migrant other into an atemporal history, concealing internal differentiations within mentioned communities, and introducing immigration from these countries concurrently and simultaneously with the homophobic attacks presents a common argument that "Muslim kids raised in Germany, who feel sidelined, who soak up hip-hop . . . might have been raised to hate homosexuals."[35] The article accepts that Germany has "native-born thugs who can't stand homosexuals," that is, the neo-Nazis; but, the argument goes, "liberal-minded Germans know how to deal with neo-Nazis," so "what's more confusing is how to contend with immigrants who are less tolerant than the Germans who want to accept them."[36]

This attitude is not uncommon. Sexuality has become a major factor in shaping dominant Western attitudes toward racialized and ethnicized cultural differences. As Volker Woltersdorff warns, the hegemonic discourse within the European Union emphasizes tolerance toward homosexuality as an allegedly European value. Thus, right-wing liberal policies give anti-homophobic struggles a nationalist and racist standpoint, "whereas queer alliances around sexuality, class, and migration are rather disarticulated."[37] A now infamous questionnaire designed to be used as part of the process of naturalization was proposed by Baden-Württemberg's *Innenminister* (Interior Minister) Heribert Rech. The questionnaire was to be answered only by citizens of the 57 member states of the Organization of the Islamic Conference (OIC) who apply for German citizenship.[38] Many of the questions focus on the stance of the respondent toward issues with regards to marriage, women's rights, roles, education, and occupation. Still others were related to sexual orientation. For instance, Question 29 asks about the applicants' would-be reaction if they find out that their son was gay. Yet another, Question 30, asks: "What do you think about the fact that open homosexuals hold public office in Germany?"[39] It is astonishing that Rech is a member of the CDU, a party that fought against the extension of marriage-like rights to gays and lesbians in 2001. Nevertheless, the presence of these questions indicates that acceptance of homosexuals is now part of being German.[40] Strangely enough, this attitude has actually been welcomed by the local sections of major gay and lesbian lobby groups. As George L. Mosse notes, "[t]he spectacle of one outsider attempting to buy his [*sic*] entrance ticket to society at the expense of another is common enough."[41] The use of racism to gain respectability was a constant theme in the beginning of the 20th century; Benedict Friedländer, for instance, a pioneer of homosexual rights in Germany, wrote in the beginning of the 20th century that attacks on homosexuals "were led by Jews determined to undermine Aryan virility and self-awareness."[42] For Friedländer, writes Mosse, the Jews were assigned the very stereotype that society had created for homosexuals. There's a certain kind of sexual politics at play here, a politics which is named by many, following Lisa Duggan, as "homonormativity." Homonormativity anesthetizes queer communities into passively accepting alternative forms of inequality in return for domestic privacy and the freedom to consume."[43] Jasbir Puar, for instance, explains in detail "the rise of a global gay right wing anchored in Europe and attaining credibility very pointedly through Islamophobic rhetoric, . . . normativizing gay and lesbian human rights frames, which produce (in tandem with gay tourism) gay-friendly and not-gay-friendly nations."[44] Puar gives the example of OutRage!, a British-based lesbian, gay, bisexual, and transgender organization, that, shortly after the London bombings of July 2005, claimed that it had received death threats from various Muslim organizations. The organization's leader called for bag and body searches in gay bars and clubs, since "Muslim fundamentalists have a violent hatred of lesbians and gay men. They think we should be killed."[45] Furthermore, Puar turns our attention to an interesting coincidence: on the day when OutRage! posted this warning, the United States convicted Eric Rudolph of the bombing of a gay bar in Atlanta, Georgia, along with the bombings of two abortion clinics. What is particularly interesting is that this conviction of a white Christian man did not provoke a similar response to that of OutRage! among U.S. lesbian, gay, bisexual, transgender, intersex, and queer (LGBTIQ) organizations. Although we are talking about different contexts, it is important to note that the assumptions that are being reproduced around the supposed causal links between violence, insecurity, and certain subjectivities are very similar.[46]

THE RELIGIOUS SUBJECT

"A century ago," says Gert Hekma, "the pederasty of the Muslims was a sign of their [Muslims'] ferocity, nowadays their anti-gay attitudes are a sign of unenlightened prejudices."[47] Indeed, it would not be incorrect to say that, today, homosexuality and Islam are seen as incongruous at best. I would now, although perhaps too briefly, like to challenge this assumption on three levels:

First, the condemnation of homosexuality via religious readings and interpretations is not exclusive to Islam. Historian George Mosse, writing about the utilization of sexuality politics in the development of nationalism, pays attention to the traditional term "sodomite" which was slowly replaced by "homosexual" during the second half of the 19th century. In the Catholic belief, "homosexual acts led to divine retribution, not only rebellions and revolutions, but natural catastrophes such as the destruction of the city of Lot because some of its inhabitants had practices this unnatural vice."[48] Catholicism, though, following Alphonso Maria de Liguori's normative eight-volume work, distinguished acts that were performed habitually from those that are accidental and therefore could be forgiven. In this sense, harsher than Catholicism was probably Protestantism, which knew no such distinctions and considered it sinful even to contemplate any sexual act for purposes other than procreation.[49]

As Sabine Schmidtke suggests, "[i]n the eyes of medieval Western writers, Islam's allegedly tolerant and even encouraging attitude toward sexual practices between people of the same sex was yet another indication of Islamic self-indulgence."[50] Similarly, according to Stephen O. Murray and Will Roscoe, characteristics that now are thought to be unique to modern Western homosexuals, such as the creation of homosexual networks and the formation of groups and subcultures, were well attested in various times and places in Islamic societies.[51] Similarly, Samar Habib shows that the medieval Arabian empire not only produced "a rich collection of material which spoke of homosexual desire" but medieval scholars were also thinking about whether or not homosexuality was innate, whether it was an illness or natural, and whether it was reversible or permanent.[52] What is perhaps more intriguing is the categorizations of diverse female homosexuality, such as the *mutathakirat*, a group of same-sex desiring women who apparently are close to modern day "butches."[53] It surely took centuries for societies to experience a shift in their negative perceptions of homosexual behavior. It is important to note, therefore, the reciprocal influence between East and West. Sexuality has commonly been used for mutual vilification; what has changed, in time, is the understanding and experience of, and the politics around, sexuality. In other words, one's perception and definition of the other (in relation to sexuality) is necessarily affected by one's own understanding of questions of sexuality, from morality to the material understanding of the regulation of sexuality (as procreative, as family-driven, etc.) Therefore, this change in one person's understanding of sexuality will not only affect another's understanding of sexuality, but with instead also reshape the way one person perceives the other. This is the reason why it is necessary to look at one's own self and self-identified community instead of focusing solely on others.

The second challenge against what we might call the "incongruity assumption," the assumption that denies homosexuality within Islam, might actually come from within Islam again. I am not an Islamic studies scholar, nor do I dare to say on this topic more than I am qualified to, however, I am aware of multiple interpretations of Islam and the work of others in this field, and particularly the scholarship published in this collection, which demonstrates that essentializing statements about Islam as necessarily homophobic are far too simplistic. Besides diverse sects and denominations, the insistence of organizations such as al-Fatiha Foundation, Aswat, Helem, and Meem all challenge the homogenization of religion. Many rightly point at the variations over space and time, as well as to sources of interpretation from prose romances and poetry to *adab* literature, from dream books to legal and medical literature.[54] Habib asserts that theologians who "were either accepting or clearly tolerant of homosexuality, sometimes reflect[ed] a culture of tolerance hidden from the traditional view of the canon—among such thinkers were Yahya bin Aktam (explicity), Tifashi and (implicitly) Ibn Hazm."[55] Indeed the multiple interpretations and expressions of religion, and the multiple anthropological settings in which religion operates, contest the fantasy of homogeneity. As Ibn Hazm and As'ad Abu Khalil suggest, "religion . . . is much more than a holy text. Religion is a holy text plus interpretations, plus local culture, plus tribal conditions."[56] Activists and scholars also stress the contradictions between different religious fatawa (opinions) on homosexual practice and homoerotic sentiments that are frequently declared in Islamic literature. Opinions also vary depending on the context and via practical reasoning; for instance, even those who claim homosexuality is a sin might vote for the legalization of gay marriage, suggesting that legalization would prevent promiscuity and help create "stable family units."[57]

Furthermore, in regards to the Muslim identity of the Turkish diaspora in Germany, one should challenge this whole process of formation of "the religious (read Muslim) subject": neither Turkey nor members of the Muslim Turkish diaspora have an easy or a homogeneous relationship with either Islam or homosexuality.

According to *The Economist,* Werner Schiffauer of the Europa Universität Viadrina, asserts that "partly in defiance, the Turkish community is becoming more Muslim." The anonymously written article, which cites Schiffauer, suggests that "profound faith is probably less widespread than its symbols: drug-dealers in Frankfurt flaunt Islam as rappers do bling.

But 29% of adult Muslims attend mosque regularly and 87% call themselves believers, according to a recent study by Germany's interior ministry."[58] The common assumption that all migrants from countries identified with Islam would be religiously observant is far from true. According to another study, although 33 percent of "German-Turks . . . define themselves as 'religious,' 40.5% of those who were born in Germany admit they do not fulfill the religious requirements, while 51.9% 'try to do so.'"[59]

However, even if we assume that the Turkish community is becoming "more Muslim," how would we define this? And why should this pose a problem? Particularly when one keeps in mind that the diversity/ heterogeneity brought to attention here, one can see that it applies not only to theoretical formulations or literature, but is also revealed in the actual experiences and encounters of everyday life. This is especially true when one takes into consideration the history of the foundation of the secular Turkish Republic and its problematic ties with the Ottoman Empire and the Islamic World in general. In this sense, "becoming more Muslim" does not suggest a singular way of understanding and experiencing sexuality or religiosity.

It is estimated that 15 to 20 percent of Turkey's Muslim population belongs to Alevism, which, after Sunnism, is the second major mode of Islam found in Turkey.[60] There are varied thoughts about what Alevism denotes as an identity; one group, for instance, emphasizes Islam as *the* determining factor for an Alevist identity, while another group defines Alevism as a belief system combining diverse aspects of different religious beliefs. In the latter case, therefore, Islam is one among many facets of Alevism. Yet another definition does not see Alevism as a religious belief at all, but a cultural philosophy unique to Anatolia.[61] In any case, what is commonly acknowledged is that Alevi practice and belief system differs from that of hegemonic Sunnism. To give a brief overview of these differences in observing the religion, one can talk about, for instance, *taqiya,* a practice permitted in the Shi'ite tradition, and a characteristic of Alevis, allowing believers to conceal their faith when under threat. Also, a more specific example discusses how "Alevis point to their hearts when discussing their faith, privileging the esoteric, inner purity of spirit over more tangible and stereotypic Sunni demonstrations of faith."[62] Alevis have their own religious ceremonies (*cem*), officiated by holy men (*dede*), at which religious poems (*nefes*) in Turkish are sung, and it is very common to see women carrying out ritual dances (*semah*) along with men. This latter case, the

situation of women, is what constitutes one of the main differences between Alevism and Sunnism. Some Sunnis "speak of [Alevi] women's promiscuity, citing specific traits and practices," while some "Alevis proudly
boast of how 'democratic, progressive, and tolerant' they are and calling
Sunnis, in turn, *yobaz* and *tutucu* (degenerate, conservative)."[63]

The meanings and the implications that have come to be attributed to
these sets of differences have resulted in the systematic discrimination
Alevis have faced in Turkey, which, in turn, must be one important reason
why this group is believed to be "disproportionately overrepresented in
the diaspora."[64] Indeed, it was only in the late 1990s that the Alevis started
to be able to "come out," demanding recognition of their religious identity
and rights, leading the Turkish state to be more tolerant of Alevi places of
worship, known as "*cemevi*," Alevi associations, and foundations.[65]

ACTS OF CITIZENSHIP: OUT IN KREUZBERG

With regards to stereotypical expectations from the supposedly homogenous and intolerant Turkish community, I would now like to focus on the
organizations formed by and for sexual minorities within this particular
group. An ongoing complaint among lesbian and gay people with Turkish
backgrounds is that Germans refuse to imagine Turkishness as being compatible with homosexuality. That is, "you cannot be a lesbian and Turkish
and Muslim at the same time. If you are, then you are assimilated."[66] In
spite of this desire to homogenize the Turkish community, and despite the
absence of the emancipatory elements of their daily life experiences, "this
'population' comprises extremely diverse individuals and groups with
widely varied experiences, based on class, regions of both origin and present residence, religion, gender, politics and age."[67] The "woman question,"
for instance, does not come along with the same answers for every Turkish
family. As Ruth Mandel reveals, some women choose not to marry, others divorce, and some others delay marriage in favor of their education
or career, while some find themselves in arranged marriages. For many,
Berlin, the city where they live, will bring even more diverse options and
possibilities, including changing identities (from Turkish to German or a
Berliner, for instance) in everyday life and the possibility of being involved
in global networks or having a transnational life. As we have seen above,
it is not surprising that the expressions of Islam and Muslimness among
Turkish Germans also differ in many ways, especially because of different

affiliations within Islam as practiced among Turks, such as Alevi or Sunni affiliations. Again, the everyday life of many community members reveal that "the assumption that all migrants from Muslim-marked countries are religiously observant is misleading at best."[68] In this context, I suggest that diverse and conflicting expressions, attitudes, and ideologies supported by Turkish gay and lesbian groups in Berlin concerning the policies on sexuality and ethnicity challenge these stereotypical assumptions and the expected homogeneity. What is more, these organizations, just like other Turkish organizations, have become crucial in the German public sphere in the sense that they have mirrored the degree in which "postwar (West) German society is deem[ed] civilized, democratic, and European."[69] Thus, looking at this mirror will be crucial for abandoning the traditional question that insistently focuses on and simultaneously recreates "the neighbor other."

The German state has funded projects aimed at spreading tolerance and addressing homophobia among migrant populations. This task is addressed by, for example, the LSVD, The Lesbian and Gay Federation in Germany (*Lesben und Schwulenverband in Deutschland e. V.*), the country's largest gay and lesbian organization. LSVD has created under its roof a center called MILES for lesbians and gays with migrant backgrounds. MILES, sponsored by the Berlin Senate's Education, Youth and Sport Administration, offers services from "psychosocial consultation" and first help in "crisis situations,"[70] to legal advice, language courses, and lectures. In 2004, they displayed two designs on sets of 12,000 posters each and 50 billboards all over Berlin, depicting a group of gay Turkish and German youths with the motto, *"Kai ist Schwul und Murat auch. Sie gehören zu uns, jeder Zeit"* ("Kai is gay, and so is Murat: They are a part of us—Always"). An alternative version in 2005 featured a group of young women. They also sponsor the annual sporting event "Respect Gaymes," which is held in Berlin during the second weekend of June, right before "Pride Week,"[71] during which teams representing immigrant associations, sport clubs, schools, youth centers, and the lesbian and gay community compete against each other. What should especially be noted is the conspicuous visibility of those with a Turkish background. Besides local soccer clubs named after Anatolian villages, soccer players of Turkish background support the Respect Gaymes by endorsing this event with their names or by appearing on the advertisements for the Gaymes. There is also an official Turkish-German patron of the event, Oktay Urkal, a boxing champion from Schoneberg. Urkal uses boxing as a metaphor for what diversity and tolerance means for those who want to "play the game," so to speak. "Only those who follow the rules have a chance. That is true in the boxing ring exactly as in life. A fighter who does not respect his opponent gets knocked out."[72]

The MILES center, and especially its project manager Bali Saygili, a Turkish-German man, indeed seems to play an important role in the lives of around 200 LSVD members with immigrant backgrounds.[73] Saygili explains that the majority of the members of Turkish descent consist of those coming from "open-minded families," academicians, and people with political aims with regards to LGBTIQ rights. I was surprised to read in another interview where Saygili claimed that he is often blamed for being a racist since he believes that "[t]here's only one German society and all immigrants need to become integrated into it. Homosexuality is a part of that."[74] When I talked to Saygili, I was happily surprised to find him, similar to my own viewpoint, in favor of the practice of organizing around the lines of sexual identifications as an "act of citizenship," traversing the illusionary borders between ethnic, religious, and sexual hierarchies. He made no mention of tolerance toward homosexuality as a proof of Germanness, or as an instrument of integration into one uniform German society as such.

The understanding and politics surrounding homophobia indeed seems to have become a dividing line between the major lesbian and gay Turkish organizations in Germany. MILES identifies the problem of homophobia in the Turkish community as cultural and insists on discussing it openly. In contrast, GLADT (Gays and Lesbians from Turkey, Berlin Brandenburg) considers that there is nothing ethnospecific in the homophobic acts by people of Turkish descent. In their view, ascribing special homophobic tendencies to Turkish culture is discriminative, if not outright racist. It hints that MILES, being a subsection of LSVD, has succumbed to the prejudices of the German gay mainstream. This disagreement came to a boiling point when, after a particular MILES publication addressed Turkish homophobia, GLADT "refused all contact" with LSVD (MILES) or "decided to distance itself" from it. Gurkan Buyurucu, from GLADT, turned onlookers' attention to the financial issues, stating that, "by presenting 80% of Turks as homophobic, they are getting more money from the state."[75] What he is referring to is a recent study that was conducted by LSVD and came up during my meeting with Ahmet Iyidirli (Social

Democratic Party member from Berlin Friedrichshain-Kreuzberg and the federal chairperson of the "Federation of Turkish Social Democrats´ Folk Associations"). According to Iyidirli, the study showed that 50 percent of youth from a German background were homophobic, in contrast to 60 percent of youth from a Russian background, and 79–80 percent of youths from a Turkish background. Similar to GLADT, Iyidirli also argues that this result is not about Turks being homophobic, but rather that it reveals there is a problem in this society, one that extends to all ethnic and national backgrounds. "Just like Germans are different from each other" Iyidirli says, "Turks also are different. If you take difference as natural, you wouldn't even ask these questions. It is because you don't actually see difference as normal, then, what is merely different turns into the 'other' . . . And I end up feeling like I have to underline my difference saying that it is natural, that it is normal. The othering process has really gained speed."[76] Having been born in Turkey but also having lived in Berlin for more than 30 years, he argues that some issues have not changed in either country. Migrants mean potential, he says, "There's no meaning in keeping them whining instead of winning these people."[77] I ask about his involvement, or that of the Turkish social democrats of Berlin, with the queer Turkish community. Iyidirli says he has supported the movement many times, "either in a private manner, or in a more public/open manner, although without marketing it."[78] "Sometimes," he continues, "some unjustified criticism comes from them [i.e., from the queer Turkish community]. But ours is a voluntary organization, we have fiscal problems, just like everybody else. Practically, you have to focus on a few things. They [the queer Turkish organizations] also are not working on all of the problems Turks are dealing with—this is normal."

I spoke to Iyidirli in a tea house and Turkish pastry shop in Kreuzberg. Throughout the 1970s, 1980s, and 1990s, writes Ruth Mandel, "it was unnecessary to know German to get by in Kreuzberg."[79] Although the majority of population residing in Kreuzberg is still Germans who are either elderly pensioners, alcoholics, or punks and nonconformists, this does not save the neighborhood from being described as "Little Istanbul."[80] One likely reason for this is that the Turkish minorities have successfully transformed the space in to "a privileged site for expressing visibly political and religious [and sexual] affiliations."[81] When I was there the last time, in the summer of 2008, my poor German language skills were not an obstacle at all: I could eat, drink, listen to *saz* (Turkish lute music), find my way around, buy a calling card, and watch soccer, all in Turkish.[82] I also realized also that it was unnecessary to try to pass as heterosexual on the streets of Kreuzberg. I was surprised to see how visible the Turkish queer (mostly women) existence was there, from the social codes present in dialogues (mostly in Turkish) or body language, to advertisements or catalogues, from the displays in bookstores to well known feminist and "alternative" cafés and clubs. I remember thinking that I had not seen this visibility anywhere I had been—not in the major cities of Turkey, or within Turkish diaspora of the United States, or in England.

SO 36, a well-known performance space and dance club in Kreuzberg, holds a monthly disco event called "Gayhane" (a Turkish compound word meaning "gay house," which, as Christopher Clark reminds, is "a rhyming pun on the Turkish *meyhane,* a traditional pub frequented mostly by men").[83] Performances there and this monthly event bring together people of diverse genders, sexual identities, orientations, and nationalities. Performers ridicule the ethnic and sexual assumptions on the scene through the their appropriation of the labels so commonly found in mainstream culture. The appropriation and thus transformation of the meaning has become central to the movements against racism and sexism. Feridun Zaimoglu, a Turkish-German author, for instance, published a book in 1995 titled *Kanak Sprak,* appropriating the derogatory term "Kanake," a term used for foreigners in German, with the deliberately misspelled verb *sprache,* meaning speak or speech. *Kanak Sprak* expresses the spoken language and dialect of Turkish-German youth. This vocabulary became so common that it led to a radical antiracist movement to include the word in their name, "Kanak Attak," arguing that "the false and pseudo-feminist position of German politicians is invoked to defend spurious 'universal' rights"[84] and that Kanak Attak "wants to break the assignment of ethnic identities and roles."[85] In a similar vein, GLADT used the motto "*wir sind kanakistan*" ("we are kanakistan") in order draw attention to "homophobia in Kanakistan."[86]

CONCLUSION

What we can do is change the very questions. We can show to what extent the very way we approach a problem, which is a very real problem, is part of that problem.

—*Slavoj Zizek, Interview by Amy Goodman*

Frankfurter Allgemeine Zeitung (the English Frankfurt general Newspaper) published two opinion polls in late 2004 about Germans' attitudes
toward religion and religious conflict. One of polls asked respondents what
they associated with "Islam. The most common concepts were "suppres-
sion of women" (93%) and "terror" (83%); only 6 percent of the respondents described the Islamic faith as "likeable." The other poll showed that
29 percent stated that a "peaceful co-existence of the Christian and Islamic
faith" is possible, while 55 percent considered the religions too different and
predicted that severe conflicts will continue.[87] Two years later, a 2006 study
conducted by the Pew Research Center showed that, even more than most
Europeans, Germans were wary of Muslims: 82 percent of Germans were
"very" or "somewhat" concerned by the rise of Islamic extremism, compared
with 77 percent in Britain and 76 percent in France. On the other hand,
51 percent of Muslims in Germany (I would have liked to say "of Germany") thought "many" or "most" Europeans were hostile to them; in France
39 percent of Muslims shared the feeling, as did 42 percent in Britain.[88]

How do we explain this double standard, one that encourages tolerance
and invites gay tourists and the "creative class" to the table on the one
hand, while calling for stricter border controls to curb immigration on the
other? How do we explain the ongoing "frustration and humiliation inherent in restrictive visa regimes, traumas of denied family union[s], and
different sets of rights for resident aliens."[89] What actually lies beneath the
representation and rhetoric of difference, diversity, and tolerance, then,
is the breakdown of *démodé* leftist discourses usually shaped around inequality. It is actually this inequality from multiple sources that enjoys a
complete freedom of movement, so to speak, formed by and touching on
the boundaries of gender, sexuality, ethnicity, and religion.

Ethnicities are always gendered and sexed not only in the sense of the
ways in which they construct sexual difference but also in terms of the attitudes expected from them depending on their position in the hierarchical
structure of diversity. In this chapter, I have suggested that it is important
to be aware of how sex is utilized as a site for conflict over various relations
and inscriptions of power. It is important to really listen to "the others
of the other," not only because this helps to reveal the fictitious homogeneity of ethnicized populations, but also because this realization of heterogeneity means questioning the taken for granted answers to questions
around belonging, identification, and citizenship, which in turn redefines
our understanding of the idea of "the state." To me, all these would make

it legitimate to take the reader's time; however, I believe there is also another crucial facet to any critique of the idea of the liberal democracies of the West. This facet, again, can only be realized by underlining the interrelationship between the politics of ethnicity and sexuality.

I suggest that queer studies can actually be cornerstone in showing how neoliberal systems of the West benefit from their performative gay-friendliness and from naturalizing their "exception" into cultural differences in creating their image as open democracies. Gert Hekma, in the context of the Netherlands, points at what he sees as the uncertainty among white, straight Dutch about Muslims and gays.[90] Thus, discourse around the homophobic attitude seen as particular to ethnic minorities functions as a way for Dutch people to discuss race and sex. This thoughtful argument reveals the need to reverse the traditional question focusing on minorities. Let us return back to Kreuzberg as an example: the *alternativen,* to use Mandel's vocabulary again (i.e., punks and countercultural "native" Germans) living in this "Turkish ghetto" do not happen to live in Kreuzberg. It is not only the state, and the city, and its native inhabitants affecting those with immigrant backgrounds. The latter, even when it is usually a stereotypical image of the ethnic, also defines, shapes, and reshapes the meanings attributed to the space, to the city, and different levels of belonging. It has been argued for a while now that "the definitions of self and other, European and non-European, have always been codependent and mutually constitutive."[91] Therefore, why insist on the old question that has apparently been unhelpful at best? Why not abandon this "elitist version of cosmopolitanism"[92] desperately refusing to see how inseparable the worlds that are codified hierarchically are? Why not question the taken for granted cohesiveness of these worlds, starting with the West? What is more, and perhaps more importantly, why not question the very necessity of this cohesion for the maintenance of identification and belonging? These worlds that are still codified as separate, as stable, and as unified within themselves, are changing while transforming each other. The "others of the others," by showing the possibility of multiple belongings, might open our eyes to this change.

NOTES

An earlier version of this chapter was presented at The Future Urban Research in Europe conference panel on the "Ethnically Diverse City," held November 1, 2008, at Bauhaus University in Weimar, Germany.

1. Speech by Angela Merkel, Chancellor of the Federal Republic of Germany, to the European Parliament in Strasbourg on Wednesday, *Germany 2007—Presidency of the European Union,* January 17, 2007 http://www.eu2007.de/en/News/Speeches_Interviews/January/Rede_Bundeskanzlerin2.html (accessed September 2, 2008).

2. The unemployment rate of "foreigners" in 2004 (around 20%) was almost twice as high as the general average (around 10%) (Germany, Federal Statistical Office (2005), Strukturdaten und Integrationsindikatoren über die ausländische Bevölkerung in Deutschland 2003, 127 cited in "Muslims in the European Union: Discrimination and Islamophobia," *European Monitoring Center on Racism and Xenophobia (EUMC),* 2006, www.eumc.at/eumc/material/pub/muslim/Manifestations_EN.pdf accessed August 10, 2008; now discontinued). Highlights from this report can now be accessed from the European Agency for Fundamental Rights, http://fra.europa.eu/fraWebsite/material/pub/muslim/EUMC-highlights-EN.pdf (accessed June 6, 2009). Martin Kronauer, a German sociology professor working on the structural changes within welfare states, gives similar statistics. According to these numbers, which relate to the year 2002, the ratio of welfare density level of Germans to those with non-German passports is as follows, respectively: in Berlin: 62/162 West Berlin:71/177 East Berlin:48/80.

Kronauer also believes that the second- and third-generation naturalized people with immigrant backgrounds would be able to change these numbers for the better (Martin Kronauer, lecture given at Humboldt University, Berlin, June 6, 2008). In line with this argument, a recent study shows that 56.5 percent of the 1,000 Turkish-origin interviewees had experienced discriminatory treatment at their work place while 48.4 percent stated that they had faced discrimination while they were looking for a job (see ZfT Foundation's Multi-Topic Survey conducted by A. Goldberg and M. Sauer, *Die Lebenssituation von Frauen und Männern türkischer Herkunft in Nordrhein-Westfalen* (Duisburg-Essen: Stiftung ZfT, 2004). Cited in "Muslims in the European Union: Discrimination and Islamophobia."

3. Simply put, the term "post-Fordism" represents the idea that, starting with the 1970s, we have been witnessing a transition from one phase of capitalism to another, threatening mass industrialization, full employment, centralized bureaucracies, and the welfare state. What comes next in terms of breaking away from the old era continues to be a matter of debate in the social sciences. While some argue, for instance, that the role of states in decision making has diminished a great deal, especially in the face of international organizations, the transnationalization of capital and so on, others see this transformation as a change in the dynamics of the relationship between capital and the state, instead of a complete dissolution of the latter. However, many agree on other matters, such as the increase in service-sector employment and the creation of more part-time jobs, as well as the increased attractiveness of careers in, for instance, advertising, information technology, and software development. See Ash Amin, ed. *Post-Fordism: A Reader* (Oxford: Blackwell, 1997).

4. Hartmund Hausserman, "United Berlin: From Division to Fragmentation" lecture given at Humboldt University, Aracata, CA, June 2, 2008.

5. Mark Landler, "Berlin Mayor, Symbol of Openness, Has National Appeal," *New York Times* September 23, 2006, http://www.nytimes.com/2006/09/23/world/europe/23wowereit.html (accessed September 26, 2008).

6. Ibid.

7. Erik Kirschbaum, "German Capital Launches 'Be Berlin' Marketing Campaign," *Reuters* March 11, 2008, http://www.reuters.com/article/lifestyleMolt/idUSL1141387220080311 (accessed September 12, 2008).

8. See "Berlin Tops Germany for 'Creative Class,'" *BusinessWeek* October 10, 2007, http://www.businessweek.com/globalbiz/content/oct2007/gb20071010_858418.htm?chan=search (accessed October 20, 2007).

9. Richard Florida, *The Rise of the Creative Class: And How It's Transforming Work, Leisure, Community and Everyday Life* (Cambridge: Basic Books, 2004), 245.

10. Anon, "Creative Cities," *Roland Berger Strategy Consultants* March 6, 2008, http://www.rolandberger.com/news/2008-03-06-rbsc-news-Creative_Cities.html (accessed September 27, 2008).

11. Gemma Pritchard, "Gay Nursing Home Opens in Germany," *Pink News* January 21, 2008, http://www.pinknews.co.uk/news/articles/2005-6623.html (accessed September 27, 2008).

12. Anon, "Lesbian and Gay Hotel Brand Launched," *Pink News* March 7, 2008, http://www.pinknews.co.uk/news/articles/2005-7059.html (accessed June 7, 2009). "Community Marketing," which specializes in gay and lesbian marketing, estimates the value of the American Market alone as $65 billion in 2007. The company's name itself is meaningful, if one thinks about the recent emphasis on the role of communities in strengthening the "Putnamian" social capital. See Robert D. Putnam, *Bowling Alone: The Collapse and Revival of American Community* (New York: Simon & Schuster, 2000).

13. Iyidirli, Ahmet personal interview June 15, 2008, Berlin. It is not only Berlin investing in lesbian, gay, bisexual, transgender, intersex, and queer (LGBTIQ) tourism; the eighth series of the quadrennial Gay Games, the world's largest sporting and cultural event organized by and specifically for LGBTIQ athletes, artists, and musicians, will be held in 2010 in Cologne, a city known for its "tradition of cosmopolitan tolerance toward dissenters and different lifestyles," according to Lord Mayor Fritz Schramma. See the official Web site of the Cologne 2010 Gay Games, http://www.games-cologne.de/en/cologne/ (accessed September 1, 2008). The Gay Games has become an international event sought after by cities worldwide. The 2006 Gay Games VII, in Chicago, was estimated to have contributed "$50 to $80 million to the local economy, with some estimating that another 10 years of positive LGBTIQ tourism visibility will generate millions more dollars in the

long term." See the Gay Games Chicago official Web site at http://www.gaygames chicago.org/media/article.php?aid=175 (accessed September 1, 2008).

14. Still, according to the Eurobarometer poll conducted in 2006, 48 percent of Germans do not agree with same-sex marriages and 58 percent do not back adoption opportunities for gay couples. "Eight EU Countries Back Same Sex Marriage," *Angus Reid Global Monitor* December 24, 2006, http://www.angus-reid.com/polls/view/14203/eight_eu_countries_back_same_sex_marriage (accessed August 28, 2008).

15. As we will see, though, Fischer also presents manifestations of homophobia in Germany. Henning Fischer, "Straight Macho Nationalism," *Interalia,* http://www.interalia.org.pl/en/artykuly/current_issue/12_straight_macho_nationalism.htm accessed (September 27, 2008). This reminds one of the 18th century German art historian J. J. Winckelmann, whose homosexuality was ignored in order to use his ideal of beauty. Winckelmann's description of the "sexless" beauty of Greek sculpture became, during his time, the symbol of masculinity, the nation, and its youth. George L. Moss points to the irony "in the fact that Winckelmann, the homosexual, made Greek art fit for the middle classes and supplied the model for the male national stereotype." George L. Moss, *Nationalism and Sexuality: Respectability and Abnormal Sexuality in Modern Europe* (New York: Howard Fertig, 1985), 14.

16. Fischer, "Straight Macho Nationalism."

17. Charles Hirschkind and Saba Mahmood, "Feminism, the Taliban, and Politics of Counter-Insurgency" *Anthropological Quarterly* 75, no. 2 (2002): 341.

18. Zygmunt Bauman, "Europe of Strangers," Oxford University Transnational Communities Programme Working Paper, available in pdf format at http://www.transcomm.ox.ac.uk/working%20papers/bauman.pdf (accessed August 27, 2008), 11.

19. Ibid.

20. Wenke Niehues and Sally Ong, "Germany's Iraqi Refugees: Saddam Is Gone, It's Time to Go Home," *Humanity in Action* 2007, http://www.humanity inaction.org/docs/Reports/2007_Reports_Germany/Niehues_Ong.doc (accessed August 30, 2008), 2.

21. Ibid.

22. Thomas Hammarberg, "Report by the Commissioner For Human Rights Mr. Thomas Hammarberg on His Visit to Germany 9–11 and 15–20 October 2006," *Council of Europe* July 11, 2007, https://wcd.coe.int/ViewDoc.jsp?id=116 2763&BackColorInternet=FEC65B&BackColorIntranet=FEC65B&BackColorLo gged=FFC679 (accessed July 20, 2008).

23. Ibid.

24. "Residence Act of 30 July 2004 (Federal Law Gazette I, p. 1950), last amended by the Act on Implementation of Residence- and Asylum-Related

Directives of the European Union of 19 August 2007 (Federal Law Gazette I, p. 1970)," *Federal Ministry for the Interior,* http://www.en.bmi.bund.de/Internet/Content/Common/Anlagen/Gesetze/Gesetze__Sprachen/AufenthG__en,tem plateId=raw,property=publicationFile.pdf/AufenthG_en.pdf (accessed June 7, 2009), 48.

25. What the application of this policy renders relevant is "'the 'inescapable, predestined commitment to homosexual behaviour or sexual satisfaction, under which the person concerned is incapable of refraining him/herself from same-sex activity.' As a consequence of such assessments, the BAMF [Bundesamt für Migration und Flüchtlinge [i.e., The Federal Agency for Migration and Refugees, I.Y.] or the courts often demand from refugees to present psychiatric evaluations of the 'extent' of their homosexuality, conducted at their own expense." "Legal Study on Homophobia and Discrimination on Grounds of Sexual Orientation—Germany," *European Union Agency for Fundamental Rights,* February 2008, http://fra.europa.eu/frawebsite/material/pub/comparativestudy/FRA-hdgso-NR_DE.pdf (accessed February 6, 2009), 20.

26. Peter Weeren, "Protests in Berlin to Save Iranian Lesbian from Deportation," *Gay Republic Daily International Gay News* September 8, 2007, http://gayrepublic.org/index.php?name=News&file=article&sid=1803&lead=1 (accessed August 20, 2008).

27. Ibid.

28. Anon. "Germany Criticised by EU over Gay Discrimination," *Pink News* February 13, 2008, http://www.pinknews.co.uk/news/articles/2005-6838.html# (accessed August 27, 2008).

29. Robert G. Moeller, "The Homosexual Man Is a 'Man', The Homosexual Woman Is a 'Woman': Sex, Society and the Law in Postwar West Germany," in *West Germany under Construction: Politics, Society, and Culture in the Adenauer Era,* ed. Robert G. Moeller (Ann Arbor: University of Michigan Press, 1997), 282.

30. Fischer, "Straight Macho Nationalism," 6.

31 Ibid., 7.

32. Wendy Brown argues that the "routine privatization of sites of difference" is always already available within the call for tolerance. This routine privatization aims to reduce the encounter with difference in the public sphere, in turn reducing the very problem of difference as an expressly political problem. See Wendy Brown, *Regulating Aversion* (Princeton: Princeton University Press, 2006), 88.

33. Fischer, "Straight Macho Nationalism," 7.

34. Michael Scott Moore, "Does Germany Have a Problem With Gay Hate Crime?" *Spiegel Online International* March 7, 2008, http://www.spiegel.de/international/germany/0,1518,562638,00.html (accessed September 2, 2008).

35. Ibid.

36. Ibid.

37. Volker Woltersdorff, "Neoliberalism and Its Homophobic Discontents [1]," *Interalia* 2007, http://www.interalia.org.pl/en/artykuly/current_issue/06_neoliber alism_and_its_homophobic_discontents_1.htm#przypis_2 (accessed August 28, 2008).

38. Concluding observations of the Committee on the Elimination of Racial Discrimination, International Convention of the Elimination of All Forms of Racial Discrimination, CERD/C/DEU/CO/18, August 21, 2008

39. "*Was halten Sie davon, dass in Deutschland Homosexuelle öffentliche Ämterbekleiden*?" translation by Jennifer Chase, " 'We know who they are, and they are not us': The Impossible Reality of Happy Turkish Queers in Germany," TSF Summer Semester 2006 œ Immigration: Shaping the Western World Culture Panel, 2006, http://www.tsf-berlin.de/publications/Culture%20and%20Immigra tion.pdf (accessed March 10, 2008).

40. Gert Hekma draws attention to the similar attitude of the right-wing in the Netherlands: "The strong reaction by politicians also amazed queer activists who had rarely seen such an outpouring of support for gay men and lesbian women, from the prime minister, the general population and imams who declared their respect for sexual diversity." It is important to note that Hekma also argues that the "[a]nti-homosexual attitudes are probably nearly as prevalent among the white majority as among ethnic minority male youth" and that "[b]oth groups sometimes even strengthen each other's homophobic attitudes." Gert Hekma, "Imams and Homosexuality: A Post-gay Debate in the Netherlands" *Sexualities* 5, no. 2 (2002): 244.

41. George L. Mosse, *Nationalism and Sexuality: Respectability and Abnormal Sexuality in Modern Europe* (New York: Howard Fertig, 1985), 41.

42. Ibid.

43. See Martin F. Manalansan, "Race, Violence, and the Neoliberal Spatial Politics in the Global City" *Social Text 84–85* 23, nos. 3–4(2005): 142; also Lisa Duggan, "The New Homonormativity: The Sexual Politics of Neoliberalism." in *Materializing Democracy,* ed. Russ Castronovo and Dana D. Nelson (Durham, NC: Duke University Press, 2002), 179.

44. Jasbir K. Puar, *Terrorist Assemblages,* xiv.

45. Ibid., 237 supra note 53.

46. Since I believe it is, again, the same assumption leading to and also being reproduced by terrorism discussions, it is worth noting that a list of terrorist attacks on the United States excludes the Oklahoma City bombing, "relegating terrorism to the unknowable and inchoate nonwhite outside" Ibid., 51. In another list, one focusing on "foreign terrorist organizations," again, the only terrorists not examined were white supremacists and Christian fundamentalists (ibid., 56).

47. Gert Hekma, "Imams and Homosexuality," 244.

48. George L. Mosse, *Nationalism and Sexuality*, 25.

49. Ibid., 26. One is reminded here, of course, of Foucault and others who emphasized the role of the sciences, especially the medical profession, in demarcating a boundary between normal and abnormal sex.

50. Norman Daniel, *Islam and the West: The Making of an Image* rev. ed. (Oxford: One World, 1993), 164, cited in Sabine Schmidtke, "Homoeroticism and Homosexuality in Islam: A Review Article," *Bulletin of the School of Oriental and African Studies* 62, no. 2 (1999): 260.

51. Stephen O. Murray and Will Roscoe, *Islamic Homosexualities: Culture, History, and Literature*, with additional contributions by Eric Allyn, et al. (New York: New York University Press, 1997), cited in Schmidtke, "Homoeroticism," 261.

52. Samar Habib, "Reading the Familiarity of the Past: an Introduction to Medieval Arabic Literature on Female Homosexuality," http://arts.brunel.ac.uk/gate/entertext/7_2/ET72HabibED.doc (accessed January 22, 2008). Also see Habib's *Female Homosexuality in the Middle East: Histories and Representations* (New York: Routledge, 2007), 47–83, for a broader discussion on sexual lives of Arabic women in that period as well as the discourses around this issue.

53. Samar Habib, "Reading the Familiarity of the Past," 169.

54. Ibid., 260.

55. Samar Habib, *Female Homosexuality in the Middle East*, 8.

56. Cited in Ibid., 143.

57. Mikail Juma Tariq, "Same Sex Marriage," November 20, 2005, http://www.geocities.com/mikailtariq/homo.htm (accessed September 2, 2008).

58. Anon. "Turks in Germany: Two Unamalgamated Worlds," *The Economist* April 3, 2008. http://www.economist.com/world/europe/displaystory.cfm?story_id=10958534 (accessed September 2, 2008).

59. Ayhan Kaya and Ferhat Kentel, "Euro-Turks: A Bridge or a Breach between Turkey and the European Union? A Comparative Study of German-Turks and French-Turks," *EurActiv* January 2005, http://www.euractiv.com/en/enlargement/euro-turks-bridge-breach-turkey-european-union/article-134586 (accessed 6 May, 2007).

60. Censuses have never registered Alevis as a distinct category; and many suggest that even if they had the outcome would be unreliable, since the Alevis, fearing discrimination, have tended to hide their identity until very recently. Although the majority of Alevis are ethnic Turks speaking Turkish, they still form a heterogeneous group made up of Kurdish-speaking and Arabic-speaking groups with diverse historical background.

61. Baskin Oran, *Türkiye'de Azinliklar: Kavramlar, Lozan, Iç Mevzuat, içtihat, Uygulama* (Istanbul: Tesev Yayinlari, 2004), 49.

62. Ruth Mandel, *Cosmopolitan Anxieties*, 252.

63. Ibid., 253. Mandel cites Alevis saying, "*kadinsiz cem olmaz*" (without women there can be no cem) and "*Kadin toplumun annesidir*" (woman is the mother of society).

64. Mandel, *Cosmopolitan Anxieties,* 251.

65. Sahin Alpay, "*Alevilik resmen taniniyor mu?*," December 4, 2007, http://www.zaman.com.tr/yazar.do?yazino=620858 (accessed June 6, 2009).

66. Ipek Ipekcioglu, explaining why the gay community in Germany only partially accepts her. Ipek Ipekcioglu, *Morning Edition,* National Public Radio: January 30, 2007.

67. Mandel, *Cosmopolitan Anxieties,* 157.

68. Ibid., 250.

69. Ibid., 12.

70. "psychosoziale Beratung, leistet erste Hilfe in Krisensituationen" See *MILES—Zentrum für Migranten, Lesben und Schwulehttp,* http://www.berlin.lsvd.de/cms/index.php?option=com_content&task=view&id=22&Itemid=64 (accessed August 20, 2008).

71. The 2008 "Pride Week" took place in almost all of June, lasting for more than three weeks.

72. See "Berlin Respect Gaymes," *LSVD,* http://www.berlin.lsvd.de/cms/index.php?option=com_content&task=view&id=232&Itemid=213 (accessed June 7, 2009). What also caught my attention when I was in Berlin was that none of the supporters of the event were gay, or at least they would not consider/identify themselves so. As in when Urkal states on the LSVD Web site "gays and lesbians are not any worse than we are." Similarly, Navina Omilade, a Football National Team player, says that "On the football field, there are clear rules: he who fouls gets thrown out and the game works only if all players have respect for each other. This is not different from everyday life."

73. LSVD has around 600 members in Berlin and more than 4,500 members nationwide. Personal interview with Bali Saygili, my translation, June 11, 2008, Berlin.

74. Julia Schaaf, "Shhh! We're Integrating," *Index on Censorship* 3 (2005): 152.

75. Umit Gurkan Buyurucu, personal interview, my translation. June 16, 2008, Berlin.

76. Personal interview, my translation, June 15, 2008, Berlin.

77. Ibid.

78. "*El altindan, el ustunden cok destek verdim. Reklamini yapmasam bile.*"

79. Mandel, *Cosmopolitan Anxieties,* 146.

80. Turkish Germans make up around 30 percent of the population in the Kreuzberg area, which has the highest population density in Berlin.

81. Mandel, *Cosmopolitan Anxieties,* 9.

82. There were a few instances when, during any of these dialogues, my Cypriot Turkish accent was found rather "amusing" by other Turkish speakers.

83. Christopher M. Clark, *Sexuality and Alterity in German Literature, Film and Performance 1968–2000*, Unpublished doctoral thesis, (Ithaca, NY: Cornell University, 2003), 222.

84. *Kanak Attak,* http://www.kanak-attak.de/ka/about/manif_eng.html (accessed September 2, 2008).

85. Ibid.

86. "Wir sind Kanakistan!" *GLADT,* 2007, http://www.gladt.de/downloads/2007-kanakistan.pdf; also see http://www.kanakistan.com/ (accessed September 2, 2008).

87. Renate Köcher, *"Die Mehrheit erwartet immer wieder Konflikte,"* December 15, 2004, *Frankfurter Allgemeine Zeitung,* in "Muslims in the European Union Discrimination and Islamophobia," 5.

88. Anon. "Turks in Germany: Two Unamalgamated Worlds," *The Economist* April 3, 2008, http://www.economist.com/world/europe/displaystory.cfm?story_id=10958534, (accessed September 2, 2008).

89. Ruth Mandel, *Cosmopolitan Anxieties: Turkish Challenges to Citizenship and Belonging in Germany* (Durham, NC: Duke University Press, 2008), 15.

90. Gert Hekma, "Imams and Homosexuality," 246.

91. Mandel, *Cosmopolitan Anxieties,* 101.

92. Ibid., 320.

19

TOUCH OF PINK: DIASPORIC QUEER EXPERIENCES WITHIN ISLAMIC COMMUNITIES

Ahmet Atay

Although the role of homosexuality in Islamic societies and the complex relationship between homosexuality and Islam have been articulated by several scholars, such as Will Roscoe and Stephen Murray,[1] Arno Schmitt,[2] and Brian Whitaker[3] (to name a few), fewer studies have focused on the lived experiences of diasporic queer individuals from Islamic countries living within Western societies. As such, the research on homosexuality in Islamic societies has been limited to how homosexuality is perceived and experienced within Islamic nation-states; for example, the role of homosexuality in Saudi Arabia, the gay movement and queer activism in Turkey, or the legal rights of gay Iraqis in the age of the war on terrorism. Since most of the past and contemporary research on homosexuality in Islamic societies focuses on how homosexuality is experienced and how it is understood, monitored, and presented within Islamic countries, the relationship between homosexuality and Islam remained limited to geographically and culturally bound definitions and descriptions. In order to present a multidimensional study of how homosexuality is practiced and understood in Islamic societies, one also needs to look at how homosexuality is experienced, understood, and policed within diasporic Muslim communities.

Due to their colonial pasts, undoubtedly, Islamic communities occupy a unique position within Western nation-states. Since there is a great religious disparity between the host culture and the diasporic community, the relationship between these two groups is often shaped by cultural and religious differences and similarities. I argue that, even though individuals from diasporic communities and host cultures share geographical and cultural locales, they experience different realities; therefore, their experiences are culturally, linguistically, and spiritually constrained. For example, homosexuality is experienced and understood differently by individuals from diasporic communities compared to individuals from mainstream host cultures because of their cultural and religious differences.

In this chapter, my goal is to focus on how queer identities are created and performed and also how homosexuality is perceived within diasporic communities from Islamic societies. To accomplish this task, I use Ian Iqbal Rashid's film *Touch of Pink* (2004) as a visual text to examine the role of homosexuality and its cultural implications in Muslim communities, in this case the Indian diaspora in Canada. As a visual text, *Touch of Pink* presents relatively complex questions about cultural identity, religion, and family, and how all these aspects intersect in everyday realities.

Before I define diaspora, more specifically, I want to emphasize that *Touch of Pink,* as a nonmainstream film, is nevertheless important because it not only focuses on relatively complex and important questions but also poses three major themes that are particularly important to the discussion of diasporic (and Muslim) queer bodies. These themes explore cultural identity formation, concepts of home and belonging, and the effects of cultural and religious differences (in this case, the impact of Islam) on how homosexuality is understood and perceived by diasporic and nondiasporic individuals and communities.

DIASPORA

The meaning of the word diaspora has continued to evolve throughout history. According to Robin Cohen, the word is derived from the Greek verb *speiro* (to sow) and the preposition *dia* (over).[4] Cohen notes that Greeks saw diaspora as migration and colonization. For Jews, Africans, Palestinians, and Armenians, however, diaspora carries a sinister and a brutal meaning. For these groups, "Diaspora signified a collective trauma, a banishment, where one dreamed of home and lived in exile."[5]

Stuart Hall defines diaspora as "the long-term settlement of peoples in 'foreign' places which follow their scattering or dispersal from their original homeland."[6] Further, Anjali Ram asserts that diaspora includes any ethnicity composed of exiles, refugees, or immigrants.[7] Similarly, Kathleen Wong (Lau) defines diaspora as "the dispersion of a minority group of people among a majority group beyond the borders of the minority's homeland."[8] For Floya Anthias, diaspora represents "the process of settlement and adaptation relating to a large range of transnational migration movements."[9] Anthias sees diaspora as a direct outcome of transnational movements of various populations that emerge from Western nations' colonial past and globalization. Anthias further argues that diaspora is an old term that was rediscovered in order to theorize growth of new experiences and identities that have resulted from globalization:

> Diaspora has also been used as a descriptive typological tool for understanding migration and settlement in the global era, and to denote a social condition and a societal process . . . [diaspora as a population category is] "a social condition entailing a particular form of consciousness."[10]

For Anthias, this form of diaspora emerges as a direct result of postmodernity, transnationality, and globalization, all of which create hybrid experiences and identities for dispersed or migrated individuals.

The presence of diasporic communities from Muslim nations in Western societies is not accidental because the formation of these communities is often a direct outcome or by-product of colonialism, transnationality, and globalization. Therefore, the political, cultural, and economic discourse that surrounds diasporic communities is influenced by historical occurrences, such as colonialism, and currents in economic, political, and cultural forces within host nation-states and home nation-states, respectively. Hence, in order to understand how homosexuality is viewed, understood, and experienced, these historical and societal dynamics need to be considered.

Touch of Pink is an exemplary text in that it successfully unmasks aspects of diasporic (Muslim) communities in both Canada and England and the social and political contexts that influence their diasporic experiences. The film provides historical information on South Asia and Africa's colonial past and reflects on history's influences on diasporic experiences and cultural identity formations by interrogating the meaning of home and belonging. *Touch of Pink* embodies interrelated social, economic, and political forces by narrating the story of a gay man whose life is shaped by colonialism, transnationality, and globalization as well as the complexities of human sexuality.

REPRESENTATIONS OF HOMOSEXUALITY AND QUEER BODIES IN FILMS

In order to understand the representation of diasporic queer bodies in films in general and *Touch of Pink* in particular, one must first examine how homosexuality has been represented in films throughout cinematic history. Because *Touch of Pink* is a British/Canadian film that also enjoyed worldwide distribution in the United States, Canada, and Australia, a close examination of the representation of minorities in general and queer bodies in Euro-American and British film in particular is important in order ascertain the reasons as to why diasporic queer bodies are widely absent from mainstream American and British film and visual culture.

Richard Dyer explains that, today, the word "stereotyping" is understood as a term of abuse and that:

> This stems from the wholly justified objections of various groups—in recent years, blacks, women and gays, in particular—to the ways in which they find themselves stereotyped in the mass media and in everyday speech.[11]

Stereotyping stems from the conscious mind's need to create categories and to mark certain groups as "others." In other words, stereotyping functions by policing on behalf of normativity. Anneke Smelik explains that stereotyping works in society both to establish and to maintain the hegemony of the dominant groups, and marginalizes and excludes other social groups, such as blacks, women, and homosexuals. As a result, stereotypes create sharp oppositions and differences between social groups in order to maintain the boundaries between them.[12]

Although homosexuality has been present in films since the earliest days of filmmaking, as Smelik explains, the representation of homosexuals was often coded subtextually, or, in the event that homosexuality made it openly into the text, homosexual characters were repeatedly represented with ridicule or as pathological killers or miserable people who inevitably kill themselves or are killed by others.[13] Larry Gross argues that, most of the time, gay people have been simply invisible from the media, including movies. He asserts that the "few exceptions were almost invariably either victim[s] of violence or ridicule or villain[s]."[14] Gross points out that producers and directors exclude and deny the existence of "normal," unexceptional, and exceptional lesbians and gay men. In addition, I argue that they also completely disregard ethnic and diasporic queer bodies.

To this day, films can be criticized for reproducing dominant stereotypes of homosexuals. For example, mainstream Hollywood movies of recent times often represent gay men as always flamboyant and effeminate, sexless best friends to heterosexual women, as sad young men, gay psychopaths, or seductive androgens, while lesbians continue to feature predominantly as vampires or murderers (or more recently, as women obsessed with reproduction). In the absence of sufficient information and counterrepresentations, most people, gay or straight, have little choice other than to accept the narrow and negative stereotypes about these representations of gay people.

For Susan Bordo, most of the early representations of homosexuals were of depressed, underground figures.[15] Bordo explains that, in the 1970s and 1980s, the homosexual characters became more sympathetic and less caricatured. Gross argues that even as late as the 1990s gay life had still not attained normality in the movies.[16] Similarly, Bordo writes:

> In the nineties there've been sympathetic dramas about those dying from AIDS. There've been daffy comedies about gays passing for straight. There've been touching coming out stories. There've been weirdo murderers, the tragically closeted, cynical bitches, flaming sissies, and leather studs. But where were the well- adjusted gays with happy lives and something else to do besides being gay.[17]

As Bordo observed, representations of gay men who have an established life and partner were missing from mainstream movies.

It was not until the latter years of the 1990s and into the 2000s that diversely queer characters made their way to mainstream cinema. *Philadelphia* (1993), *In & Out* (1997), *The Birdcage* (1996), *My Best Friend's Wedding* (1997), and *To Wong Foo, Thanks for Everything, Julie Newmar* (1995), *The Object of My Affection* (1998), *Boys Don't Cry* (1999), *Bound* (1996), *The Talented Mr. Ripley* (1999), *Brokeback Mountain* (2005), *Capote* (2005), and *Transamerica* (2005) were among prominent movies featuring a major or minor gay character. Mainstream cinema started to open up for diverse homosexual characters and to give them the voice that they had been missing for many years.[18]

> After decades of exclusion and negative stereotyping television and the other mass media, for a variety of reasons, have entered a phase where they are contributing to a various spiral of progressive change in sexual culture. They have done this by making homosexuality more visible than before,

and by allowing representations to become more diverse and representative of the reality of lived (gay) experience, in all its flawed and imperfect complexity.[19]

Alexander Doty and Ben Gove assert that, until "the last decade or so, lesbians, gays and queers were generally represented in media contexts explicitly catered to a large heterosexual audience."[20] Doty and Gove's argument, though it is a decade old, remains valid because gay and lesbian characters are still portrayed through the ideological filters of straight society. Even these recent representations are not "authentic" representations of homosexuality, because they are not representations created by homosexuals, but rather representations of homosexuals as they are perceived by a heteronormative culture finally beginning to accept them.

REPRESENTATIONS OF DIASPORIC QUEER BODIES (THE NEW QUEER CINEMA)

The emergence of the new queer cinema provided new opportunities and possibilities to tell alternative narratives about homosexuality and queerness. B. Ruby Rich points out that films from this new era have common characteristics that have been labeled as "Homo Pomo." Rich further explains that new queer cinema uses appropriation, pastiche, irony, and a "reworking of history with social constructionsim."[21] Queer cinema also blends discordant genres and rejects the notion of an essential gay sensibility. New queer cinema emerges as an alternative of representation of homosexuality or queerness in mainstream cinema. Quickly this new approach to queer filmmaking has expanded its influence and found a space in film festivals, alternative film theatres, and, more importantly, in academia.[22]

Identity politics, coming out stories, and stories about the struggles and happiness of queer individuals dominate new queer cinema narratives. Since attention to identity formation is one of the major themes of new queer cinema, I would like to examine the definition of cultural identity and specifically the definition of queer identity.

According to Rueyling Chuang, our identities are shaped and reshaped in interactions, so our identities have an emergent quality.[23] Chuang asserts that:

The categories of race, gender, nationality, religion, and age deteriorated and the assumptions of self-identity become problematic. We no longer have a clear sense of self; what we have now is relational self. Who we are and our identity are dependent on our relationship with others and "the web of interdependencies."[24]

Chuang points out that segments of our identities are not isolated; instead, they are intertwined. For example, we cannot isolate the queer aspect of the self from racial and ethnic aspects. In the diasporic queer body, we would have to look at queerness in relation to cultural identities. Identity, therefore, is abstract, complex, multidimensional, and fluid.[25] Intersecting identities become the major theme of *Touch of Pink,* as Alim, a postcolonial and diasporic queer man, and his in-betweenness experiences emerge as a complex phenomenon.

It is also important to point out that we create a sense of identity through interaction and communication with others. Our cultural identities are nothing more than fluid entities created and recreated through everyday encounters. Therefore, they are shaped and reshaped by economic, social, and political forces, visual culture forms, and everyday performances. For our purposes, it is worth noting that representations and identities of diasporic and Muslim queer bodies in Western societies are often impacted by two interrelated social and cultural forces: how homosexuality is perceived within Islamic communities, and how homosexuality is portrayed in mainstream Western visual culture. Moreover, these representations and identities are also affected by the complex relationship between host nation-states and diasporic communities.

TOUCH OF PINK

Touch of Pink, independent filmmaker Ian Iqbal Rashid's tale of Alim, a diasporic queer man born in Africa, raised in Canada, and now living in London, is a Canada–U.K. coproduction. It was distributed by Mongrel Media (Canada), Redbus Film Distribution (in the United Kingdom), and Columbia Pictures (in the United States). The film features Jimi Mistry (Alim), Kyle MacLachlan (Spirit of Cary Grant), Suleka Mathew (Nuru), and Kristen Holden-Ried (Giles) in major roles.

The film opens with Cary Grant delivering a monologue. In this film, Grant is Alim's imaginary friend and idol who guides him through his journey to find his diasporic queer self. At the same time, Grant's character functions as a role model for masculinity. In addition, because of the controversy that surrounds Grant's sexuality, his character embodies a queer sensibility for Alim. Ironically, Cary Grant was often featured in romantic comedies and adventure movies that were centered on colonial experiences. As a Kenyan-born Indian man, Alim idolizes white bodies, which often appear as images of the colonizer in these films. This situation begs for more attention, considering that it is infused with the historical and cultural contexts that surround it. Even though Grant is an imaginary friend and icon for Alim, the character functions as the main figure that guides Alim and helps him to unmask aspects of his diasporic queer identity. Moreover, it is arguable that Grant's character represents not only Alim's colonial past, but also England's. In this sense, Grant represents the colonial past. When Alim decides to let Grant go at the end of the film, he finally has finally made peace with his postcolonial identity. In a way, he begins to understand his postcolonial queer body in relation to other bodies, particularly to another white British man, Giles.

In the film, we learn that Alim created his imaginary friend when he was a child. During that time, Nuru, Alim's mother, was away in London, and this imaginary friend functioned as a vehicle to ease his loneliness. In a way, Grant also replaced Alim's father, who died when Alim was a young boy. In the monologue scene, Cary Grant explains that, although he has been dead more than 20 years (in actuality), he is still alive for Alim. He addresses the audience by saying "you look after us [actors], and we look after you [audience]."

Shortly after the film opens, we learn that Alim was born into an Indian family living in Kenya. Alim and his mother relocated to Canada after the death of Alim's father. We also learn that when Alim was still a small child, Nuru left him with his aunt and moved to London. The death of Alim's father changed Nuru's feelings toward Alim and life in general. Even though she returned after some time, her relationship with Alim was already significantly weakened. When the film begins, however, Alim is the one living in London, while his mother has moved back to Canada, where she lives in the company of her sister and her family.

The film mainly focuses on Alim's life in London and his relationship with a Caucasian, non-Muslim man (Giles). Even though their interracial relationship remains one of the foci of the film, the second half of the film is mostly devoted to Alim's relationship with his mother. Therefore, the latter portion of the film functions as a coming out story. The film simultaneously provides insights into diasporic experiences in Canada and the United Kingdom by focusing on Alim and Nuru's intersecting lives.

By focusing on Alim's sexuality, *Touch of Pink* goes beyond race and transcontinental identities in order to interrogate the ways in which queer sexualities are perceived by Muslim communities existing in Western nations.

In order to make sense of his cultural identity, Alim searches for answers about his roots, home, and queerness throughout the film. He negotiates not only his sexual identity, but also his idea of home, roots, and belonging. In a way, Alim is the embodiment of in-between experiences.

The first part of the film reveals that Alim is in a committed relationship with Giles, his British boyfriend, and but he is hiding both his sexuality and his boyfriend from his family in Canada. At the same time, Alim lives an openly gay life in London. He works as a film photographer and lives with Giles in a nice neighborhood. Soon, his life drastically changes, upon the arrival of his mother. The reason behind Nuru's visit is her desire to arrange a marriage for Alim, whose cousin of a comparable age is soon to wed in Canada. Moreover, Nuru also hopes to find a way to convince Alim to return to Canada. However, Nuru is not aware of Alim's sexual orientation or of his relationship with Giles. Before her arrival, as an audience, we are made aware that Nuru is a Muslim woman. She lives in Toronto and works for her sister's husband. Her life drastically changes when she discovers Alim's sexual identity and his relationship.

After spending the day with Giles, Nuru returns home drunk. Because Alim disapproves of Giles and Nuru's closeness, and out of a sudden sense of jealousy, he tells her the truth about his sexuality and his relationship with Giles; as a result, even though *Touch of Pink* focuses on Alim's diasporic queer identity, it also centers on Nuru and her identity transformation.

THE SEARCH FOR CULTURAL IDENTITY

Early in the film, we are introduced to Nuru's sister, Dolly, who is preparing for her son's wedding. During the preparations, Dolly interrogates Nuru about whether Alim will be marrying soon as well. In order to save face, Nuru lies about Alim and tells all present, including Dolly, that Alim is seeing a woman, a brain surgeon. The emphasis on weddings and romantic relationships successfully illustrates the importance of marriage in this diasporic Muslim community. After several rounds of congratulatory visits from many friends and relatives, Nuru helps Dolly clean the house. During the cleaning process, Hassan, Dolly's husband, starts to play an old Indian song and the couple begins to dance. The song functions as another indicator that highlights their diasporic roots and the importance of certain emotions, such as connection to the home culture. In this scene, Hassan articulates that it is time for them to rest because they have done everything required to succeed. Clearly, the marriage of their son is the pinnacle of their success story. As an immigrant family, their success is measured by their son's education, his vocation as dentist, and his impending marriage to a successful and beautiful Indian woman. Theirs is a success story because receiving a higher education and surviving in Western societies as diasporic individuals (with cultural customs intact) are not easy tasks to accomplish. While Nuru sees their family and accomplishments as a success story, she feels a renewed societal and cultural pressure to succeed in the same way as the others in her community.

When the camera captures Nuru's tears, the audience is led to sympathize with her struggle and loneliness. Clearly, the scene shows that she misses Alim and her deceased husband. She says that it is time for her to win. In reality, she is far from being a winner because she is clueless about Alim's sexual identity and his relationship with Giles. This urge to become successful by marrying off her son is only the catalyst for Nuru's transformation and her journey with Alim as they explore their cultural identities and desires that are constructed through an amalgam of Muslim Indian experiences in tension with Western ideals.

RELIGION

Immediately after we see Nuru crying over her lack of success, the camera cuts to Alim. The scene is Alim and Giles's anniversary party, which was organized by Giles's sister, Delia. Unlike Nuru, Giles's parents are among the guests. Alim appears a bit restless; it is apparent that he is not really comfortable with the present situation. He is surprised by the party and he is even more surprised to see one of Giles's former boyfriends partying attendance.

One of the most interesting dialogues takes place when Alim goes to get a drink and is accompanied by his imaginary mentor. Alim says "Imagine my mom in here," and Cary Grant replies, "Your mother is different. She is a Muslim woman from the third world. She would not understand." Alim continues, "I am Muslim. I am from the third world." Even though he appears comfortable with his sexual identity, at the same time, he has deeper questions about his Islamic queer body and his diasporic roots. In addition, Grant's comment about Nuru also begs for further analysis. As Grant points out, Nuru is a Muslim woman and likely has not been exposed to Western ideas about homosexuality and queer politics. This remark positions Islam as a religion and culture that excludes same-sex attraction. Alim is quick to point out that he, too, is Muslim and from the third world, yet also gay, challenging the assumption that being Muslim is antithetical to being gay.

Alim's simple statement that he is a Muslim gay man from the third world is true, but at the same time, he is also a diasporic man who grew up in Canada and is currently living in London. Therefore, he is also a cosmopolitan man whose experiences are infused by ideals that are an amalgam of colonial, postcolonial, and diasporic experiences; he experiences constant translations between the host cultures and diasporic communities. Moreover, his experiences are multifaceted because he has to deal with his ethnicity and sexuality simultaneously. In short, he functions as an embodiment of in-between experiences.

This scene is also important because it reflects Alim's hesitations about coming out to his mother. He suspects that Nuru would not understand his sexuality and his in-between experiences because of her religious and ethnic background. He assumes that she has not been exposed to gay culture; therefore, he assumes that she is not open to different articulations of human sexuality and relationships. In the scene, Cary Grant functions as Alim's inner psyche and explains exactly what Alim thinks about his mother, perhaps even repeating the colonial discourse that associates whiteness with individualism and ethnicity with the stereotype of traditionalism and homogeneity.

IN-BETWEEN EXPERIENCES

As soon as Nuru arrives in London, she begins asking questions about Alim's girlfriend, jobs, apartment, and other important issues. Alim ignores most of these questions and briefly answers the others. In the meantime, Giles is introduced as Alim's roommate. Although Nuru does not look happy about Alim's living conditions and she constantly complains about them, Giles finds her relatively attractive and, more importantly, edgy; he likes her. On the other hand, Nuru's behaviors are not really friendly; they are rather judgmental. It becomes apparent later on that Nuru associates

Giles with their shared colonial history. Furthermore, Nuru ruins Alim and Giles's plans by refusing to take Giles's room, the guest room, and she wants to take Alim's room instead. As an alternative, Nuru makes new arrangements. According to these new arrangements, Alim must sleep on the sofa while Giles remains in the guest room.

THE CONCEPT OF HOME

The concept of home is one of the major themes of the film; this becomes apparent where Nuru and Alim go to an Indian grocery store. After a brief chat with Alim, the storeowner asks "where are you from?" This remains one of the most important and critical questions of the film. Alim's answers reflect his confusion about where home is for him. He responds by saying that he lives down the street; however, the shopkeeper keeps asking the same question. Then Alim answers, "I am from Toronto." Again, the storeowner asks, "Where are you from *originally*?" This time, Nuru answers the question. "He was born in Kenya." This dialogue captures the complexity of Alim's identity because, as a diasporic Muslim queer man, he was born in Kenya to an Indian family. Although he grew up in Toronto, he currently resides in London. He is not from India, since he was neither born there nor has ever visited the country, and yet his Indianness is inscribed on his body as a biological imperative. Although he was born in Kenya, he does not consider Kenya to be his home either, because he grew up in Canada. When we add the religious and sexuality aspects into his complex diasporic identity, the audience realizes that Alim is an amalgam of Islamic diasporic cultures and Western lifestyles, cultural practices, and ideologies. He also belongs to a diasporic community that bides normative Muslim values in Canada. Therefore, he is in between places. For him, home is not a clear, unproblematic entity signifying unconditional belonging, because he has yet to find a home capable of housing all of the often-conflicting aspects of his identity. Perhaps home is across the street, where he lives with his lover, but this home lacks his connection to his ethnicity; or maybe home is Toronto, where his extended family and mother live, but that home lacks a meaningful connection to his sexuality; maybe home is in Kenya, where he spent his early childhood; or maybe home is India, the country he has never seen, but to which he owes his ancestral heritage. Perhaps home is all of these places, or none of them. As a postcolonial diasporic queer man, he is dislocated. His identity is in crisis because he is caught in between cultures and experiences. Alim's crisis becomes even more apparent with Nuru's arrival. The scene in the grocery store marks the beginning of Alim's journey to find home and to understand the complexity of his cultural, racial, and sexual identities. The scene also serves as a good example of how identities are created and recreated through communication with others. Alim's ideas about home are reshaped through this dialogue. As an audience, we see his confusion, restlessness, and pain when the conversation with the shopkeeper ends.

RELATIONSHIPS, DIASPORIC VALUES, AND RELIGION

In the next scene, Nuru interrogates Alim about getting married, starting a family, and his future plans about living with Giles. As soon as Alim tells Nuru that he is in a relationship, Giles and his sister Delia walk in. As soon as Nuru asks further questions about Alim's relationship, Cary Grant appears and encourages him to introduce Delia as his fiancé. Without evaluating the potential consequences, Alim introduces Delia as his fiancé. This unexpected reply surprises and upsets Nuru and Giles equally. Nuru is upset because Delia is not Muslim; therefore, she does not satisfy the criteria of what Nuru seeks in a daughter-in-law. As this scene illuminates, religious background and beliefs, in this case belonging to the same religion, play an important role and are often considered as desirable assets for most diasporic marriages. In addition, Giles is upset because of Alim's decisions to hide their relationship and to cover the truth about their sexualities.

Instead of making her happy, this unexpected news upsets Nuru, and she announces that she will be leaving in the morning. However, after talking to her sister Dolly in Canada, Nuru decides to say in London until she can convince Alim to return with her permanently. In order to put her plans into motion, Nuru decides to organize a dinner and asks Alim to bring Delia so the women can have an opportunity to bond. In the meantime, Nuru shows her dissatisfaction with Giles by making his life difficult. For example, during breakfast, Nuru accuses Giles of eating Alim's food. During their conversation, Nuru reveals her postcolonial identity and illuminates her diasporic experiences by attacking Giles and Britain for being colonizers. She accuses Giles of eating Alim's breakfast and accuses Britain of colonizing India, the Middle East, and Africa. In a way, her humor reflects guerilla attacks that Helen Hok-Sze Leung talks about in her article "The New Queer Cinema and the Third Cinema." Leung explains that the Third Cinema, as a movement, emerged in colonized countries as a reaction to Western ideals.[26] In *Touch of Pink,* Nuru's edgy comments represent her reaction and opposition to Britain's colonial past.

Although Giles and Nuru's relationship begins with a troubling start, their relationship improves when Giles asks her out and shows her around. While Giles takes her shopping, and to tourist attractions like the London Eye, parks, lunch, dinner, and dancing, they find an opportunity to bond. After a fine day, when they arrive at the apartment, they find Alim asleep. In this scene, the audience sees a different side to Alim. When Giles asks Alim to dance with him, he refuses because he is mad at Giles and Nuru for drinking and spending the night together. Angry now, Giles tells him that the situation is "not what he signed up for." The awkwardness and confusion between Giles and Alim increases after this bitter exchange. Because of this episode, Giles decides to go to for a swim with Delia's handsome friend. His decision makes Alim even more frustrated. All of the sudden, Alim decides to tell Nuru the truth and reveals his homosexuality. He shows Nuru Giles's naked picture, which he had taken a while ago. After seeing the picture, Nuru realizes that Alim and Giles are lovers. Upon this realization, Nuru decides to leave immediately.

When Nuru departs, returning to Toronto, Giles accuses Alim of being harsh with her. As a response, Alim says, "She is a Muslim woman from the third world and she cannot understand." Giles's response illustrates their confusion. He says, "If she is a Muslim woman from the third world, what does that make you? A Paki?" While this scene illuminates the role of religion in the lives of diasporic queer men, it also captures the complexity of Muslim men's relationships with men from nondiasporic communities. Since Alim is in search for his identity, he does not know how to position himself when it comes to his ethnicity and religion as a gay man. As a result, it becomes apparent that Alim faces cultural and religious difficulties on many levels. Because of his sexuality, he experiences cultural rejection, as evidenced by his mother's rejection upon his articulation of his queerness. While he is dealing with his sexuality, Alim also has to negotiate the role of his homosexuality in the diasporic Muslim community and must negotiate his ethnic and cultural roots to make sense of everyday experiences as a diasporic queer man.

After Nuru's brief visit and confrontation with Alim, he decides to return to Toronto to sort things out with his mother. During the flight, an

African American woman who is sitting next to him asks if he is going home or visiting. Alim replies, "I am going to visit." This illustrates Alim's position. He does not see Toronto as home anymore. He is going to visit. His stay there will be temporary. When Nuru and Dolly find out that Alim is back, his arrival makes both women happy. At the same time, the wedding preparations for Alim's cousin are almost finalized. Alim decides to join his mother at one of the receptions, where he meets his successful and soon-to-be-wed cousin, Khaled. Alim leaves after the reception and goes home to sleep, but his sleep is interrupted by Khaled. He is drunk and looking for more to drink. When Khaled tries to kiss him, Alim tells him that he has changed; he is in a relationship with Giles. The dialogue between the two men reveals that Khaled and Alim had engaged in sexual activity when they were growing up. As the two young men exchange harsh words, Nuru arrives. She is surprised to hear Khaled's comments about getting married *and* continuing to sleep with men. Alim apologizes for what Nuru has heard and this encounter breaks the ice between the mother and son. Further, Nuru confesses that, after her husband's death, she lost her ability to experience emotions, including love and the desire to care for Alim. She explains that this is the reason why she left for London. She went in pursuit of her dreams, to become an Indian Doris Day, but, as she says, she failed because London was not ready for Indian Doris Days.

This scene illustrates another postcolonial moment that captures the characters' in-between experiences. Her departure was also one of the major reasons why, as a child, Alim cast Cary Grant in the role of mentor and imaginary friend. Grant's character not only explains Alim's desire to find a sense of stability in his life but also symbolizes Alim's colonial past. In addition, the character also illuminates certain masculine traits and sexual sensibilities. Like Alim, Nuru is also incomplete because she is also searching for her roots and a place where she can belong.

Although Nuru has some hesitations about the wedding, she chooses to go and Alim accompanies her. During the reception, Nuru reveals the truth to Dolly; however, she realizes that Dolly is aware of their sons' past (and present) sexual tendencies. Instead of talking about and solving the problem, Dolly decides to live a lie and concentrate on false dreams. As she says, she is fine with her son's sexual desires, as long as he provides her with grandchildren, an indication of his "straightness." Dolly wants to continue to live a lie. Before Nuru leaves, she asks her, "Flowers will brown and ice sculptures will melt, then what?" This critical question critiques the compulsory heterosexuality enforced within such societies, and

Nuru comes to realize that Alim's "straightness," on which her "success" depends, can only come about if he is willing to compromise both of their integrities by hiding from the truth.

While all these events are taking place, Giles comes to the wedding to see Alim. Both Nuru and Alim are surprised by his arrival. Without thinking about their ethnic and religious backgrounds, and not caring too much about what the other guests might think, the two men kiss in front of the guests. Alim realizes that it is time for him to say goodbye to his imaginary friend as the same time that his sexuality and ethnicity come to occupy the same space. Cary role is completed with Nuru's acceptance and Giles's return. As soon as Grant disappears, they all leave to go home, to the final stop on their long and painful journey. Cary Grant's disappearance is connected to Alim's recognition of his new identity. He is finally able to understand his ethnic and religious selves in relation to his diasporic queer body; therefore, he is able to bring into union the more disparate aspects of his self, which looked rather disconnected earlier in the film. At this point, Alim does not need an imaginary friend to help him to cope with the ideal of compulsory heterosexuality. Therefore, letting Cary Grant go signifies his transformation and acceptance of his multifaceted cultural identity.

NOTES

1. Will Roscoe and Stephen Murray, *Islamic Homosexualities: Culture, History, Literature* (New York: New York University Press, 1997).

2. Arno Schmitt, *Sexuality and Eroticism among Males in Muslim Societies* (London: Routledge, 1992).

3. Brian Whitaker, *Unspeakable Love: Gay and Lesbian Life in the Middle East* (Berkeley: University of California Press, 2006).

4. Robin Cohen, *Global Diaspora: An Introduction* (Seattle: University of Washington Press, 1997), ix.

5. Ibid.

6. Stuart Hall, "New Cultures for Old," in *A Place in the World?* ed. Doreen Massey and Pat Jess (Oxford: Oxford University Press, 1995), 193.

7. Anjali Ram, "Memory, Cinema, and the Reconstruction of Cultural Identities," in *Communicating Ethnic and Cultural Identity*, ed. Mary Fong and Rueyling Chuang (Lanham: Rowman and Littlefield, 2004), 121–34.

8. Kathleen Wong (Lau), "Migrations Across Generations: Whose Identity Is Authentic?" in *Readings in Cultural Contexts*, ed. Judith N. Martin, Thomas K. Nakayama, and Lisa. A. Flores (Mountain View, CA: Mayfield, 1998), 130.

9. Floya Anthias, "Evaluating Diaspora: Beyond Ethnicity?" *Sociology* 32 (1998): 557.

10. Floya Anthias, "New Hybridities, Old Concepts: The Limits of 'Culture,'" *Ethnic and Racial Studies* 24 (2001): 631.

11. Richard Dyer, *The Matter of Images: Essays of Representation* (London: Routledge, 1993), 11.

12. Anneke Smelik, "Gay and Lesbian Criticism," in *Film Studies: Critical Approaches,* ed. John Hill, Pamela Church Gibson, Richard Dyer, and E. Ann Kaplan (Oxford: Oxford University Press, 2000), 133–44.

13. Smelik, "Gay and Lesbian Criticism," 133–44. Seminal works, such as Harry Benshoff's *Monsters in the Closet: Homosexuality and the Horror Film* (Manchester: Manchester University Press, 1997) and Vitto Russo's archival work on representation of homosexuality in cinema, *The Celluloid Closet: Homosexuality in the Movies* (New York: Harper and Row, 1987) widely focus on Hollywood's early censorship and "moral decency" codes. These works also suggest that, in order to represent queer bodies in their films, filmmakers during most of the 20th century found cinematic ways to code their characters. As Russo suggested, these characters often appeared non-queer to mainstream audiences; however, queer audiences were able to decode these codes and unmask the hidden stories.

14. Larry Gross, "Out of the Mainstream: Sexual Minorities and the Mass Media," in *Gay People, Sex, and Media,* ed. Michelle Wolf and Alfred Kielwasser (Thousand Oaks, CA: Sage, 1991), 19–46.

15. Susan Bordo, *The Male Body: A New Look at Men in Public and in Private* (New York: Farrar, Straus and Giroux, 1999), 168.

16. Larry Gross, "Out of the Mainstream," 19.

17. Susan Bordo, "The Male Body," 168.

18. See Larry Gross, *Up From Invisibility: Lesbian, Gay Men, and the Media in America* (New York: Columbia University Press, 2001); also see Brian McNair, *Striptease Culture: Sex, Media and the Demonstration of Desire* (London: Routledge, 2002).

19. McNair, *Striptease Culture,* 147.

20. Alexander Doty and Ben Grove, "Queer Representations in the Mass Media," in *Lesbian and Gay Studies: Critical Introduction,* ed. Andy Medhurst and Sally Munt (London: Cassell, 1997), 84–98.

21. B. Ruby Rich, "New Queer Cinema," in *New Queer Cinema: A Critical Reader,* ed. Michelle Aaron (New Brunswick, NJ: Rutgers University Press, 2004), 15–22.

22. Michael DeAngelis, "The Characteristics of New Queer Filmmaking: Case Study- Todd Haynes," in *New Queer Cinema: A Critical Reader,* ed. Michelle Aaron (New Brunswick, NJ: Rutgers University Press, 2004), 41–52.

23. Rueyling Chuang, "Theoretical Perspectives: Fluidity and Complexity of Cultural and Ethnic Identity," in *Communicating Ethnic and Cultural Identity,* ed. Mary Fong and Rueyling Chuang (Lanham: Rowman and Littlefield, 2004), 52.

24. Ibid., 54.

25. Gust A. Yep, "My Three Cultures: Navigating the Multicultural Identity Landscape," in *Readings in Intercultural Communication,* ed. Judith N. Martin, Thomas K. Nakayama, and Lisa. A. Flores (Mountain View, CA: Mayfield 1998), 60–66.

26. Helen Hok-Zse Leung, "New Queer Cinema and Third Cinema," in *New Queer Cinema: A Critical Reader,* ed. Michelle Aaron (New Brunswick, NJ: Rutgers University Press, 2004), 155–67.

20

—·◆·—

SEXUALITIES AND THE SOCIAL ORDER IN ARAB AND MUSLIM COMMUNITIES

Rabab Abdulhadi

Among the articles included under the chapter "Oppressions" in *Coming Out: An Anthology of International Gay and Lesbian Writings,* edited by Stephan Likosky,[1] is Rex Wockner's article, "Iran, the Middle East, and North Africa: Homosexuality in the Arab and Moslem World." Wockner's piece raises serious issues for both academics and activists. In his article, Wockner makes four claims about Arab and Muslim communities: first, he claims that "virtually all men have sex with other men throughout their lives";[2] second, he argues that practicing homosexuals, in particular, have been singled out for the harshest punishments by today's political regimes;[3] third, he suggests that such punishment can be traced back to the Islamic Sharia, or religious code;[4] and, finally, Wockner proposes that coming out is the only path for homosexual salvation.[5] Since no evidence exists to support or verify Wockner's claim that each and every man (and woman) in Arab and Muslim communities has had (and may continue to have) same-sex sexual experiences, this claim does not warrant a discussion. The other claims, however, are serious in that they paint a picture of Arab and Muslim communities as "brutal," "uncivilized," inherently homophobic, and as irredeemable in themselves, unless and until they catch up with the "more enlightened" Western[6] model of gay liberation, and until the time comes when homosexuals in the region are finally rid of false consciousness.

Wockner's ahistorical, Orientalist,[7] and oversimplified claims fall apart against a historically grounded analysis of the ways in which sexual orders emerged in contemporary Muslim and Arab communities. Below I delineate how the Islamic scripture framed sexuality, including homosexuality, and the development of such a framework during the era of Muslim reign, the impact of colonialism on the region's sexual order, and the processes in which homosexuality is treated today.

HISTORICIZING MUSLIM AND ARAB PERSPECTIVES ON SEXUALITY

Under the heading, "in their own words: overview," Wockner quotes and accepts the statement made by the general secretary of the International Lesbian and Gay Association, Lisa Power, in which she claims that "most Islamic cultures don't take kindly to organized homosexuality, even though male homoeroticism is deep within their cultural roots."[8] Power's quote is not an anomaly in Wockner's piece; in fact, Wockner himself makes such claims throughout the article. The only exception is the single instance in which he cites Dr. Jeanette Wakin, a lecturer in Islamic Studies at Columbia University, who suggests that "the Quran itself doesn't say anything about homosexuality." Dismissing Wakin's qualification to speak authoritatively on the topic, Wockner goes on to argue that legal prohibition against homosexuality "can be traced to the Islamic Sharia code, a Quran-and-revelation-based legal system roughly comparable to the Talmudic tradition in Judaism."[9] Is it true that Muslim communities have not, in fact, taken kindly to homosexuality? Does the Quran have nothing to say about homosexuality, as Wakin claims? And if Wakin is right, what accounts, then, for the contradictions between Wockner's claims and the statement of the scholar he quotes?

SEXUALITY IN ISLAMIC SCRIPTURE

Before attempting to deal with Power's claim, let us go to what is viewed as the most authoritative sources in the Islamic Sharia: the Quran and the *hadith,* or the Prophet's sayings. *Surat Ash-Shu'ara, ayat* 166 says: "Will you fornicate with males and abandon your wives, whom God has created for you? Surely you are great transgressors." Another warning made to both male and female transgressors is issued in *surat an-Nisa', ayat* 15: "If any of your women commit *al-fahishah* [flagrant lewdness or fornication] bring in four witnesses from amongst you against them; if they confess, confine them to their houses until death overtakes them or until God finds a way for them. If two men among you commit it [al-fahishah], punish them both. If they repent and mend their ways, let them alone. God is forgiving and merciful." As Habib argues, reading the Arabic original of these two verses does not make it readily clear that the *fahisha* (lewdness) in question is homosexuality; instead, Habib suggests that the verse could be interpreted as referring to one theoretical woman involved with two theoretical men (a *ménage a trois*). Habib further refers to tolerant Shiites who see the verse as a reference to orgy-like activity, rather than homosexuality, particularly given the broad and ambiguous semantics of *fahisha*.[10]

Conversely, the Quran is not uniform in its treatment of homosexuality. *surat At-Tur, ayat* 24 describes life in heaven: "and there shall wait on them young boys (*ghilman*) of their own, as fair as virgin pearls," while *surat al-Waqiah, ayat* 17–18 says: "and there shall wait on them immortal youth (*wildan*) with bowls and ewers and a cup of purest wine that will neither pain their heads nor take away their reason." How do we explain the contradictory judgments of the Quran? Two possibilities exist. The first can be attributed to the notion of gradualism, as advanced by, among others, Aziza al-Hibri, who argues against the imposition of the hijab (headscarf) by contemporary Islamist groups. For example, al-Hibri claims that Quranic references to such a dress code was intended only for a specific period of time and for a particular group of women, namely, the wives of the Prophet and other Arab elite.[11] Although no such interpretation has been made in the case of homosexuality, parallel analysis can be applied to this issue.

The second possible explanation lies in the attempt of Islam as a new religion to reach as many adherents as possible by promising—as other religions have done in their early stages—would-be Muslims that their afterlife would be more lax and enjoyable than their worldly one. Support for this claim can be extrapolated from similar promises concerning wine and young boys.

As far as the *hadith* is concerned, the literature surveyed fails to produce major references to homosexuality. Only a few quotes by disciples of the Prophet Mohammed concern cross-dressing. Abu Hurayra (viewed as one of the most authenticated sources of Muhamad's sayings) cites a *hadith* as saying that, "God's messenger condemned men who wear women's clothes and women dressed in men's attire."[12]

Notwithstanding the ambiguous references to homosexuality in the Quran, and the absence of such references in the authenticated *hadith*,[13] it is possible to argue that underlying the Islamic scripture (much like the other two monotheistic religions, Judaism and Christianity) is a sex-gender system that is grounded in the dominance of heterosexual practices and in which men are the central players. This becomes evident as one reads the Quran. For example, *surat Al-Baqarah, ayat* 223, says: "Your women are your tilth: go then into your tilth in any way you wish." Similar themes are invoked in the *hadith*; Abu Hurayra quotes the Prophet as saying: "If a man calls his woman to his bed and she refuses, she will be cursed by the angels until she agrees."

Unlike Judaism and Christianity, however, Islam does not shy away from the topic of sexuality, but recognizes the sexual desires of both women and men,[14] as is evident in a dialogue with Muhamad, narrated by Abdullah Ben Amrou, wherein Islam instructs men to fulfill women's sexual needs: "God's messenger once asked me: 'Abdulla, wasn't I informed that you fast days and pray the nights away?' I said: 'yes, God's messenger.' He said: 'Don't! Fast and break your fast, wake up and sleep; your body claims a right to you . . . and your wife has a right to you.'"[15] Along the same lines are the Quranic *surat Al-Baqarah, ayat* 187, the *hadith* quoted by Awn Ben Aby Juhayfah, and the authenticated sayings of Muhamad's favorite wife, Aisha.[16]

Two qualifications, however, exist in Muslim scripture regarding sexual intercourse: women must be married to the men with whom they are having sex; and such intercourse is forbidden during women's menstruation. When Muhamad's disciples asked him about it, the *ayat* was revealed. The Prophet added: "Do everything except *Nikkah*." Islamic scripture defines *Nikkah* as the sexual intercourse that is sanctioned by marriage.[17] Some Muslim scholars, utilizing *ijtihad,* or interpretation of Islamic scripture (a pillar of the Sharia), add another qualification to male–female sexual intercourse. In discussing "The Rights of the Married Couple: The Right of Initiation and Pleasure in Sexual Intercourse," Abu Shaqqa argues that "no harm arises in any position the couple favors in their enjoyment, whether in sexual intercourse or in other [acts], as long as they avoid what God prohibited: menstruation and the backside."[18] Abu Shaqqa does not cite any Quranic verses or quotes from the Prophet; thus, he fails to provide a convincing argument against anal intercourse. In fact, other Muslim scholars cite the same *ayat* to substantiate their claim that the Islamic scripture allowed diversity in sexual positions, including anal intercourse. The leading Muslim theologian, Imam Malik, argues in *Kitab As-Sirr* (*The Book of Secrecy*), that *al-liwat al-asghar,* or anal intercourse between men and women, is not prohibited.[19] The confusion can, perhaps, stem from the similarity in the spelling and pronunciation of the two expressions.

SEXUALITY IN THE POLITICAL AND SOCIAL ORDER: 14 CENTURIES OF ISLAMIC RULE

While the Quran and Muhamad's *hadith* leave us with a certain degree of ambiguity regarding homosexuality, Muslim leaders who succeeded the Prophet exhibited more clarity, albeit with varying degrees of emphasis. This arose from two interrelated issues: first, the context in which these leaders operated differed from that of the Prophet's times, especially as they sought to consolidate their command of Islamic rule after his death; and second, the social control of sexuality seemed to some to be one of the most potent ways in which they could accomplish their goal of consolidating their hold on power.

Immediately after Muhamad's death, the first caliphate, Abu Bakr (623–624) took over. Known for his strictness and rigidity on one hand, and threatened with a few attempts to challenge not only his caliphate, but also the authority of Islam in general on the other, Abu Bakr ordered the burning of homosexuals, the first documented occurrence of ostracization in the history of Islam.[20] The second caliphate, Omar Ibn al-Khattab (634–644), however, was more tolerant. Known as "the Just Caliph," Omar's attitudes toward sexuality resonated with the rest of his views and thus were more lax. The third, Othman Ibn Affan (644–656), did not last long enough to deal with such matters, as his rule was contested by Ali Ibn Abi Talib (656–661). According to Abu Khalil, Ibn Abi Talib "once threw a homosexual—with his head pointing down—from atop a minaret, saying: 'This is how he will be dumped in the fire of hell.'"[21] Ibn Abi Talib's actions were not inconsistent with the mark of his shaky rule. Ali was rejected by many of Mohammed's followers, including the latter's favorite wife, Aisha.

During the Umayyad era (661–680), Islamic rule was no longer threatened with collapse. As a result, Muslim leaders embarked on the conquest through which they sought to control, with much success, vast areas extending from China in the East to what became al-Andalus in the Iberian

Peninsula. Thus, Umayyad's preoccupation with the conquest played a significant role in diverting these rulers from attempting to exercise state control over sexual practices. Umayyad Caliph, al-Walid bin Yazid in al-Andalus (743–744), whose rule lasted only a year, had a reputation of enjoying both "wine and *at-talawwut* [from *liwat*, or sex with other men]."[22]

The Abbasid dynasty (749–1258) controlled an empire stretching from Central Asia to the Atlantic Coast, and their rule became known later as the "golden age" of Islam, during which economic prosperity, rich cultural life, and medical developments were enjoyed by the citizenry.[23] These developments affected the Abbasid sexual order in more ways than one could possibly imagine. On one level, while the administration of the vast empire had demanded the Caliphs' complete attention, the Abbasid dynasty hardly faced any serious challenges, short of a few attempts that were crushed almost as soon as they flared up. On another level, to maintain their rule over different peoples, linguistic groups, and cultural norms, the Abbasids had to refrain from controlling the cultural life of their subjects. Furthermore, by the time Harun al-Rashid (786–809), best-known as the Abbasid Caliph, assumed the reigns of power, almost 200 years had passed since the death of the Prophet Muhamad; Islamic rule was being normalized, bureaucratized, and had moved further away from the literalist adherence to the teachings of the scripture.

These three factors contributed to the Abbasids' tolerance of diverse sexual practices, including the overt discussion of such desires and practices. It was during this period that some of the most graphic textual works on sexuality, including same-sex desires and practices, proliferated. It was also under the tutelage and the protection of Harun al-Rashid that the famous Arab poet Abu Nuwas lived. Although credited today as being the most prominent author of works replete with heterosexual innuendos, Abu Nuwas was equally interested in men, and especially young boys. Immediately after Harun al-Rashid's death, al-Amin (809–813) became the Caliph. al-Amin "rejected women and concubines," preferring eunuchs instead.

Despite numerous references to male same-sex desires and practices in the Abbasid era, however, there is limited data concerning women's sexual preferences,[24] notwithstanding the recent writings and translations by Samar Habib.[25] In Keddie and Baron's anthology *Women in Middle East History,* Paula Sanders writes on "Gendering the Ungendered Body: Hermaphrodites in Medieval Islamic Law," in which she argues that medieval Islam constructed a "bipolar [sexual] view of the world" as "a place with only two sexes, male and female." In this, Sanders posits that medieval Islam was distinct from the "single-sex model" of the Ancient Greeks.[26]

If the world of medieval Islam was rigidly composed of two sexes, male and female, how can we account for the diverse sexual practices and how can we explain the absence of the "female" voice? Egyptian feminist scholar, Leila Ahmad, offers a possible explanation: "the practices and living arrangements of the dominant classes of the Abbasid era were such that at an implicit and often an explicit level, the words *woman, slave,* and *object for sexual use* came close to being indistinguishably fused."[27] Arguing that the more egalitarian and less androcentric "ethical voice" of Islam was institutionally silenced in the Abbasid era,[28] Ahmad partly attributes this transformation to Muslim philosophers' adoption of the Aristotelian theory of conception, according to which "the male secretion was [considered] superior to the female secretion and contributed the soul while the female secretion provided the matter."[29] While I do not totally dispute the argument advanced by Sanders, I would argue that the "bipolar [sexual] view of the world" of medieval Islam was influenced by the "single sex model" that Laqueur described for the Greeks.[30] This becomes evident if we accept that, in Medieval Islam, "Aristotle's influence was widespread and enduring,"[31] including the notion that women being "as it were an impotent male, for it is through a certain incapacity that the female is a female."[32] Furthermore, if women were subsumed under the same category with slaves and objects for sexual use, it should not be surprising that the Abbasid rule adopted Greek attitudes that viewed free men as the dominant and all others as the dominated. This also explains why Abbasid Caliphs permitted (and engaged in) diverse sexual practices, yet such practices were only tolerated as long as they did not disrupt the sexual order in which elite men were the doers, or aggressive partners, and everyone else (women, eunuchs, boys, and slaves) were the ones done unto, or the passive recipients.

During the Ottoman dynasty (1281–1922), diverse sexual practices were not only widespread, but also well-documented. This is partly because of the relatively recent advent of the regime, and partly due to the increasing interest of European travelers to the Arab world during this period. Among those flocking to the region were missionaries, archeologists, would-be colonists, and some who sought to explore "exotic" and "oriental" cultures of the Arabs and Muslims.[33] Thus, numerous accounts of the harem, eunuchs, same-sex practices, slaves, and women's sexuality emerged in the literature,[34] many of which were more reflective of European fantasies than the actual experiences of Arabs and Muslims.

Despite the proliferation of "Orientalist" textual production in which Arab and Muslim societies were dichotomously constructed as either completely decadent, immoral, and permissive,[35] or as strict and oppressive to women,[36] however, nowhere in the literature can we find serious analyses of the sex and gender power hierarchies that only deepened during the Ottoman rule. For Ahmad, accounts of "sexual excesses of all sorts . . . attributed to members of the ruling family," should not have been used as the basis for speculation about the "use of power and the breaking of boundaries" in the broader society,"[37] nor, I would add, about the complexity of sexual hierarchy that operated in a particular context; what transpired among the ruling elite in itself demands more than a superficial analysis, let alone the verification of its applicability to the majority of the population. Thus, short of the few cases cited on the sexual desires and practices of some elites, we have no way of knowing whether "male homoeroticism is deep within [Arab and Muslim] cultural roots," as Power argues in Wockner's piece.[38]

Nonetheless, a specific Arab and Muslim sexual order prevailed. Were similar practices, though, maintained as Arabs and Muslims began to experience colonialism? In what ways did this intervening factor influence and shape Arab perspectives on sexuality?

THE ADVENT OF COLONIALISM

While the Ottoman dynasty lasted for more than 750 years, during which it controlled most of the Arab world. It drew its legitimacy, in part, from being Muslim, and thus was not seen as a colonial power in the eyes of Arabs until the early 1900,[39] when the latter was approaching defeat in World War I. The war, however, produced a victory for Western European powers who sought to divide the war's spoils among themselves and embark on their colonialist projects. The colonists brought with them their morality, social codes, and religious teachings as they understood them at the time. Equally important was the colonial construction of dual and oppositional images: a dominant and superior one of itself, and an inferior image of the dominated Arabs.

To facilitate their control over the Arabs, and so that they could justify such domination, France and England, not unlike other colonial powers,

and especially European settlers in North America[40] and Africa,[41] constructed a binary system in which the colonial European was "civilized,"
masculinized, and gentlemanly, intent on a moral crusade to rescue the
oppressed colonized women.[42] As Fanon argues, "the governing race" is
"first and foremost those who come from elsewhere, those who are unlike the original inhabitants, 'the others.'"[43] Conversely, the image of the
"other," embodied in that of the colonized Arab man, was constructed as
"emasculated," "brutish" and "savage"[44]—a negation of what the colonist
stood for. As Fanon puts it: "The native is declared insensible to ethics; he
represents not only the absence of values, but also the negation of values,"[45]
and lives "in a town of n——s and dirty Arabs."[46]

Not only did colonial powers construct this dual imagery, they also influenced and shaped the Arab world' views of sexuality, especially because
the Victorian code of morality prevailing in Europe at the time[47] confined
the acceptability of sexual intercourse to reproduction, while defining any
other sexual desires not leading to such ends as sinful, dirty, and deviant.

As they forged a politics of resistance, Arab anticolonial nationalists,
not unlike other marginalized groups, incorporated aspects of their colonizers' values and internalized the latter's image of themselves. On one
level, colonized Arabs adopted many of the tenets of the European ideology of nationalism, which emerged, along with "respectable" sexuality at
the end of the 18th century.[48] Adopting the European model of nationalism as a male-centered and heteronormative ideology translated in different ways. First, through the incorporation of the Victorian code of
morality, Arab anticolonial discourses began to erode a basic concept of
Islamic scripture that guaranteed sexual rights to women. Perhaps placing
the erosion of women's rights in parts of the Arab and Muslim communities in the historical and socioeconomic context would act as a correc-
tive to explain that the "extreme institutionalized sexism," mentioned by
Wockner.[49] The notion did not emerge in a vacuum, nor was an inherent
phenomenon in this setting, but was rather a direct result of the colonial
project. Second, to be rid of the "emasculated" image produced by colonial
logic, anticolonial Arab nationalists equated anticolonial militancy with
hypermasculinity. As Victorian morality settled in, displaying emotions
or sentiments in public was increasingly frowned upon. Third, despite the
fact that "the nation" represented "a passionate brotherhood," colonized
Arab nationalists found themselves "compelled to distinguish . . . 'proper'
homosociality from more explicitly sexualized male–male relations, a

compulsion that requires the identification, isolation and containment of male homosexuality."[50] Neither women (irrespective of their sexual preferences) who were excluded, nor men who did not subscribe to the hypermasculinized imagery could be part of the picture.

CONTEMPORARY REALITY

The rupture in Arab and Muslim cultural norms regarding sexuality, a byproduct of colonial rule, was further consolidated as colonization and occupation by foreign forces deepened their intervention in this region of the world well into the latter part of the 20th century.

Emerging was a dominant concept of what constituted proper sexual conduct. This idea produced discourses and practices by governments and liberation movements in which any deviations from the accepted code of morality were treated with isolation and ostracization at best, and with death, at worst. Wockner quotes Ayatollah Musavi-Ardebili, a key political and spiritual leader in Iran, in stressing the need to develop an "anti-vice culture," and in stating that "there cannot be the slightest degree of mercy or compassion toward those who observe inadequate Islamic dress or toward prohibitions. There should not be the slightest degree of mercy toward these criminals."[51]

ANTICOLONIAL RESISTANCE AND THE MORALITY QUESTION

The moral code of sexual conduct, enforced by the Post-Shah, anti-Western government of Iran, is not an anomaly. My argument that anticolonial national projects blurred the lines between morality and anticolonial politics is supported by what transpired during the struggle waged by the Algerians against French colonialism and by evidence from the evolving concepts of proper conduct of the Palestinian national movement against the Israeli occupation.

At the height of the Algerian war of independence, 1954–1962,[52] French General Mathieu gathered Algerian maids in a central square on May 13, 1958 and forced them to take off their veils. Responding to this incident, the National Liberation Front (FLN) called on Algerian women to wear the *hayek* (a traditional Algerian garb for women exposing only their eyes) as evidence of the Islamic and Arab heritage of Algeria.[53] In *A Dying Colonialism*, Frantz Fanon discusses the incident and hails what he sees as the revolutionary use of the *hayek* as a symbol of anticolonial resistance.[54] Similarly, the Palestinian national movement formed a gendered and a sexualized discourse in which the lost land, Palestine, was imagined as the body of a woman whose victimization by Zionist settlers must be avenged by young men. This image of Palestine was extended to Palestinian women, who were further conceptualized as fertile mothers, and as super-women enduring the pain and suffering of their people.[55] These iconized images of Palestinian womanhood, however and perhaps not surprisingly, did not translate into equal status for women in nationalist discourse. The Palestinian National Charter (1968), for example, defined the Palestinian identity in such a way as to privilege fatherhood, not motherhood. Article Four of the Charter says "the Palestinian identity is an authentic, intrinsic and indissoluble quality that is *transmitted from father to son*," while Article Five states "Anyone born to a *Palestinian father* after that date [1947], whether inside or outside Palestine is a Palestinian [emphasis added]."[56] This signals not only a male-centric discourse, but also an implicit policy in which only males who reproduced and who engaged in heterosexual intercourse were seen as legitimate models of what Palestinian masculinity was all about. It should be added that attempts to impose a hegemonic discourse never go without challenges or contestations; women's contestation of such constructs were as old as the Palestinian National Charter. In 1965, the same year of the adoption of the Charter, the General Union of Palestinian Women (GUPW) was founded. GUPW members refused to accept the dominant definition of Palestinianness, and instead insisted that a Palestinian was one whose father or mother was a Palestinian.

In such a context of colonial legacies and a limited anticolonial imagination, women whose behavior undermined hegemonic morality would often be labeled lesbians by the leadership of their movement[57] and Western media and security officials[58] alike, the latter being as complicit in the demonization of both women militants and lesbians. Labeling women as lesbians to discredit them is not only homophobic, it is also a reaffirmation of the "biology is destiny principle" in which "real" women are constructed as having a "natural" predisposition to motherhood, soft and oversensitive as if they were genetically built so as not to participate in militant movements.

It is not unexpected that accusations of spying for adversaries[59] would be directed against women (and men) who were perceived as behaving in a contradictory manner to the "culture of modesty," which, according to

Rema Hammami,[60] emerged during the first Palestinian intifada when the campaign by Hamas to impose the hijab on women in Gaza did not elicit a response from the Unified Leadership of the Intifada until a year after the fact.[61]

The defeat of nationalist and Marxist ideologies in the Arab world in the aftermath of the collapse of the USSR and Communist Block in 1989, and the U.S. intervention in the Gulf in the early 1990s, combined with the earlier victory by the 1979 Islamic Revolution in Iran, gave rise to Islamist movements that constituted a new ideological and political trend in the region. The rise of these movements influenced the sexual order in three distinct, yet interrelated ways. First, the emphasis Islamist movements placed on the segregation of men and women, on the "modesty" of the women's dress code[62] and on the prohibition of diverse sexual practices made it extremely difficult for anyone to deviate from such restrictions. Second, movements and governments that view themselves as "secular," such as Fatah in Palestine and the National Liberation Front in Algeria, which were threatened by the Islamist popular ideology and found themselves on the defensive, especially given how corrupt they were, and adopted more conservative positions on "public morality" as if they were competing with the Islamist trend over who could be more conservative, as demonstrated by the Palestinian Authority in the self-rule areas[63] or the Algerian government when it lost the elections to the Islamic Salvation Front, FIS, in the early 1990s. Third, the emphasis of the upper class and educated elite on adopting what they perceived of as Western lifestyles alienated the majority of the population on a grass-roots level, as they saw such lifestyles as decadent, excessive, un-Arab, and un-Muslim. The deteriorating socioeconomic conditions, experienced in rising unemployment and poverty, coalesced with neglect and corruption by governments made up of those Western-oriented elite, expanded the popular grassroots support for the Islamist movements led to further rigidification of the most conservative interpretations of Islamic scripture.

Further contributing to the rigidification of social codes in Arab and Muslim communities was the concerted campaign by colonial and neo-colonial forces to "save" brown queer people from other brown heterosexual people, to paraphrase Laila Abu Lughod.[64] Joseph Massad is correct in arguing that the discourse of the "Gay International" has fed into the colonial project[65] in the Arab world, much like the U.S. Feminist Majority discourse regarding the liberation of Afghan women supplied the George W. Bush Administration with a pretext to invade and occupy Afghanistan.

A similar strategy has been applied by Israel and the global Zionist movement, especially during periods of intense isolation of Israel in response to its escalating violations of Palestinian rights. Building on the Zionist master narrative that constructs a mythical Israel as the "only modern," "democratic," and "civilized" country in the region, this fairy tale strategy has the "noble hero," Israel, is on a "human rights" mission impossible to "rescue" Palestinian homosexuals (especially men) from a homophobic and evil Palestinian society and whisk away the victims to a refuge of safety in the "open" and "gay friendly" Israeli society.

Targeting the lesbian, gay, bisexual, transgender, intersex, and queer (LGBTIQ) public, this discourse was very much in circulation following the 2002 Israeli invasion and the destruction of West Bank cities. Israel was widely condemned as its forces killed hundreds of Palestinians and held under siege the headquarters of the late Palestinian President, Yasser Arafat.[66] At that particular historical moment, when Israel needed to mobilize all the tools at its disposal, major American Jewish organizations offered student groups at college campuses funding support for Pride Month events in return for hosting a speaker's tour that, according to students involved in Pride Month activities in October 2004, featured a Palestinian homosexual escapee to Israel who "only wanted to share his story of horror at the hands of the Palestinians and his tale of survival" with American college audiences.

This campaign was heightened once again in preparation for the World Pride festival that was to be held in Jerusalem during the summer of 2005, but the festival was rescheduled as a result of the Israeli unilateral withdrawal from Gaza and what the organizers of the festival claimed to be their concerns for the safety of international delegations. However, security issues fade as a reason for rescheduling the festival when we take into consideration the widespread protests around the world against the apartheid wall Israel was building on the West Bank, including queer activists who urged queer organizations and individuals to boycott the Jerusalem festival. This movement included Kate Raphael, elected that year to serve as the Grand Marshall of the world's largest (and oldest) Gay Pride parade in San Francisco. In turning down such a great honor, Raphael explained that she was preoccupied with fighting the apartheid wall as a token of her solidarity with the Palestinian people. As an active member and cofounder of QUIT

(Queers Undermining Israeli Terrorism), Raphael continued on with her activism to oppose Israeli injustices and joined the BDS (Boycott, Divestment, Sanctions) movement most recently during the Israeli war on Gaza.

OPPOSITIONAL MOVEMENTS—CULTURES OF RESISTANCE

Despite the widespread conservative wave engulfing the Arab world (and the rest of the world), several challenges to the prevailing sexual order have emerged. Feminist activism and popular movements for social and economic justice and self-determination have offered alternatives to established sex-gender status quo, such as women's grassroots organizations in Palestine, Egypt, Lebanon, and elsewhere in Arab and Muslim communities. Another significant site where contestation to official male-centric and heterosexist discourse is in the literary world.

With very few exceptions, such as Thani al-Suwaydee's *al-Diesel* and Elham Mansour's *Ana Hiya Anti*,[67] textual challenges, nevertheless, retain certain dominant discursive notions. In *Misk el-Ghazal*, or *Women of Sand and Myrrh* (1988), for example, Lebanese novelist, Hanan al-Shaykh narrates an incident in which two married women, a Lebanese, Suha, and a (presumably) Saudi, Nour, engage in sexual intercourse. The incident, however, remains a one-time affair, as Suha's sense of guilt and shame drives her to cut off all her ties to Nour. In another, *Al-Khoubz al-Hafi*, or *Naked Bread*, the 1935–1965 autobiography of Moroccan writer Mohammed Shukri, Shukri paints a picture of his childhood growing up poor in miserable dwellings, finding out that his father had murdered his brother, and running away from the father he hated. In his subsequent adventures, Shukri narrates an experience during which a rich older man, speaking Spanish, fellates the young boy and offers him 50 pesos in return.

Although "deviant" sexual experiences are seeping into contemporary Arab literature, such as the works discussed here, the conceptualization of such acts, nevertheless, is not freed from dominant discourses which relegate non-normative sexual practices to the shady, secretive, and shameful side of social life. Furthermore, whether it is the "moral" values embedded in Shaykh's account, or the sexual violence (the rape and child molestation) in Shukri's, neither of these works offer a vision of sexual freedom.

Other literary works exemplify opposition to official Arab regimes and attempt to hint at the possibility of a more humane social structure, yet a contradiction exists in them, given that sexuality is constructed in such a way as to privilege male domination and heterosexual intercourse while dismissing all other possibilities.[68] The brilliance of *Cities of Salt,* by the late Saudi writer Abdelrahman Munif, for example, is undermined by an overt homophobic and sexist tone.

THE GLOBALIZATION OF KNOWLEDGE PRODUCTION: CONTRADICTORY CONSEQUENCES

Influences on Arab and Muslim social conceptions of sexuality are not limited to colonial legacies, neocolonial intervention, or the rising popularity of Islamist movements. A significant structural factor that must be thrown into the pot as well is the globalization of information networks and the domination—on an international scale—of Western thought patterns and discourses. This factor accounts for contradictions in contemporary Arab attitudes toward sexuality on different levels. On one level, we need to take note of the fact that, with the exception of Munif, all the Arab writers discussed here produced their works while living in areas where Western influences are the greatest: Shukri in Morocco and al-Shaykh in London.[69] It is possible to argue that, because of the location in which these texts are produced, Arab readers with no stake in the matter can choose to view them with amusement, but not necessarily take them seriously. For the advocates of a strict and "moralistic" sexual order, however, these writers can easily be dismissed as agents of imperialism, or at the very least as playing into the hands of the colonial world.

On a second level, these Arab writers (and other challengers to the prevailing sexual order) are generally located in a privileged position in comparison with the majority of Arab peoples. Usually middle or upper class and Western-educated, these writers have more space than others to contest dominant discourses, especially when such an attitude allows them to present themselves as modern subjects and as completely opposite to the "backward" and "undeveloped" peasants in their home countries. In so doing, however, these writers tend to gloss over class (and other) markers of distinction in people's lives, and thus end up speaking to—and for—the few who share their socioeconomic, political, and ideological positions. Furthermore, the fact that these writers depict sexual acts as shady, hidden, and underground activities may be (and is at times) counterproductive, inviting a backlash and negative reactions against those who may potentially wage a struggle for sexual freedoms. If LGBTIQ activists are waging a struggle for sexual freedoms, constructing same-sex desires and practices as shady immediately places the activists in the "pervert" category, thus depriving them (and the sexual freedoms movements they form) of any sense of seriousness and making a mockery of their activism and struggles. Furthermore, by equating what they define as Western values with civilization and by denigrating their homelands, these writers have little space for the emergence of oppositional genuine movements who see struggles for sexual freedom as important as their struggles for other political and socioeconomic freedoms.

On another level, the globalization of information is carried out by multinational corporations and mostly controlled by the elite in Western societies. As such, these corporations reproduce and disseminate information on specific dominant discourses in the Western context that constructs members of marginalized communities, such as indigenous and other communities of color as well as immigrants from the global South, as dangerous, suspect, and prone to crime. Rarely do LGBTIQ people appear, but if they do, they are generally shown in police and mystery dramas as child molesters, extortionists, rapists, or as psychologically disturbed; such representations also aid in the negative perceptions of non-normative genders and sexualities in the non-Western world.

On a final level, it must come as no surprise to anyone that Arab boys and girls—who used to be seen holding hands, hugging, and enjoying the homosocial company of each other—have now become more rigid in their relations with persons of the same-sex gender. This is especially noticeable among those youngsters with more access to and familiarity with Western heterosexual practices. So far, I have addressed three of the four questions raised earlier in the chapter, but what about the final question of whether homosexual identities have emerged among Arab and Muslim communities? The importance of this issue warrants a full discussion, which I undertake in the next section.

ARE THERE HOMOSEXUAL IDENTITIES IN THE ARAB AND MUSLIM COMMUNITIES?

As far as Arabs and Muslims are concerned, Wockner's article includes several quotes which hint that no such thing as a gay or lesbian identity exists in their communities. Jehan Agrama, an Egyptian lesbian and former president of the Los Angeles chapter of the Gay and Lesbian Alliance Against Defamation, told Wockner that, while:

> there is significant woman–woman sex in the Arab world . . . a practice of this sort certainly [was] not considered 'lesbian' . . . that women can have sex with other women and feel friendship and not necessarily identify as a lesbian . . . I know people in Egypt who have these relationships and wouldn't even consider themselves bisexual . . . In all countries [of the region] . . . nobody goes around saying that they are a lesbian—or gay either.

Agrama attributes the absence of such identity to the fact that "it is not part of the consciousness. Maybe the women are just enjoying their anonymity and having a ball."[70] In another interview conducted in Stockholm, Wockner quotes Mansour, an Iranian gay man, as stressing that "being gay and having a gay identity is a Western phenomenon."[71]

Add these quotes to the evidence delineated in the preceding pages and it is clear that sociopolitical context has everything to do with identity politics. Perhaps the historically developed Arab and Muslim sexual norms that prevailed prior to the consolidation of the Muslim state and before the advent of colonialism was more beneficial to sexual freedoms, in that it did not force individuals to choose a specific sexual identity that would stick to him forever, but neither did it recreate a binary sexual order in which sexual activities are restricted to either hetero- or homosexual.

There are two things worth noting about Wockner's interviews. First, while the gays and lesbians interviewed came from Muslim and Arab backgrounds, they lived in the West at the time during which they expressed their opinions. Can we contemplate the possibility that the process of identifying as gays and lesbians may not have emerged in their home countries, but only after they have interacted with LGBTIQ[72] movements in their new homes? If we accept the notion that the sex-gender order herds most of us into "compulsory heterosexuality,"[73] it would not be a leap to suppose that the seemingly alternative order has merely replaced one set of binary opposition with another. Now we have to choose what our sexual identities are, but we cannot be both at the same time. This is not to say that the Arab and Muslim individuals Wockner interviewed were not sexually inclined to same-sex practices when living in their countries of origin, as ample evidence has been presented throughout this chapter to underline the existence of same-sex practices since time immemorial, rather it is simply to emphasize that sexual desires and practices take different shapes and forms, and what applies in (white upper/middle class) Western contexts may not apply in another.

The second point begs the question as to why Wockner refuses to listen to the Arab and Muslim gays and lesbians who insist that a homosexual identity does not exist in the region. These statements might seem contradictory. However, arguing against the existence of identifiable (homo) sexual identities back home while simultaneously stressing that Arab and Muslim gays and lesbians identify as such while living in the West is not a contradiction at all; speaking of different contexts and different strategies of survival when the cost is too high for coming out makes perfect sense. People generally do not tend to pass unless not passing is associated with immediate danger. The explanation, in my view, lies in the assumption grounding Wockner's discussion that any same-sex practice, regardless of its context, deserves to be rescued and hailed. Wockner's superficial work, however, leads him to avoid sifting through the many cases he cites in order to determine, on one hand, which of them qualify as same-sex practices (even though support and solidarity should be extended to any case where freedom—sexual or otherwise—is denied). On the other hand, Wockner glosses over the distinctions and conclusions that must be made when sexual acts (hetero- or homo- alike) involve power, domination, violence, and human rights violations. These relations imply a power dynamic in which some men dominate not only their female partners but also the men with whom they have sexual liaisons.

In addition, Wockner lists a number of atrocious and violent sexual acts without ever commenting on their brutal nature. In half a page dedicated to the discussion of homosexuality in Iraq, Wockner quotes Amnesty International's report as stating that "widespread incidents of male rape, especially of young men" by "Iraqi soldiers" took place during the Iraqi occupation of Kuwait. The report further details "such tortures as 'inserting bottle necks, sometimes when broken, into the rectum; tying a string around the penis and pulling it tightly; [and] pumping air using a pipe through the anus, particularly of young boys.'"[74] While citing such brutality, the author fails to treat it as evidence of violence and domination, regardless of whether the site of such atrocity was the same part of the anatomy where male homosexual intercourse occurs.

Puzzling, however, is the fact that Wockner singles out Iraq, of all the countries in the region, as a gross violator of human rights. Why is it that

Iraq is noted as such, while U.S. allies in the region, such as Egypt, Kuwait, Saudi Arabia, Oman, Qatar, the United Arab Emirates, and Israel (all discussed in the article), are exempted from the same treatment even though a spokesperson from Amnesty International pointedly told him that "the horrific rape of men detailed in this report is consistent with what we see all over the world."[75] In other words, Arab and Muslim communities are not more exceptionally brutal toward same-sex practicing individuals than other parts of the world. Is it possible to conclude that, in his enthusiasm to demonstrate the miserable conditions of Arab homosexuals, Wockner picked the country that had just been bombed by U.S. forces?

Wockner accepts on face value racist statements made by both American media and officials that are loaded with buzz words, but he makes no attempt to contemplate the possibility raised by Miller in her statement: "according to the Iranian government, the three men were convicted of raping two [male] youth while drunk and the two women were convicted of spreading corruption, prohibited things and adultery."[76] Miller's statement raises three issues symptomatic of Wockner's analysis. First, Wockner does not even entertain the possibility that the Iranian government may have been telling the truth. Second, evidence cited throughout Wockner's article attests to the fact that the five may have been executed for violating the rigidly constructed code of morality and not exclusively because of their homosexuality. Third, molesting children of the same or other sex is indicative of violence and domination, but definitely not of sexual pleasure, and thus, should be treated as such.

TOWARD A LIBERATING VISION: CHALLENGING THE STATUS QUO

Ending the discussion by rejecting Wockner's conclusions does not solve the problems facing individuals and communities of individuals with same-sex desires and practices, nor does an intellectual exercise offer an alternative vision for human liberation, including the ability to enjoy sexual pleasures without fear of retribution. In this sense, Massad's argument, while correct, leaves LGBTIQ communities in a straight-jacket with two bad choices: mobilize around sexual freedoms and be seen as an agent of the Gay International, or don't mobilize and be seen as part of the community, but suppress a movement that has to emerge alongside other movements for justice. An alternative model that challenges the dominant rigid sexual order in Arab and Muslim communities, however, must go beyond Wockner's narrow vision. "If we only export the Western model of gay liberation to the Middle East and super-impose the act of 'coming out of the closet' to this setting," he seems to say, "Arab and Muslim homosexuals will immediately enjoy sexual freedoms." This is exactly what Massad is arguing against, and in that he is absolutely correct.

If the discussion above demonstrates the failure of Wockner's model, then what is the solution? Offering criticism without options for liberation, which is missing from Massad's argument, is not a choice. Sexual freedom cannot be unlinked from other aspects of human liberation, nor can such rights be guaranteed in the absence of the social setting in which all other rights are respected. To achieve such a vision, people in the Arab and Muslim communities must be freed from colonial legacy, neocolonial interventions, foreign occupation, socioeconomic hierarchies, and dictatorial and monarchical authority. Furthermore, for LGBTIQ people in Arab and Muslim communities—as more of such identities emerge—the solution lies not in building alliances with those who denigrate their communities and their religion, but rather, they must build ties with forces struggling for comprehensive social change, first on a regional level, and then internationally. As the Arab proverb reminds us, "one hand cannot clap!"

NOTES

This chapter has gone through many revisions since I first wrote it as a paper for a graduate class. I wish to thank Joshua Gamson, who encouraged me to pursue research on this topic in his graduate class, Joseph Massad, for reading the first draft back in 1994 and offering feedback and resources, including the article by As'ad AbuKhalil, and Samar Habib, who read several drafts and responded with amazing speed, detailed input, and thoughtful comments. I am grateful for the smart and supportive graduate research assistants who have made the completion of this paper a reality: Elisa Oceguera, Vanessa Saldívar, and Sriya Shrestha. This chapter is dedicated to Josh and Richard, Helen and Rina, Anjali and Leili, Ken and Perry, and Jacqui, Wilson, and Leslie. Above all, this is my labor of love for Jaime; you opened my mind with your persistent arguments and insistence on the indivisibility of justice and you kept it real.

1. Rex Wockner, "Iran, the Middle East, and North Africa: Homosexuality in the Arab and Moslem World," in *Coming Out: An Anthology of International Gay and Lesbian Writings,* ed. Stephan Likosky (New York: Pantheon Books, 1992).

2. Ibid., 103.

3. Ibid., 104.

4. Ibid.

5. Ibid., 105.

6. While the "West" continues to refer to the geographic sites at which colonial projects were born and later flourished at the expense of the rest of the world, especially in Asia, Africa, and Latin America, and thus warrants the continued use of the West to refer to the centers of power of imperialism and neocolonialism, I do not share two assumptions associated with the term: first, that social groups living in what has become to be geographically known as "the West" (North America, Europe, Australia, and New Zealand), such as white ethnic groups, immigrants from the global South, and communities of color in the global north, are far from constituting a single monolithic unit without distinction or variations. Second, I question the notion that assumes that contemporary hegemonic thought is only circulated in and by the geographic West and exonerates the rest of world, including those who directly reproduce unjust and hegemonic discourses as innocent of the impact of these hegemonic and colonial projects.

7. See Edward Said, *Orientalism* (New York: Pantheon Books, 1978).

8. Wockner, 105.

9. Ibid., 104.

10. Samar Habib, *Arabo-Islamic Texts on Female Homosexuality 850–1780 A.D.* (New York: Teneo, 2009), 18; personal communication, February 20, 2009.

11. Aziza al-Habri made this argument at a lecture in Marnia Lazreg's class on Women and Development at Hunter College, spring 1992. Also see Aziza al-Hibi, ed., *Women and Islam* (Oxford: Pergamon Press, 1982).

12. Other explanations in "weak" or less authentic *hadith* suggest that the Prophet, referring to gender ambiguous persons, may have said, "cast them out of your houses."

13. Habib, however, argues that there were more references in weakly authenticated *hadith* in which the prophet instructs to "kill the doer and the done to" in a male homosexual act, or that women having intimate relations amounted to fornication.

14. As'ad AbuKhalil, "A Note on the Study of Homosexuality in the Arab/Islamic Civilization." *Arab Studies Journal* 1, no. 2 (1993): 32–34.

15. A. Abu Shaqqa, *Tahrir al-Mar'a fi Asr El-Risala [The Liberation of Women in the Era of the Message], Volume IV, The Muslim Woman's Attire and Adornment* (Kuwait: Dar al-Qalam, 1991), 196.

16. Ibid., 194–96.

17. Ibid., 194.

18. Ibid., 193.

19. J. Jum'ah, *Nuzhat al-Albab fi Ma La Yujad fi Kitab [Pleasures of Hearts Not Found in Books]* (Beirut: Riad El-Rayyes., 1992), 31.

20. AbuKhalil, "A Note on the Study of Homosexuality," 33.

21. Ibid.

22. As-Suyuti, *Tarikh al-Khulafa' [History of the Caliphs]* (Cairo: Ahmad al-Babi al Halabi, 1305 A.H.), 97, cited in As'ad AbuKhalil, "A Note on the Study of Homosexuality."

23. A. Hourani, *A History of the Arab People* (New York: Warner Books, 1991), 33, 44, 52, 197, 103, and 202.

24. Although there has been good and solid scholarship on queer female sexuality recently, such as the work by the editor of this volume, the number of works on female sexuality pales in comparison with male sexuality. See Samar Habib, *Female Homosexuality in the Middle East, Arabo-Islamic Texts on Female Homosexuality* (New York: Routledge, 2007) and "Queer Friendly Islamic Hermeneutics" in *ISIM Review* 21(2008): 30–31.

25. Samar Habib, *Arabo-Islamic Texts on Female Homosexuality 850–1780 A.D.* (New York: Teneo, 2009), 16.

26. Paula Sanders, "Gendering the Ungendered Body: Hermaphrodites in Medieval Islamic Law," in *Women in Middle Eastern History,* ed. N. Keddie and B. Baron (New Haven, CT: Yale University Press, 1991), 88.

27. Leila Ahmad. *Women and Gender in Islam* (New Haven, CT: Yale University Press, 1992), 67.

28. Ibid., 88.

29. Ibid., 65.

30. Thomas W. Laqueur, *Making Sex: Body and Gender from the Greeks to Freud* (Cambridge: Harvard University Press, 1990).

31. Ahmad, 29.

32. Aristotle, "GA: Generation of Animals," trans. Arthur Platt, in *Works of Aristotle,* ed., J. A. Smith and W. D. Ross (Oxford: Clarendon Press, 1912), 1.20.728a.

33. See J. Mabro, ed., *Veiled Half-Truths: Western Travellers' Perception of Middle East Women* (London: I. B. Tauris and Company., 1991) and Edward Said. *Orientalism* (New York: Pantheon Books, 1978).

34. See Alev Lytle Croutier, *Harem: The World Behind the Veil* (New York: Abbeville Press, 1989); W. Walther, *Women in Islam: From Medieval to Modern Times* (Princeton, NJ: Markus Wiener Publishing, 1993); M. E. Combs-Schilling, *Sacred Performances: Islam, Sexuality, and Sacrifice* (New York: Columbia University Press, 1989); and B. Utas, ed., *Women in Islamic Societies: Social Attitudes and Historical Perspectives* (New York: Olive Branch Press, 1983).

35. AbuKhalil, "A Note on the Study of Homosexuality," 32.

36. Mary A. Wollstonecraft, *A Vindication of the Rights of Women* (New York: W.W. Norton and Co., 1988), 27.

37. Ibid., 186.

38. Ibid., 105.

39. Hourani, *A History of the Arab People*; Sami Hadawi, *Bitter Harvest: A Modern History of Palestine* (New York: Olive Branch Press, 1989).

40. R. Green, "The Pocahontas Complex: The Image of Indian Women in American Culture," in *Unequal Sisters: A Multicultural Reader in US Women's History,* ed. E. Carol DuBois and V. Ruiz (New York: Routledge, 1990), 15–21.

41. W. Jordan, "First Impressions: Initial English Confrontation with African," in *White Over Black: American Attitudes Toward the Negro* (New York: W. W. Norton, 1977), 7.

42. Cynthia Enloe, *Bananas, Beaches, and Bases* (Berkeley: University of California Press, 1989), 49.

43. Franz Fanon, *The Wretched of the Earth* (New York: Grove Press, 1963), 40.

44. Ibid., 211.

45. Ibid., 41.

46. Ibid., 39.

47. Enloe, 48.

48. George Mosse, *Nationalism and Sexuality: Middle Class Morality and Sexual Norms in Modern Europe* (Madison: University of Wisconsin Press, 1985).

49. Wockner, 104.

50. Andrew Parker, et al., eds., *Nationalisms and Sexualities* (New York: Routledge, 1992), 6.

51. Wockner, 109.

52. Sir Alistair Horne, *A Savage War of Peace* (New York: Penguin Books, 1987).

53. S. Dayan-Herzburn, "Women: A Political Gamble," in *Femininity in Islam,* ed. Mawaqef (London: Al-Saqi Books, 1991), 49.

54. Franz Fanon, *A Dying Colonialism* (New York: Grove Press, Inc. 1965), 42. While a further discussion of this topic is necessary, it is beyond the scope of this chapter. I discuss the dialectics of gender and anti-colonial resistance in my forthcoming book, *Revising Master Narratives: Gender, Nation, and Resistance in Palestine.*

55. Rabab Abdulhadi, "The Limitations of Nationalism: Gender Dynamics and Emergent Palestinian Feminist Discourses" (B.A. Honors Thesis, Hunter College, New York, 1994), 32–42.

56. Hadawi, 310.

57. Enloe, 61.

58. Eileen MacDonald, *Shoot the Women First* (New York: Random House, 1992), xv.

59. Evelyne Accad, "Sexuality and Sexual Politics: Conflicts and Contradictions for Contemporary Women in the Middle East," in *Third World Women and the Politics of Feminism,* ed. Chandra Mohanty, et al. (Bloomington: Indiana University Press, 1991), 242.

60. Rema Hammami, "Women's Political Participation in the Intifada: A Critical Overview," in *Women's Studies Committee, The Intifada and Some Women's Social Issues* (Ramallah: Bisan Center for Research and Development, 1991), 78.

61. While conducting my field work in the Israeli-occupied West Bank and Gaza Strip in 1993, I interviewed a male leader of Fatah, the largest Palestinian group, led by PLO Chairman, Yasser Arafat. Throughout the interview, Mr. B., who insisted on anonymity, lumped women, accused of collaborating with the occupation authorities, with prostitutes and with women who did not behave "properly." Mr. B. also equated Palestinian men's collaboration and drug dealing with *lutis,* or men engaged in same-sex intercourse.

62. Abdulhadi, 59.

63. I have not been able to enter Gaza since the Israeli closure in 2000 and the complete blockade after Hamas began to rule Gaza in 2006. However, to my knowledge there have been no reported incidents of gay bashing under Hamas rule, despite a concerted campaign by Israel, the Palestinian Authority and the United States to discredit Hamas that would greatly benefit from reporting and publicizing homophobic attacks condoned or enabled by Hamas in Gaza.

64. See Lila Abu-Lughod, "Do Muslim Women Really Need Saving? Anthropological Reflections on Cultural Relativism and Its Others," *American Anthropologist* 104, no. 3 (2002): 783–90.

65. See Joseph Massad, "Re-Orienting Desire: The Gay International and the Arab World," *Public Culture* 14 no. 2 (2002): 361–85.

66. Israel's siege extended to denying Arafat access to water to flush the toilets in his compound, in an attempt to humiliate him as a symbol of Palestinian statehood.

67. See Habib, *Female Homosexuality in the Middle East,* 87–112. Also see Thani al-Suwaydee *Diesel* (Beirut: Dar al-Jadid, 1994); Elham Mansour, *Ana Hiya Anti* (Beirut: Riadd el-Rayyess, 2000). For the English translation of this novel, see Elham Mansour, *I Am You* trans. and intro. Samar Habib (New York: Cambria Press, 2008).

68. See Abdelrahman Munif, *al-An Huna Aw Sharq al-Mutawaset Marratan Oukhra [Here Now or Revisiting the East of the Mediterranean]* (Beirut: The Arab Establishment for Studies and Publications, 1991); Abdelrahman Munif, *Cities of Salt* (New York: Vintage Books, 1987); Abdelrahman Munif, *al-Tieh [Labyrinth]* (Beirut: The Arab Establishment for Studies and Publications, 1983).

69. See H. al-Shaykh, *Misk el-Ghazal [Women of Sand and Myth]* (Beirut: dar al-Adab, 1988); M. Shukri, *al-Khoubz al-Hafi [Naked Bread]* (London: Dar al-Saqi, 1990); Tahar Ben Jelloun, *La nuit sacree* (Paris: Seuil, 1987), trans., as *Laylat Al-Qadr* (Casablanca: Toubqal Publishing Co, 1990); and Tahar Ben Jelloun, *The Sand Child* (London: Quartet Books, 1987).

70. Wockner, 105.

71. Ibid., 110.

72. LGBTIQ stands for Lesbian, Gay, Bisexual, Transgender, Intersex, and Queer, recognizing and including Two-Spirited and Trans-Identified persons.

73. A. Rich, "Compulsory Heterosexuality and Lesbian Existence," in *The Lesbian and Gay Studies Reader,* ed. H. Abelove, M. Barale, and D. Halperin (New York: Routledge, 1993).

74. Wockner, 112.

75. Ibid.

76. Ibid., 109.

ABOUT THE EDITOR AND CONTRIBUTORS

Samar Habib is a lecturer in Gender and Islamic Studies at the University of Western Sydney (Australia). She is the author of *Female Homosexuality in the Middle East* (2007) and has translated and introduced the Arabic novel *Ana Hiya Anti/I Am You* by Elham Mansour (2008). Her criticism and translations of *Arabo-Islamic texts on Female Homosexuality* was published by Teneo Press in 2009. She is the chief editor of *Nebula: A Journal for Multidisciplinary Scholarship* and has published and forthcoming articles in *Entertext, Nebula,* and *Gay and Lesbian Quarterly.* In addition to her scholarly work, Habib is the author of *A Tree Like Rain* (a novel) and *Islands in Space: Selected Poems,* both published by Nebula Press in 2005 and 2008, respectively.

Rabab Abdulhadi is associate professor at the College of Ethnic Studies at San Francisco State University. Her publications include newspaper, magazine, and scholarly articles in Arabic and English that take up questions of Palestinian feminisms, gender and exilic existence; racial and ethnic profiling post-9/11; social movements and social change; and dynamics of race, class, nation, and citizenship as they interact with gender and sexuality. Two of her manuscripts are currently undergoing revisions for publication: *Cultures of Resistance and the "Post Colonial" State: Altering the Question of Palestine* (working title), and *Revising Narratives?*

Gender, Nation, and Resistance in Palestine (working title). Her work-in-progress focuses on "Carving Spaces, Building Communities: Palestinian Women's Activism in North America 1983–1995."

Ibrahim Abraham is a Ph.D. student in the sociology department at the University of Bristol. He has published in various journals and edited books on the relationship between religion and culture, gender, sexuality, psychoanalysis, politics, punk, and Palestine.

Ayisha A. Al-Sayyad received her Master's degree in 2008 from the University of Arizona Women's Studies program and will continue her studies at the Ph.D. level in the fall of 2009. In 2007, she won the National Women's Studies Association Lesbian Caucus award to support her research on queer Muslim women living in the diaspora.

Ahmet Atay is a Ph.D. candidate in the Speech Communication Department at Southern Illinois University-Carbondale, where he teaches Communication Across Cultures, Visual Culture, and Oral Communication classes. His present research centers on cultural identity formations of diasporic queer bodies in the context of globalization. He is currently working on articles that focus on issues of cultural identity and new media technologies.

Tilo Beckers is a postdoctoral researcher and has earned his Ph.D. in Sociology at the University of Cologne. He has studied at the Heinrich-Heine-Universität Düsseldorf and the New School for Social Research in New York City. He has published on "Coquetry and Cruising as Two Forms of Simmel's Wechselwirkungen," in *Georg Simmel in Translation*, ed. David D. Kim (Cambridge Scholars Press: Newcastle, 2006: 50–77). He is currently preparing a research project on attitudes toward other moral issues (bioethics and beginning- and end-of-life issues).

Junaid Bin Jahangir is a final year doctoral student of Economics at the University of Alberta, Canada. He works toward initiating dialogues between the LGBT community and representatives of the mainstream Muslim clergy. He is a recipient of the 2007 Pride Certificate Award in Edmonton for outstanding services to the LGBT community.

Christopher Grant Kelly is a graduate student in the sociology department at Boston College. His research interests include qualitative research methods, the sociology of knowledge, social psychology, interpretive, and constructionist approaches to sociology and Islam and sexuality.

Badruddin Khan is the *nom de plume* of a Pakistan-born writer who lives in North America. In his day job, he is an established business professional with broad global interests. Khan is the author of *Sex, Longing and Not Belonging: A Gay Muslim's Quest for Love and Meaning* (Oakland, CA: Floating Lotus, 1997) and "Not-so-gay Life in Pakistan in the 1980s and 1990s," in *Islamic Homosexualities: Culture, History and Literature,* ed. Stephen Murray and Will Roscoe (New York University Press, 1997), 275–96.

Mahruq Fatima Khan received the Arthur J. Schmitt Fellowship to complete her dissertation in Sociology in 2007 on queer and feminist Muslims in the United States. Her research focuses on the intersections of faith, gender, and sexuality in the lives of second-generation American Muslims. She currently teaches a "Sociology of Muslims" course at Loyola University in Chicago.

Max Kramer is guest professor of French literature at Sarah Lawrence College (New York). He holds a Ph.D. in Comparative Literature from Columbia University and the Sorbonne (Paris IV). He is a former Fellow of the Studienstiftung des deutschen Volkes and former Pensionnaire Étranger of the École Normale Supérieure in Paris. His research focuses on queer issues in modernist poetry (French, German, Spanish, English), postcolonial North African and Middle Eastern society and literature, on-line media, and on the question of human rights vs. cultural rights. He has a book forthcoming with L'Harmattan entitled *Poésie et Inversion: La métaphore queer dans la poésie moderniste,* and has published various articles on queer sexuality in the Muslim world.

Michael T. Luongo is a well-published writer, editor, and photographer. He has published articles in *The Advocate***,** *The New York Times, The Chicago Tribune, National Geographic Traveler* and many other publications. He is the co-editor of *Gay Tourism: Culture, Identity and Sex* (London: Continuum Press, 2002); the author of *Between the Palms* (New York: Haworth Press, 2004); and the editor of *Looking for Love in Faraway Places*

(New York: Southern Tier Editions, 2007) and *Gay Travels in the Muslim World* (New York: Harrington Park Press, 2007).

Nur 'Adlina Maulod and **Nurhaizatul Jamila Jamil** are graduate students in the Department of Sociology at the National University of Singapore. Their research interests include queer theory, the sociology of the body, feminist theory, gender and sexuality, and theories of agency and subjectivation. They constantly strive to address ontological and epistemological questions related to "Malay-ness" in their research.

Rusmir Musić (pronounced "moose-itch") originally hails from Bosnia and Herzegovina, but now lives in the United States, where he arrived on his own at age 17. Rusmir received his B.A. in Chemistry from the College of the Holy Cross and his M.A. in Humanities and Social Thought from New York University. He has written and presented on such diverse topics as higher education, Harry Potter, and religion and homosexuality. A full list of Rusmir's publications and a biographical overview can be found at http://rusmir.music.googlepages.com.

Omer Shah received his B.A. in Anthropology from Bard College in 2007. His senior thesis, "Spectacles of Difference: Class, National, and Gendered Structuring on the Hajj," was awarded the Franz Boas/Ruth Benedict Prize in Anthropology. His writing has appeared in *SAMAR* (*South Asian Magazine for Action and Reflection*). Omer currently works for a nonprofit organization in New York. He hopes to pursue an advanced degree in anthropology, someday.

Jocelyn Sharlet is an Assistant Professor of Comparative Literature at the University of California, Davis. She co-translated with Kamran Talattof the Iranian novella *Women Without Men* by Shahrnush Parsipur (Syracuse University Press, 1998 and Feminist Press at the City University of New York, 2002). She has published "Voracious Men Meet their Match: Masculinity and the City in Wattar's *The Earthquake*," in *Masculinity in Middle Eastern Literature and Film,* ed. Lahoucine Ouzgane (New York: Routledge, 2008) and has recently completed a book project on social mobility and patronage in medieval Arabic and Persian literature. Sharlet's "Inside and Outside the Pleasure Scene in Poetry about locations by al-Sari al-Raffa' al-Mawsili" is forthcoming in the *Journal of Arabic Literature.*

Walter L. Williams is Professor of Anthropology, History, and Gender Studies at the University of Southern California. He is the author of *Javanese Lives: Women and Men in Modern Indonesian Society* (New Brunswick, NJ: Rutgers University Press, 1991) and *The Spirit and the Flesh: Sexual Diversity in American Indian Culture* (Boston: Beacon Press, 1986, rev. ed. 1992), co-author of *Overcoming Heterosexism and Homophobia: Strategies That Work* (New York: Columbia University Press, 1997, with James T. Sears), and *Gay and Lesbian Rights in the United States: A Documentary History* (Westport, CT: Greenwood Press, 2003, with Yolanda Retter).

Ilgin Yorukoglu is a doctoral candidate in sociology at the Graduate Center of the City University of New York. She has been teaching urban sociology as well as sexuality. She received her M.A. in Cultural Studies with a thesis on the recent transformation of the hegemonic representation of contemporary history in the Turkish part of Cyprus. Her doctoral dissertation, focusing on the everyday lives of queer women of Turkish background in Berlin, examines the everyday understandings of belonging and citizenship in Western democracies.

Aleardo Zanghellini is Senior Lecturer in Law at Macquarie University, Sydney. His research interests lie in the area of legal, moral, and political philosophy, socio-legal studies, and cultural studies of law, particularly in relation to the regulation of sexuality and sexual orientation. He has published widely in these areas, especially on gay parenting.

Barbara Zollner is a Lecturer in Islamic Studies at Birkbeck College, University of London. She currently also serves as the British Society for Middle Eastern Studies' Network Coordinator on Faith, Society, and Politics. Apart from her continuous interest in the intersection of gender rights, human rights, and Islamic law, her main field of expertise is on the Muslim Brotherhood. She has published a number of articles and chapters on this topic and is the author of the book *The Muslim Brotherhood: al-Hudaybi and Ideology* (London: Routledge, 2008).

INDEX

Abbasid: dynasty, 468; Empire, 40; Period,
   330, 339, 469
Abu Ghraib, 29, 109, 376, 377
Abu Hiffan, 43
Abu Hurayra, 465, 466
AbuKhalil, As'ad, 65, 66, 67, 92, 340, 428,
   467, 482
Abu Nuwas, 38, 40, 43, 44, 46, 47, 284, 468
Abu Shaqqa, 466
Abu Tammam, 40, 45
Active, 68, 135, 138–39, 143, 147–48,
   150–51, 157, 171, 173, 199, 210, 212,
   278–79, 281, 283, 286, 292. *See also*
   Top/s
Actualization, 70, 174
Adab, 38, 428
Affan, Othman Ibn, 467
Afghanistan: gay in, 101, 104; occupying,
   108, 109, 157, 366; refugees, 111, 396,
   475; Taliban, 8; women in, 422, 475
Ahadith, 200, v2 330, 334. *See also* Hadith
Ahmad, Leila, 469
AIDS, 27, 80, 87, 270, 449
AIPAC, 35
al-Amin, 468
al-Andalus, 467

al-Buhturi, 40, 45–47
al-Diesel, 476
Alevism, 429–31
Al-Fatiha, 30, 136, 352–54, 356–57, 362,
   364–65, 369, 377, 428
Algeria/Algerians, 143, 145, 149 158,
   472; government in, 474; war
   of independence, 472; women
   in, 472
Ali, Kecia, 194, 203, 274
American Civil Liberties Union, 30
Ammerman, Nancy T., 240–41, 348
Amnesty International, 17, 480, 481
Ana Hiya Anti, 476, 486.
Anal Sex, 140, 210–11, 213–14, 249, 251,
   253, 255, 261, 275–88, 293, 299–302,
   310, 316
Ancient Egypt, 306
Ancient Greece, 277–78
Ancient Greeks, 469
Ancient Rome, 277
Anglophone, 148–49, 161, 293
Anthias, Floya, 447
Anwar, Ghazala, 298
Anwar, Ibrahim, 9–10, 12, 269
Apartheid Wall, 475

Arab Mind, The, 376

Arabo-Islamic Texts on Female Homosexuality, 850–1780 AD, 303, 325, 484

Asian Law Caucus, 30

Aswat, 428

Australia, 395–415, 448

Axel, Brian Keith, 113

Ayatollah Musavi-Ardebili, 472

Bakr, Abu 467, 340

Bambale, Yahaya Yunusa, 275–6

Barlas, Asma, 327–8, 330–1, 344

BDS (Boycott, Divestment, Sanctions), 475, 476

Bedouins, 282–85

Ben Amrou, Abdullah, 466

Berger, Peter L., 365

Berlin Institute for Population and Development, 420

Be With Me, 172

Beyond Flesh: Queer Masculinities and Nationalism in Israeli Cinema, 102

Bible, 24, 92, 241, 335, 344, 376

Bint el Nas, 374

Bisexual, 30, 87, 134, 148, 150, 223, 343, 349, 352, 356, 358–60, 364–65, 479

Boisvert, Donald, 349, 358, 365

Bollywood, 173

Boswell, John, 98, 136

Bottom/s, 137–38, 280, 293. *See also* Passive

Bouhdiba, Abdelwahab, 332–33, 335–36, 340, 345

Buddhism, 58, 160

Burton, Richard, 33, 114, 119

Bush, George, 20, 28, 34, 404, 475

Butler, Judith, 51, 133, 166–68, 180, 269

Cairo, 52 case, 102, 342

Canada: LGBTIQ persons in, 354, 378; Muslim communities in, 27, 140, 350, 378, 381, 446, 451–53, 454; Supreme Court of, 301

Capitalism/capitalist, 395–6, 398, 404, 410, 412, 414, 437

China, 3

Chinese Government, 2

Chinese LGBT, 4–5

Christianity: Abrahamic, 24, 62, 160; Arab Christians, 43–44, 399, 409; Catholics, 28; European, 7, 90; Fundamentalist, 2, 34, 249, 290, 441; Judeo-Christian, 58, 63, 136, 334, 375; Puritanism in, 65, 66; Queer Christians, 224, 358; story of Lot, 61, 307; Zionists and, 28, 34

Chuang, Rueyling 450–51

Cinema. *See* Film

Cities of Salt, 477

Citizenship, second class, 30

Clash of civilizations, 269, 396, 404, 409

Classical Arabic language, 208

Closet/closeted, 24, 87, 144, 145, 352, 355, 363, 399, 401, 402, 408, 449, 482

Cohen, Robin, 446

Colonial, 7, 115, 119, 384, 447, 452, 455, 471, 474, 482; anticolonial, 471–73; colonialism, 64–66, 121, 422, 445, 464, 470, 479; postcolonial, 377, 411, 452, 455–57, 459

Coming Out: An Anthology of International Gay and Lesbian Writings, 463, 482

Communism, 241, 474

Comstock, Craig, 354

Concubine, 125, 322

Conservative, 170, 172, 203–4, 212, 249, 255, 298, 331, 336, 363, 376, 380, 382–83, 396, 399, 404, 430, 474, 476

Constructionism and sexual identity, 1, 135, 144, 152, 154, 168, 200; and gender, 182

Cooley, Charles Horton, 229

Crime and Punishment in Islamic Law, 209

Cross-dressing, 170, 339, 465

Cultural elite, 37–39, 42–47, 49–50

Death penalty, 8, 16, 64, 193, 200, 211, 253, 255, 261–62, 265, 340, 414

Delaney, Carol, 113

Democracy, 9, 59, 71–2, 74, 78, 80–82, 299, 419. *See also* Responsive Democracy

Desiring Arabs, 102, 155, 161, 384. *See also* Massad, Joseph

Deviance, 26, 136, 174, 342, 384

Deviant, 76, 171, 175–77, 182, 227, 381, 396, 471, 476

Diaspora, 58, 113, 121, 348, 373, 374, 375, 380, 386, 389, 390; defining diaspora, 391, 446–7; *diasporic imaginary,* 113–14; doubled diaspora, 383, 385; Indian, 446; Pakistani, 23; Palestinian, 67, 103, 378; South Asian, 381–382; Turkish, 113, 428, 430, 434

Don't Ask, Don't Tell, 103, 172, 203

Drag queen, 167–8, 264, 375

Duran, Khalid, 60, 90

Dyer, Richard, 448

A Dying Colonialism, 472

Dyke, 392, 400

Economist, The, 428

Egalitarian homosexuality, 68

Egypt: attitudes toward anal sex, 277; feminism in, 476; human rights violations, 9, 11; Western homophobic intervention, 66; www.gayegypt.com, 148

Eid, 181

Electronic Frontier, The, 30

El-Rouayheb, Khaled, 159, 195, 263, 278, 281, 305, 312

Esack, Farid, 195, 257–258, 298, 329

Essentialism/essentialist, 151, 154, 157, 165, 181, 195–96, 228, 259, 333, 337, 386, 419

Ethnocentric, 271

Fakhr al-Din al-Razi, 205

Familialism, 62, 64, 67–69, 76, 85

Fatah, 474, 486

Fatawa, 194, 196–97, 199–200, 204, 216, 290, 378, 428

Fatwa, 13, 123

Female Homosexuality in the Middle East, 98, 102, 293, 295, 393, 484

Female Masculinity, 164

Feminism, 271

Feminist movement, 476

Feudalism, 169

Film, 30, 102, 117, 129, 172, 447–50, 452–3, 456, 458, 460

Fiqh, 197, 199, 201, 204. *See also* Fuqaha

Foucauldian, 166, 415

Foucault, Michel, 136, 156, 165–66, 191

Francophone, 135, 148–49, 161

Franz Fanon, 471–72

Fundamentalist Muslims, 13

Fuqaha, 194, 197

Gay: activism, 1, 3, 4, 24, 31, 32, 87, 136, 145, 258, 302, 352, 383, 385, 388, 390, 397, 432, 445; after 9/11, 28, 30, 403; asylum seekers, 5, 87; gayness, 27, 200, 342; identity, 26, 60, 67, 88, 114, 134–37, 149, 157, 198, 223, 224, 241, 260, 262, 350, 355–58, 406, 411, 478–80; in film, 448–53, 458; Iraq, 99–109; in Islam, 262–63, 298, 316, 352, 365; marriage, 210, 214; oppression, 4, 18, 134, 153, 265, 300–301, 310–11, 315, 421, 423–26, 432; Quran on, 214, 252, 254–55, 260, 264, 311, 363; Western, 144, 152, 203, 232, 241, 271–2, 290, 354, 362, 375, 377, 384, 479, 482

Gay and Lesbian Alliance Against Defamation, 479

Gay and Lesbian Arab Society (GLAS), 136

Gay City News, 99

Gay marriage, 135, 210, 214, 424, 428

Gay Mecca (San Francisco), 6

Gay men 354

Gay tourism 103, 136, 426, 435

Gay Travels in the Muslim World, 102

Gaza, 35, 474–6, 486

Gender equality, 72–4, 77, 80–2, 85–8, 202

Generalized Other, 229–30

General Union of Palestinian Women (GUPW), 473

German Asylum Procedure Act, 421

Germany: asylum in, 12, 422, 423; Germans, 153, 435–36, 439; Nazis, 14, 421, 425; politics in, 421, 422, 424–5; Turkish experience in, 419, 428–34, 443

Globalization, 127, 135, 152, 159, 169, 447, 477–8,

Global Zionist movement, 475

Goffman, Erving, 180

Gorsline, Robin, 340–41
Governmentality, 166
Gramsci, 399, 404
Guantanamo Prison Colony, 29

Habib, Samar, 41, 102, 103, 195, 200, 270, 280, 295, 303, 393, 427, 428, 465, 468, 483
Hadith, 64, 92, 170, 185, 189, 199–200, 464–67, 483, 224, 253, 255–57, 287, 290, 297–98, 309, 310–13, 316, 324, 328, 330, 334, 337, 339, 340, 378, 364–67, 483
Hai, Wan Yan, 1
Hajj: Burton, Richard at, 114, 119; literature about, 117–122; queer Hajj, 128; ritual at, 112–16; women in, 124–126
Halberstam, Judith. *See Female Masculinity*
Hall, Stuart, 446
Hamas, 29, 35, 474, 486
Hamdun, Ahmad b. Ibrahim b. Isma'il b, 42
Hammad 'Ajrad, 46
Hammami, Rema, 474, 485
Hammarberg, Thomas, 422
Hamori, Andras, 38, 39, 46
Hanbali, 198, 208, 210–11, 253, 288
Hanifi, 198, 208–10, 214, 251, 253, 259, 261, 312
Haram, 122, 171, 178, 184,
Haumann, Gunter, 59–60, 62
Hayek, 472–3
Headscarf, 177–8, 271, 289, 465
Helem, 428
Hendricks, Muhsin, 298
Heteronormativity (heteronormative), 163–64, 169, 172, 183–84, 251–52, 261, 366, 377–78, 400–402, 450, 471
Heterosexual, 63, 67, 76, 86, 135, 137, 139, 143, 149–52, 166–7, 171, 174, 183, 200, 208–12, 226–28, 360, 364, 366–67, 376, 381, 396, 399–401, 409, 424, 434, 449–50, 459, 460, 473–74, 477–79
Hezbollah 28, 100
al-Hibri, Aziza, 465

Hijab, 120, 270–73, 289, 280, 300, 400, 465, 474
Hili, Ali, 100, 104–5
History of Makkah, The, 121
Holocaust, 230
Homoeroticism (in classic Arabic literature), 37–42, 44–50, 51, 171, 174
Homonormativity, 404, 426
Homophobia: challenging homophobia, 2–3, 412–14; impact of colonialism on, 11, 66, 92 n.37; in the West, 263; Islamic basis for, 9, 345, 349, 396, 407; nationalist discourses, 9, 144, 431–32, 434; persecution due to, 366; religious, 385, 411
al-Hubab, Walibah b., 44
Human development, 59, 70, 71, 72, 73, 74, 78, 80, 81, 82, 85, 87, 88
Human rights: activism/organizations, 18, 87, 136, 384, 385; abuses of, 9, 10, 11, 13, 15, 249, 475, 480; discourse, 149, 152, 154, 203, 271, 272, 299, 367, 383, 389, 390, 412, 426
Human rights law, 271, 301, 421
Human Rights Watch, 11, 153
Hussein, Saddam, 99–101, 108
Hybridity, 395, 410–14

I Am You. *See Ana Hiya Anti*
Ibn al-Mudabbir, 43, 47
Ibn al-Mu'tazz b. al-Mutawakkil b. al-Mu'tasim b. Harun al-Rashid, 'Abd Allah, 40, 52, 54
Ibn Bistam, 47
Ibn Hazm, 42, 45, 307, 312, 428
Ibn Khafajah, 39
Ibn Mufarrigh, 46–47
Ibn Quzman, 42
Identity: politics, 270, 271, 272, 274, 290, 450, 479; sexual 24, 26–27, 135, 238–40, 243
IGLHRC (International Gay and Lesbian Human Rights Commission), 136, 162
Ijtihad, 61, 90, 197, 216, 288, 466
Individualism, 373, 386, 455
Institute for the Study of Human Resources (ISHR), 2

Institutionalization, 71, 228
International Lesbian and Gay
    Association (ILGA) 464
Internet: blogs 30, 136, 223–4; Muslim
    LGBTIQ activism/organization on
    the, 31, 32, 136, 354, 355, 363; Muslim
    LGBTIQ internet communities, 26, 31,
    99, 101, 106, 134–39, 148–49
Intersex, 298, 312–16, 392. *See also*
    Web sites
Intifada, 157, 474
*Invisible Lives: The Erasure of Transsexual
    and Transgendered People,* 168
Iran: and the West, 153, 249, 481; *Homan,*
    8; LGBTIQ persons in, 8, 89, 153,
    479; president of, 30, 129; Sharia
    in, 153, 423
Iraq: gay men in, 99–109, 445;
    insurgencies in, 99, 101, 108; U.S.
    invasion and occupation of, 32, 101,
    103, 106, 157, 366, 422, 480
Ireland, Doug, 99
al-Isbahani, Abu al-Faraj, 43
al-Isbahani, Ibn Dawud, 43, 46, 51
Islamicate Sexualities, 62
Islamic Homosexualities, 102, 172
Islam in Australia, 400
Islamic jurisprudence, 184, 250, 253,
    261, 263, 265, 286 (section), 298,
    310, 312, 315
Islamic law: classical, 204, 209, 214,
    315, 468; interpretation 148, 172, 196–
    99, 208, 328; principles, 61, 193–94,
    201, 204; reform, 204, 213, 255–56, 201
Islamic rule, 467–68
Islamic Salvation Front, 474
Islamic Studies, 428, 464
Islamic theology, 249
Islamism, 270
Islamophobia: after 9/11, 23, 29–30, 34,
    396, 405, 409; anti-Muslim, 347, 351,
    413–14, 379, 409; and terrorism, 24,
    29–33, 34, 375, 391, 396, 403–4, 435;
    queer Islamophobia, 395, 399, 404,
    410–12, 415
Israel, 249, 335, 472, 475, 476, 481,
    486; advocating for 119, 249; Jewish
    identity and, 126; lobby, 28, 34, 35;

occupation of Palestinians, 472, 475,
    468; politics in, 35, 119
Iyas, Muti' b., 46

Jamal, Amreen, 159, 195, 298, 316, 330–
    31, 334, 337–38
Jami', Muhammad b., 46
Jihad. *See* Queer Jihad
A Jihad for Love, 30, 172, 190
Judaism, 464, 466; Abrahamic religions
    24, 62, 160; and homosexuality [Rabbi
    Schulweis, Harold] 316; Jews 14, 27;
    Torah 330

Al-Kassim, Dina, 62
al-Kawakibi, 312
Khaminai, Ayatollah, 314
Khaqan, al-Fath b., 42
al-Khattab, Omar Ibn, 6, 467
al-Khoubz al-Hafi, 476
Kitab As-Sirr, 467
Kugle, Scott Siraj al-Haq, 61, 69, 90, 160,
    194, 195, 200, 224, 225, 237, 247–48,
    250–55, 237, 247–48, 250–55, 257,
    258–66, 298, 304, 308, 316, 319, 323,
    339, 353, 362, 363
Kulayb, Ahmad b., 42, 44, 47, 53
Kurds, 100, 105, 442
Kuwait, 142, 480–81

Lady boy, 142
Lahiqi, 43
A Leader of Men. See Idris, Yusuf
Lebanese, 383, 396, 399
Lebanon, 108, 476
Legitimation, 226–29, 231–32
Lesbian: activism, 3, 4, 87, 136, 258, 302,
    352, 365, 396, 404, 425–26, 473; asylum
    seekers, 5, 87, 423; discrimination
    against, 265, 300–301, 310, 315, 419,
    448, 373, 375; identity, 60, 67, 88, 198,
    223–24, 260, 262, 356, 358, 373–75,
    378–79, 382, 385, 390–91, 478–80;
    in Islam, 262–63, 298, 316, 352; in
    Yemen, 389; lesbianism, 199, 203, 299;
    Malaysia, 7–8, 10–15, 19; Palestinian,
    249; Quran on, 214, 252, 254–55, 260,

264, 311; Turkish, 430–32; Western, 271–72, 290, 362, 421   ·
Lesbian and Gay Federation in Germany, The (LSVD), 431–32
Lewis, Bernard, 28
LGBT, 1
LGBTIQ, 87, 100, 225, 258–59, 262, 270, 272–73, 358, 426, 432, 438, 475, 478–79, 481–82, 486
LGBTQ, 30, 369, 384
LGBTQ movement, 373–4, 377, 378, 383–91
Liberalism, 64, 202–3, 408
Likosky, Stephan, 463
Liwat, 193–94, 196, 204–5, 207–14, 275–77, 285–8, 293, 468
Looking-glass Self, 229
Lot, people of, 61, 106, 159, 274–77, 281, 284, 285, 287–301, 304–11, 332–41, 343, 427. See also Lut
Lughod, Laila Abu, 474
Lut, people of, 61, 193–94, 199, 205–8, 211, 213–14, 249, 252–54, 260, 262, 305, 333, 363

Maghrib, 183
Mahdi army, 99
Mahmood, Saba, 167–68, 385, 389
Makiya, Kanan, 103
Malay Mail, The, 14
Malaysia: laws, 8, 10–11; LGBT 6, 7; Malays in Singapore, 164, 168–73, 176, 178, 181, 186; penal code in, 7; persecution in, 14–19, 469; Suaram (human rights group), 13
Malcolm X, 114
Malik, Imam, 467
Maliki (school/thought), 198, 208, 210–11, 253, 288
al-Ma'mun, 47
Manji, Irshad, 119 129, 302, 404, 409
Mansour, Elham, 476, 479
Marxism/Marxist, 149, 397, 411, 414, 474
Masculinity: female, 163–67, 169–74, 177, 180–86; male/maleness, 30, 67, 279, 377, 439, 451, 473
Maslow, Abraham, 70
Massad, Joseph, 102–3, 149–52, 155, 157, 160–162, 474, 481–82, 482, 270,

341–42, 384, 386, 386, 389–91: and the Gay International, 102, 150, 151, 270, 481
Mathieu, General, 472
Mead, George Herbert, 229
Mecca, 6, 111–24, 128, 129, 282, 284. See also Hajj
Medina, 112, 114, 117–19, 123–24, 127, 282, 284, 310–11
Meem, 428
Menstruation (menstruate), 179–81
Mesopotamia, 277–79, 284, 306
MILES, 431–32
Misk el-Ghazal, 476
Mithliyyah, 144
Modernity, 86, 125, 258–59, 342, 381–82
Modernization, 59, 60, 68–9, 72–3, 89, 70
Modesty, 175, 260, 265, 316, 473–74
Mohamed, Mahithir, 10–12
Mohanty, Chandra Talpade, 383
Mormons, 28
Morris, Benny 34
Mosque, 34, 112, 124, 167, 176–77, 197, 237, 239, 265, 348, 354, 378, 429; Grand Mosque, 118, 120, 122–24
al-Mu'adhdhal, Abd al-Samad, 48
Mudrik b. 'Ali, 43, 47
Muhammad, the Prophet. See Prophet Muhammad
Mujun, 39
Mulia, Siti Musdah, 298
Multiculturalism, 395–96, 408–9, 411
Multilevel analysis, 81, 85
Munif, Abdelrahman, 477
Muqtada al-Sadr, 99
Murray, Stephen O., 24, 39, 67, 102, 172, 195, 278–79, 292, 303, 427, 445
Murray and Roscoe's collection, 303, 59
al-Mu'tasim, 47
al-Mutawakkil, 42

Namaste, Viviane, 168, 181
Narratives: metanarrative, 232–33, 241, 367; ontological 232–33; public, 228, 232–23, 240–41
Nationalist masculinity, 144
National Liberation Front (FLN), 472, 474

Nature, 12, 40, 60–64, 75, 76, 82, 85, 86, 90, 162, 172, 183, 201, 261, 333, 334, 408, 480
Nazis, 14, 19, 153, 421, 424–25
Niftawayh, Ibrahim b. Muhammad, 46
Neo-orthodox scholars, 193–200, 203–4, 212–13, 216
New Testament. *See* Bible
Nigeria, 9
Nihilation, 227–228, 231, 240–41
Nomani, Asra Q, 114, 120–21, 124–25
Nuwas, Abu, 38, 40, 43, 44, 45, 46, 47, 284, 468
Nuzhat al-albab, 41

Obama, Barack, 30–31, 109
Oklahoma City bombing, 441
Old Testament, 309, 335. *See also* Judaism
Oman, 481
ONE Institute (ONE), 2, 3, 4
Operation Clean, 16
Orientalism, 152, 376, 385, 390
Orientalist, 155, 157, 278, 374, 375, 376, 377, 382, 464, 470
Ostracism, 299
Ottoman dynasty, 102, 470
OutRage! 426
Out Traveler, 119
Overcoming Heterosexism and Homophobia: Strategies That Work, 2

Paganism, 264, 335
Pakistani, 26, 32
Palestine, 34, 378, 473
Palestinian National Charter, 473
Palestinian national movement, 472, 473
Palestinians (Israeli occupying), 249, 475
Palestinians, 29, 35, 102, 126, 446, 475
Parsah, 12
Passive, 68, 138–39, 143–44, 147, 150–51, 171, 199, 210, 212, 278–79, 281, 283–84, 286, 292, 469. *See also* Bottom/s
Passport, 119
Patriarchy, 67, 68 121, 172, 352, 358, 365, 400, 412
Performativity, 166–68, 188
Pilgrimage. *See* Hajj
Pipes, Daniel, 28
Platonic, 332

Plausibility structures, 229–31, 233, 237, 240–41, 243, 348
Politics of Piety: The Islamic Revival and the Feminist Subject, 167
Polytheism, 264
Pornography, 278, 301
Positivist, 201, 225
Postmaterialism, 76
Postmaterialist, 70, 76, 82
Power, Lisa, 464, 470
Prayers. *See* Salat
Pre-Islamic Arabia, 276, 281–85
Presentation of Self in Everyday Life, The, 180
Pride month, 475
Prophet Muhammad, 61, 35–35, 67, 112, 114, 118, 123, 224, 249, 253, 256, 329–30, 344, 351, 465–68
Puberty, 179–81

al-Qaeda, 29, 32, 99
Qaradawi, Yousuf, 200–203, 217, 262, 290, 299
Qatar, 217, 481
Queer, 114, 119, 121–29, 144, 151, 167, 224, 241, 328, 331, 341–43, 376, 407–15, 424, 436, 446, 474
Queer bodies, 121, 122, 125, 127, 446, 448, 450, 451
Queer Hajj, 128
Queer jihad, 31, 354
Queer Muslims, 125, 128, 129, 224–25, 229, 233–34, 243, 327, 329, 342, 348–67, 376, 385, 396, 398, 400–401, 407, 409, 415
Queerness, 115, 122, 157, 331, 379
Queer theory, 181, 400
QUIT (Queers Undermining Israeli Terrorism), 404, 476
al-Qummi, Muhammad b. 'Ali, 45
Quran: Exegesis, 205, 207, 328, 330–32, 335–36, 339–40; Kugle on, 224, 237, 250–55, 258–66, 298, 304, 308, 316, 319, 323, 339, 353, 362–63; on sexual behavior, 24, 66, 90, 143, 159, 185, 194, 196, 199, 206, 259, 272, 304, 336–37, 339, 464–67; on translation, 115, 321, 328–33; people of Lut in, 61, 193, 205,

209–12, 249, 274, 276–77, 285–88, 299, 307, 334, 336, 340–41, 363

Racism/racist, 128, 137, 155, 265, 402–3, 405, 423, 425, 432, 434, 481
Rahman, Fazlur, 195, 252, 256–58
Ramadan, 176, 415
Raphael, Kate, 475, 476
al-Rashid, Harun, 468
Rashid, Iqbal, 446, 451
Reno, Janet, 1
Respect Gaymes, 431
Responsive democracy, 85–89
Robert Bosch Foundation, 420
Roscoe, Will, 39, 102, 195, 280, 303, 427, 445
Rowson, Everett, 39, 51, 195, 304, 339, 341
Russia, 424

al-Safadi, 42
Sa'id, Ahmad b, 42
Said, Edward, 152, 156
Salaam Canada, 353
Salat (Prayers), 124
Same-sex acts, 196, 198–99, 204, 206, 209–12, 214, 249, 251, 255, 263–64, 269–74, 276–77
Same-sex desires, 68, 202, 203, 468, 478, 481
Same-sex practices, 133–34, 140, 159, 469, 479–80
al-Sanawbari (d. 945), 40, 45
Sanders, Paula, 468, 469, 315
al-Sari al-Raffa' (d. 973), 40
al-Sarraj, 42
Saudi Arabia: Punishing same-sex relations, 8, 11, 97, 481
Schmitt, Arno, 148, 157, 161, 195, 208, 215–16, 278–79, 445
Schulweis, Harold, 316. See also Judaism
Seidman, Steve, 397, 401–2
September 11th, 157, 239, 240, 251, 367, 375, 422
Sexism, 434, 471
Sex, Longing and Not Belonging (SLNB), 23, 25–28, 32, 33
Sexual Expression, 24, 89, 250
Sexuality in Islam, 332

Sexual liberalism, 64
Sexual liberation, 134, 375, 385
Sexual orientation, 5, 8, 26, 37, 58–59, 134–35, 148–52, 161, 204, 234, 252–55, 259–65, 311, 340, 350, 354–61, 421–25, 453
Shafi'I, 198, 208, 210–12, 253, 288
Sharia, 9, 13, 58, 193, 255–56, 263, 272, 301, 464, 466
al-Shaybani, Mudrik b. 'Ali, 43
al-Shaykh, Hanan, 476, 477
Shiite, 58, 90, 313, 397, 465
Shukri, Mohammed, 476, 477
Singapore: Malay community in, 164, 168–73, 176, 178, 181, 186; LGBTIQ persons in 187, 190
Slave boys, 45–47
Socialization, 72–73, 181, 187, 203, 231, 370
Sodom, 305, 340
Sodomite, 8, 426
Sodomy, 7–12, 19, 136, 148, 153, 196, 199, 200, 210, 275, 280, 281, 284, 286, 333, 342, 376
Sodomy law, 7, 9, 12, 270, 288
Soviet Union, 32
Spider Lilies, 172
Spirituality, 353, 356, 407–8, 412–14
Standing Alone [in Mecca]: An American Woman's Struggle for the Soul of Islam, 114, 120
Stereotype/stereotyping, 25, 34, 239, 273, 301, 251, 266, 390, 401, 422, 425, 430–31, 436, 448–49, 455
Stolen Generation, 396
Straight, 27, 105, 119, 137–38, 150, 352, 378, 384, 436, 449–50, 459–60
Subject of Freedom, The, 383
Sun, The, 14
Sunna, 198, 199, 209, 212, 214, 256, 257, 270
Sunni, 58, 61, 90, 209, 247, 251, 261, 286, 287, 300, 314, 429, 430–31
Surveys, 57, 59, 60, 77, 78; European Values Study, 77; For Iraqi and Afghani men, 104–5; World Values Survey, 57, 77, 82
al-Suyuti, 42

Sydney Gay and Lesbian Mardi Gras, 396, 401

al-Tabari, Abu Ja'afar Muhammad ibn Jarir, 205–7, 212, 219
Tafasir (Quranic commentary), 196, 207, 212
Talib, Ali Ibn Abi, 329, 467
Terrorist Assemblages, 375, 383
Third gender, 170–71
al-Tifashi, Ahmad b. Yusuf, 41
Tomboy, 171–72, 174, 179, 190
Top/s, 135, 137–38, 141, 280, 293
Touch of Pink, 446–48, 451, 453, 458
Transgender, 13, 128, 164–65, 168, 181, 187, 314, 359–61, 365, 370
Trans Muslim, 354
Tribadism, 171, 172, 183
Tunisia, 138, 158, 265
Turkey, 80, 102, 113, 139, 265, 368, 424, 428–34
2007 Zogby Poll, 30

Umayyad Caliph, 468
Umayyad era, 467
Unified Leadership of the Intifada, 474
United Arab Emirates, 481
United Nations Commissioner for Human Rights, 422
United States: asylum in, 18; foreign policy, 29, 35; Immigration code, 1, 5; Immigration policy, 18; invading/occupying, 100, 101, 106–7, 366, 422, 474, 481; military, 103, 105, 109; Victorian code, 471
Unspeakable Love: Gay and Lesbian Life in the Middle East, 102, 162, 290
USSR, 474

Voices of Islam, 253

Wadud, Amina, 195, 257–58, 330, 332–33, 343, 353
Wafer, Jim, 339–40

Wahabbism, 115, 118
War on Terror, 34, 118–119, 157, 401. *See also* Islamophobia and Terrorism
Warring Souls: Youth, Media, and Martyrdom in Post-Revolution Iran, 115
Waun, Maurie, 352
Weber, Max, 65, 74
Web sites, 132; "Eye on Gay Muslims" blog, 223, 225; Gay.com, 106; Gaydar.com, 101, 106; Gayegypt.com, 148; habibak.net, 148; Kelma.org, 148; Manjam.com, 106; "Mere Muslim," 247
West Bank, 475, 486
Westernization, 150, 410
Whitaker, Brian, 102, 319, 445, 490
Wockner, Rex, 67, 463–64, 470–72, 478–82
Women in Middle East History, 468
Women of Sand and Myrrh, 476
Women's sexual preference, 468
Wong, Kathleen, 447
World Pride festival, 475
World Report 2002, Special Issues and Campaigns, 11
Wowereit, Klaus, 420

Yaqut al-Hammami al-Rumi, 52
Yasser Arafat 486, 475
Yazid, Al-Walid bin, 468
al-Yazidi, Ahmad b. Muhammad, 47
Yip, Andrew K. T., 358, 363, 365, 397, 400, 402, 405, 409–10
Yosef, Raz, 102

al-Zamakhshari, Abu al-Qasim Mahmud ibn 'Umar, 113, 205–7, 212
al-Zayyat, Muhammad b. 'Abd al-Malik, 48
Zionism, 270, 473, 475
Zionist, 28, 34
Zionist settlers, 473
Zuhd, 39